The publisher gratefully acknowledges the generous support of the Music in America Endowment Fund of the University of California Press Foundation, which was established by a major gift from Sukey and Gil Garcetti, Michael P. Roth, and the Roth Family Foundation.

At the Jazz Band Ball

NEA Jazz Masters, 2004, left to right from back row: George Russell, Dave Brubeck; second row: David Baker, Percy Heath, Billy Taylor; third row: Nat Hentoff, Jim Hall, James Moody; fourth row: Jackie McLean, Chico Hamilton, Gerald Wilson, Jimmy Heath; fifth row: Ron Carter, Anita O'Day; sixth row: Randy Weston, Horace Silver; standing next to or in front of balustrade: Benny Golson, Hank Jones, Frank Foster (seated), Cecil Taylor, Roy Haynes, Clark Terry (seated), Louie Bellson, NEA Chairman Dana Gioia. Photograph by Tom Pich.

At the Jazz Band Ball

Sixty Years on the Jazz Scene

Nat Hentoff

Foreword by Lewis Porter

UNIVERSITY OF CALIFORNIA PRESS

Berkeley   Los Angeles   London

University of California Press, one of the most distinguished university presses in the United States, enriches lives around the world by advancing scholarship in the humanities, social sciences, and natural sciences. Its activities are supported by the UC Press Foundation and by philanthropic contributions from individuals and institutions. For more information, visit www.ucpress.edu.

University of California Press
Berkeley and Los Angeles, California
University of California Press, Ltd.
London, England

Every effort has been made to identify the rightful copyright holders of material not specifically commissioned for use in this publication and to secure permission, where applicable, for reuse of all such material. Credit, if and as available, has been provided for all borrowed material in the credits section of the book. Errors or omissions in credit citations or failure to obtain permission if required by copyright law have been either unavoidable or unintentional. The author and publisher welcome any information that would allow them to correct future reprints.

Library of Congress Cataloging-in-Publication Data

Hentoff, Nat.
    At the jazz band ball : sixty years on the jazz scene / Nat Hentoff.
        p.   cm.
    Includes bibliographical references and index.
    ISBN 978-0-520-26113-6 (cloth : alk. paper)
        1. Music—History and criticism.   2. Jazz—History and criticism.
I. Title.
    ML60.H4982   2010
    781.6509—dc22   2009038153

Manufactured in the United States of America

19   18   17   16   15   14   13   12   11   10
10   9   8   7   6   5   4   3   2   1

This book is printed on Natures Book, which contains 50% post-consumer waste and meets the minimum requirements of ANSI/NISO Z39.48–1992 (R 1997) (*Permanence of Paper*).

*To the musicians who keep putting new life into mine, and to Mary Francis,
but for whom this book would not have been born—
and to her similarly extraordinary colleagues at University of California Press,
who, in a Duke Ellington phrase, are also "beyond category"*

CONTENTS

FOREWORD

If you've ever had the chance to speak with Nat Hentoff, you won't be surprised to learn that he has a background in radio—he speaks clearly and decisively, with never an "um" or "uhh." As he recounted in a 2007 interview with jazz musician and historian Loren Schoenberg:

> By luck I got into radio. I had worked in a candy store with a guy named Ed Blackman, who later became an announcer before he became a professor of religion, and there was an opening at this radio station. I was a staff announcer. I also covered politics. . . . But I got them to let me do a jazz program on time they couldn't sell [i.e., when they had no sponsors]. That led to my inviting up [Duke] Ellington, Rex Stewart and all those people. [I] got to know them somewhat . . . It was called *The Jazz Album*. . . . A lot of the tapes are now at the University of New Hampshire. . . . A woman, Dorothy Cook, who came to live there, she and her husband had taped the shows.*

Those taped shows must be a gold mine, and reading this collection gives one some of the flavor of what Nat has to offer as a jazz commentator. But before we say more about that, a little background on Nat's life might be in order. Nat was born on June 10, 1925, in Boston, and, as he recounts in his memoir *Boston Boy,* his parents were Russian Jewish immigrants, Simon Hentoff and Lena Katzenberg. His younger sister went to Girls' Latin School. She's now Janet Krauss, a professor at Fairfield University and a published poet. Nat came to New York in 1953 to work as the city's editor of the jazz magazine *Down Beat* until 1957. He has been in Manhattan ever since.

*See www.smithsonianjazz.org/oral_histories/pdf/Hentoff.pdf.

His memoirs are continued, informally (as a collection of stories, rather than as a chronological account), in *Boston Boy* and *Speaking Freely*. As his devoted readers will know, Nat has led another career as a civil libertarian and political reporter. He received his B.A. with highest honors from Northeastern University and did graduate work at Harvard. In 1950, he was a Fulbright Fellow in Paris at the Sorbonne. He has won awards for his coverage of the law and criminal justice in his columns, notably during his fifty-year tenure at the *Village Voice*. In 1985, his alma mater, Northeastern University, awarded him an honorary Doctorate of Laws. We won't list all of his many awards here, but Nat is rightly proud that in 1995 the National Press Foundation gave him their award for lifetime distinguished contributions to journalism.

It was Nat's personal politics that got him into writing about the world of politics. He was fired from *Down Beat* in 1957 for hiring a staff person of color, against the rules of the then owner of the magazine (somewhat shocking to us today, for a magazine about music of black Americans!). It took a few months, into 1958, before he landed another steady job. Again quoting from the interview with Loren Schoenberg, Nat recalls, "So finally a guy from the *[Village] Voice* said, 'We'd like you to do a column.' I said, 'Okay, only on one proviso, that I will not write about jazz.'" Nat insisted on this condition and accepted the offer, even though at first there was no pay, because it allowed him to broaden his purview and reputation as a writer on topics beyond jazz. So began his celebrated career as a political commentator, particularly focused on the First Amendment, the freedom of speech. He stayed at the *Village Voice* for fifty years, until December 2008, when his many readers were shocked to learn that he had been let go, along with other casualties of budget cuts.

But Nat landed on his feet, as they say. In a press release dated February 13, 2009, the Cato Institute welcomed Nat as Senior Fellow, describing him as "one of the foremost authorities on the First Amendment. . . . No American in recent history has done more in defense of free speech and the First Amendment than the great civil libertarian Nat Hentoff. All of us at Cato are honored to have him as a colleague." The Cato Institute is a nonprofit public policy research foundation headquartered in Washington, D.C. The institute is named for *Cato's Letters,* a series of libertarian pamphlets that helped lay the philosophical foundation for the American Revolution. The mission of the Cato Institute is to increase the understanding of public policies based on the principles of limited government, free markets, individual liberty and peace. In his role as a Senior Fellow, Nat continues to write commentaries for the United Media Newspaper Syndicate (which reaches about 250 papers) and is featured in an occasional podcast and video.*

*See www.cato.org/people/nat-hentoff.

Of course, even while at the *Voice,* he had continued to write regularly on jazz for the *Wall Street Journal* and for the *JazzTimes,* as well as for Jazz.com. Many of the pieces in this collection come from the two publications. Nat never attempted to keep separate his interests in jazz and politics. No mature discussion of jazz can avoid the topics of race relations and civil rights, and this collection has a section, "Finding the First Amendment Groove," in which Nat explicitly makes those connections. And during his short but notable career as a record producer, Nat started with Contemporary Records and then was asked by Archie Bleyer (owner of Cadence Records) to create his own jazz label, which Nat named Candid, and which is still celebrated for the uncensored freedom that Nat allowed to such artists as Charles Mingus and Cecil Taylor.

Articles, columns and recordings aside, Nat has also published many books in his two fields of note, but how many readers know that he has also authored a number of books for young readers? Their titles indicate that here, too, his two main interests prevail: he authored *Jazz Country* and *Journey into Jazz,* but also *The Day They Came to Arrest the Book* and *Does This School Have Capital Punishment?* (among others).

Nat is a parent, with two sons and two daughters. (Their activities as of 1997 are recalled in *Speaking Freely.*) Nat's two daughters are from his first marriage. One daughter, Jessica Hentoff, known internationally as "the Circus Lady," is a circus performer, a cofounder of New York's Big Apple Circus and director of Circus Harmony in St. Louis. She organizes innovative multicultural circus projects and has involved, for example, local Jewish and black Muslim children. Her performances include musics from yet more cultures. She is the mother of three home-schooled children who are also talented performers—Elliana, Keaton and Kellin Hentoff-Killian. Quincy Jones entered her into the jazz canon by writing the piece "Jessica's Day" for her. (Nat himself has been immortalized by Ernie Wilkins in "Grooving for Nat" and by Booker Little in "Man of Words.")

Nat's other daughter, Miranda, is a musician—composer, teacher, pianist and singer—and mother to a young daughter, Ruby. She has taught at Juilliard and the Manhattan School of Music (where she earned her Bachelor's and Master's degrees), written themes for *Frontline* and other TV series and taught students of all ages as well as their teachers.*

Nat is currently married to Margot Hentoff, whose writings have long been published in the *Voice* as well as the *New York Review of Books* and other publications. Their two sons are both lawyers. Tom Hentoff is a senior partner at the prestigious firm of Williams and Connolly in Washington, D.C., specializing in

---

*See www.mirandahentoff.com.

intellectual property and, yes, First Amendment law.* Tom's children are named Hugo and Story. Nat's other son, Nick Hentoff, is a criminal defense and civil liberties lawyer who practices in Arizona but is now traveling under the auspices of the American Bar Association's Rule of Law Initiative, teaching lawyers in Kyrgyzstan and expecting to move on from there to other countries. Readers might be surprised to learn that this Hentoff son also has a sharpshooter's designation as a life member of the National Rifle Association (NRA), but, like his father, who is famously pro-life, Nick follows no predictable party line.†

Like many who write about jazz, Nat is not himself a musician, but he played soprano saxophone as a youth and had clarinet lessons as well. As Nat recounts here in "My Debt to Artie Shaw," it was a chance encounter with clarinetist Shaw's music that started him seriously exploring jazz. He compared it with "passionate, mesmerizing, often improvisatory singing of the hazan, the cantor in Orthodox synagogues."

Curiously, cantors figure in the present collection as well. In "Old Country Jewish Blues and Ornette Coleman," Nat notes his surprise upon learning that Coleman was a fan of Yosef "Yossele" Rosenblatt, perhaps the most celebrated cantor of all time. I think he was almost as surprised to learn that my great-aunt Nettie Rosenblatt, who died just before her 101st birthday in October 2005, was the daughter of Yossele. Ornette was impressed as well, and I burned a CD for each of them of some of Rosenblatt's singing. I especially recommend to the reader the 1916 recordings *Omar Rabbi Eleazar* and *V'Lirushalayim Irchu*, which display his amazing range and virtuosic embellishments.

In fact, Nat has retained a powerful Jewish identity. He has called himself "a member of the Proud and Ancient Order of Stiff-Necked Jewish Atheists." And he's not joking about this. Nat is rightly proud of the Jewish intellectual tradition of which he is a part and to which he has contributed mightily. As a Jewish atheist myself, I like to say that atheism is a Jewish choice, just like Reform, Conservative or Orthodox are. In fact, I understand that Jews are more likely to be atheists than any other ethnic group in America, though I haven't seen statistics on this. On this topic, Nat and I have a little inside joke which he won't mind my sharing with you: I was helping him to find a publisher for this collection (though, as it turned out, Mary Francis of University of California Press came to the rescue without my intervention), and in return Nat called me his rabbi!

My name turns up in one of the pieces included here that deal with jazz and race, "Is Jazz Black Music?" so I'd like to say a little more about the event described there. I chose the topic and the guests for this panel for Jazz at Lincoln

---

*See www.wc.com/attorney-ThomasHentoff.html
†For more on Nick Hentoff, see www.citizenlawyer.com.

Center (I led the discussion series entitled "Jazz Talk" from fall 2006 through May 2009)—the other two guests were clarinetist Don Byron, whom I've known on and off since 1978, when he was a student at the New England Conservatory, and Daniel Carter, a multi-instrumentalist (sax, clarinet, trumpet, etc.) who is highly regarded in "free jazz" circles and with whom I've performed on piano a number of times. I got some flak from people who weren't there, because they assumed that I was questioning whether jazz is indeed black music. If they had been there, my comments, some of which are cited by Nat, made it clear that I don't doubt this. The point of asking the question is that there are people (invariably white) who do dispute this, and it's a question that periodically deserves to be discussed and clarified. For example, some non-blacks question this because they assume that to acknowledge it as a black music would mean that they should not, or could not perform it—but none of the panelists felt that that is necessarily an implication of accepting it as black music. On this panel, as in every situation, Nat's wit, wisdom and experience were invaluable. "Stiff-necked" or not (and he's not, really), we're lucky to have him around.

Lewis Porter
Rutgers University, Newark
May 2009

ACKNOWLEDGMENTS

My thanks, most especially, to the musicians here: for their time, friendship and the education they have given me not only about jazz but about life itself.

I am grateful to Eric Gibson, editor of the *Wall Street Journal*'s "Leisure and Arts" section, and his colleagues; Lee Mergner, publisher of *JazzTimes;* Ted Gioia of Jazz.com; Frank Alkyer of *Down Beat* magazine; and Tony Ortega, editor of the *Village Voice,* for permission to include certain profiles in this book that appeared, in their original form, in their publications. Also, Jonathan Kantor of New York's Blue Note jazz club for enabling the television interviews of jazz creators I conducted there. And to Phoebe Jacobs, the embodiment of the jazz spirit.

For many years, my literary agent, Richard Morris (Janklow and Nesbit) has been a continual source of confidence and encouragement. And in memory of my friend, the late Norman Granz, who based his choice of recording artists—including many in this book—not on potential sales figures but on the insistent integrity and life force of their music. Also, to Artie Shaw, who first brought me into the resounding glories of this music.

INTRODUCTION

Cecil Taylor, an exhilaratingly uncategorizable pianist, whom I've known for more than half a century, has said of the musicians who first showed him what he was here for—Duke Ellington, Fats Waller, Chick Webb, Jimmie Lunceford—"They were beacons. There was a way they looked, a way you felt when you heard what they did, that you wanted to become part of. And you *strove* to become a part of it. It's a question of trying to capture that magic in sound, in thought, in feeling, in *being*."

Since the day Artie Shaw's "Nightmare"—from the open door of a record store in Boston—stopped me on the street when I was eleven years old, jazz became a part of me. It still makes me shout aloud in pleasure, as I did then. Or, when I'm so far down nothing else can lift me up, Charles Mingus, Duke, Lester Young, Dizzy Gillespie and so many other carriers of the life force bring me back alive.

I never was a good enough musician (clarinet) to strive to be with them in sound; but first in radio, and then on the typewriter, they became my mentors—in life itself—as well as in the boundless self-discoveries through hearing their music.

It wasn't until I was nineteen, with a jazz program on a Boston radio station, that I got to know them off the stand, even hanging out with sidemen passing through—and, astonishingly, getting Duke Ellington as an occasional mentor. "Never get caught up in categories," he told me. "It's individuals who make the difference."

And his tenor saxophonist, Ben Webster, gave me another lifetime credo: "If the rhythm section ain't making it, go for yourself!"

I came to know many more of these jazz makers when I became New York

1

editor of *Down Beat,* then the leading national jazz magazine, in 1953. Since they were telling their life stories in their music, my interviews with them were about their lives—not the techniques they used and originated in their music. That was for other critics and historians much more versed in that language than I am.

What I've learned from their lives—that became their music—is in much of this book. And although it took me too long to realize the vital creative force of women in jazz—instrumentalists, not only singers—I have focused on the long marginalized, and just plain ignored, women originals at the jazz band ball.

The life force of jazz across the world—resisting banning even within Nazi Germany and Stalin's Russia—energized my day job: from reporting on keeping the Bill of Rights alive here to genocide in Darfur. Another area of reporting I'm increasingly pursuing is that of *individualizing* education in this country—in the schools and in the public square—to enable more of us to know why we're Americans, each with the fundamental right to be as free in our beliefs and expressions as the jazz originals in this book.

There is a connection. Max Roach once showed me the interaction between jazz and the Constitution. He was teaching at the University of Massachusetts at the time, and between classes he told me: "What we do musically as we tell our stories is based on each individual's listening intently to one another, and thereby creating a whole experience that has its own identity. Isn't that how we and the Constitution are supposed to work together?"

Those of us who are musicians and lifetime listeners to jazz remember how the first discovery of this music, at whatever age, was so exciting and self-enlarging, that we had to become part of it.

This happened to a number of fifth graders in Sarasota, Florida, when the Jazz Club of Sarasota convinced the city's public school system to teach fifth graders American history simultaneously with the history of jazz. As far as I can find out, and I keep searching, no other school system has connected these currents of the American experience.

Chronicling this swinging approach to educational reform—in "Jazz Links: Jazz Connections to History"—for the *Wall Street Journal* in 2001 and in the years since—I found that at its beginnings some 2,500 Sarasota fifth graders in twenty elementary schools—in both the regular fifth-grade classrooms and the music classrooms—were learning from recordings and visiting jazz musicians.

Said Denise Roberts, managing director of the Venice Foundation, one of the initial funders of the program, "I have never seen children so engaged by a program. The material that teachers were trying to get across was alien to these kids. The Jim Crow laws might as well have been in place centuries ago instead of just decades ago as far as these kids knew, but the music brought it all together for them."

And fifth-grade teacher Fran Valencic reported: "As a classroom teacher, I learned so much I didn't realize about our history. My students and I also came to love the music. Some of the boys and girls decided to form small jazz bands of their own. Every student in this class was either in the band or in the chorus."

A social studies lesson, as described in the curriculum, "traces the great migration of African Americans from the South to the North through the art of painter Jacob Lawrence and the development of 'urban' jazz."

My great hope is that in other cities around the land, these links will be reverberatingly explored in middle and high schools, as well as in elementary school. In a fourth-grade class in New York City, I once played a vintage New Orleans jazz recording by George Lewis's band, and the kids started dancing. Soon the teacher joined in.

Jazz, of course, is hardly the only way to make our history, including the Bill of Rights, come alive in schools. Years ago, I both witnessed and was a part of the surge of excitement as a large assembly of high school students in Miami discovered America.

It was at a book fair in that city, and authors had to perform for publicity. Since my newly published book was *Living the Bill of Rights* (since republished by University of California Press) I was asked to speak to these black, white and Hispanic students. Just as I was about to go on stage, one of their teachers whispered to me, "Don't be disappointed. They won't be interested in what you say. All they really care about is music and books."

For about an hour I told them stories about why we have a Constitution and some of the many battles there have been by We the People to get various presidential administrations to keep it fully alive. I brought back Samuel Adams and his Sons of Liberty who, before the American Revolution and before the Internet, created the Committees of Correspondence that spread the word around the colonies about the British forces' "general search warrant" that in Boston turned the colonists' homes and offices—and these Americans themselves—upside down in search of contrabands.

From that news soon came the Fourth Amendment to our Constitution to safeguard our privacy. I also told them that hearing of the Committees of Correspondence, Thomas Jefferson and Patrick Henry—at a secret meeting in a tavern in Williamsburg, Virginia—started their own branch of the Committees of Correspondence.

And I told them about the struggles through the centuries to keep our freedom of the press and the right to talk back to our government officials (including going to court against public high school principals who censor student newspapers).

After I finished my journey through what makes us the freest nation on earth—though we have to keep battling to keep it free—I received a standing ovation. Not because I was so eloquent; but, having in most cases heard these stories for the first time, these students had discovered why they were Americans.

As for those fifth graders in Sarasota, who already know much more than I could pack into an hour, I was thinking of the impact of jazz on them when I was at Louis Armstrong's home in Queens, New York, when it was dedicated officially in 2003. The crowds outside included kids from the neighborhood elementary and middle schools (both named for Louis Armstrong) and listeners and musicians throughout this country and around the world.

Suddenly, above us on the balcony next to the room where Louis used to listen to music, tape record his conversations, write letters and fill his scrapbooks, Jon Faddis suddenly appeared with his trumpet. Thrillingly—I use the word literally—he serenaded us with Louis's choruses on "West End Blues."

Then he told all of us—of all ages and backgrounds—a story of why we were there. In 1953, there was a ruthless civil war in Africa's Belgian Congo. Suddenly the leaders of both armies suspended hostilities. They had just heard that Louis Armstrong had been booked for a concert in a city in the Congo that was away from the battlegrounds. They wanted to hear those glorious sounds and stopped the fighting until he left.

I had to tell the story again in this book because it reminded me of when I was fourteen and heard Ruby Braff (a kid a year younger than I) play his cornet. Young as he was, he was telling a pure jazz story. We became lifelong friends when Ruby began to play professionally, winning a New Star competition where he won Louis Armstrong's vote, and eventually he turned into an international jazz star.

"You see," Ruby used to tell me, "I went to the Louis Armstrong University, from which you never graduate." I am also a fellow perpetual student there, still learning about music and life from such faculty members as Duke Ellington, Lester Young, Clark Terry and Billie Holiday.

To get further into the jazz scene, I've also produced jazz recordings—not just reviewed them. Among those I made for the Contemporary and then for the Candid labels were sessions by Willie "The Lion" Smith (a mentor of Duke Ellington, Fats Waller and, late in his life, me), Charles Mingus, Booker Little, Cecil Taylor, Abbey Lincoln, Pee Wee Russell and Coleman Hawkins, blues bards Otis Spann, Lightning Hopkins and Memphis Slim, and Max Roach directing his "Freedom Now Suite," quickly banned in apartheid South Africa.

Since making a living is part of the lives of the players, I've been investigating for years the business practices of the jazz life—including the predatory nature of some of the club owners, booking agents and record company executives. An essential corollary focus for me continues to be on the often bleak autumnal years of sidemen whose names are known internationally and are still being featured on the abundance of reissue recordings. Since most of these aging players often did not receive royalties from subsequent recordings—and were nearly always paid in cash for their club gigs—they usually have no medical insurance or pensions. They try to survive, usually alone and vulnerable, in their "barren days" (see chapter 49).

I regard these forgotten lives as an important part of living jazz history, overlooked in many of the books on the music. Accordingly, I have continually written about the Jazz Foundation of America, based in New York, which takes care of musicians in need—paying their rent, providing food, finding gigs and enabling them to obtain free medical care, including surgery, at the Englewood Hospital and Medical Center in New Jersey.

It was there that Dizzy Gillespie—one of the most caring people I've ever known—while dying of cancer, asked his doctor "to make sure there's going to be care for musicians who can't afford what I'm getting." And so it came to be.

At the Jazz Band Ball encompasses many dimensions of the jazz life I've witnessed and reported—including the remnants of racism in its economics and a period, not entirely gone, of reverse racism, as when Miles Davis was sharply criticized by some black musicians for hiring white pianist Bill Evans.

"I don't care if he's purple with green polka dots," Miles told me, "so long as he can play."

Unlike some writers on this music, I am not pessimistic about whether there will be enough committed listeners in future generations. New listeners, and the emerging players among them, are being nurtured in schools, including elementary and middle schools, and, most important, in colleges and music schools, where an increasing number of jazz elders are teaching eyewitness jazz history.

Also broadening and deepening the reach of future American and international audiences and musicians is the vision—explored in this book—of Adrian Ellis, the primary force, along with Wynton Marsalis, at the New York-based Jazz at Lincoln Center.

The profiles of musicians at this jazz band ball, including when they're not on the stand, have not appeared previously in book form, and they have been updated when based on previous versions in such publications as the *Wall Street Journal* and *JazzTimes*.

Key parts of this book have not appeared anywhere else. Among the new essays is one on how deeply my life has been affected and shaped in the company of players who to me, as a youngster, were larger than life—or at least larger than the lives of the other adults I knew, with the exception of my father, Simon, whose generosity of spirit was as deep as Dizzy Gillespie's.

In my day job as a writer on the law, politics, civil liberties, civil rights and human rights around the world, I've gotten to know well a range of singular people who, as Henry David Thoreau put it, march to their own drum—from a Supreme Court Justice (William Brennan) to Malcolm X, New York's John Cardinal O'Connor and high school journalists learning, against formidable odds, to practice the First Amendment by defying principals and school boards.

But by and large, I have most enjoyed the company of these musicians who put their lives, memories and expectations into the penetrating immediacy of their music, which often stays in the mind long after being played.

Listening to Dixieland bands long ago, one of my favorite joyous songs was "At the Jazz Band Ball," where there was always an open invitation. My life would have been so much poorer had I not been a continual participant in this grooving jazz scene.

The nonpareil country music singer and composer Merle Haggard, who knows a lot about jazz and plays it when the audience is right, once told me: "There are times when I'm so far down that nothing can lift me up—except music." That's what jazz has always done for me. My intent and hope are that this book will lead you to experience more of the signature sounds and stories of these spirit forces, as Cecil Taylor calls them, who keep reaching into so many lives all over the world.

One of my sources when I need reviving is pianist Hank Jones, now in his nineties. His sound and touch are like the first day of spring. I once told him that, as often as I've heard him play some of the songs in his repertory, it's always as if I'm hearing them for the first time.

"There's always something new to explore in music," he told me. "That's why every night, I begin again." Like life itself.

PART ONE

What Am I Here For?

The Rules of My Jazz Odyssey

1 | Who Owns Jazz?

Clark Terry, a vital presence for so much of jazz history, is one of the most unswervingly honest and truly democratic persons I've ever had the privilege of knowing—in and outside of jazz. There is a story he tells that illuminates his continuous involvement as an educator, in and out of the classroom, in helping to form new generations of jazz musicians.

For Clark's story, I am indebted to Hank O'Neal—another multiple influence on the jazz scene as record producer at Chiaroscuro, photographer, educator and historian. In 1997, the French publisher Editions Filipacchi released O'Neal's book *The Ghosts of Harlem*. An English edition will eventually be available, but O'Neal was kind enough to give me the following quotes from Clark.

In the 1970s, Terry worked in Harlem with his own seventeen-piece band at the Club Baron. "It just so happens that it was about half and half, blacks and whites," Clark said. "One night, three black Mafia guys, Black Muslims with guns, come into the club, corner me and said, 'What are you doing playing with all these whities in Harlem?' I'm a little bit frightened, but I know I've got to be stern, so I say, 'I think you're aware of the fact that Harlem has always been responsible for great jazz, big-band jazz, individual jazz, and that's been missing from the scene for a number of years. I feel it's my duty to bring big bands back to Harlem. I just choose the best musicians I can find and I don't listen with my eyes.'"

The Black Muslims seemed to be getting the message. One of them said, "Well, we got a kid here, a little black kid, and he wants to play and we want to hear him play."

Clark nodded and said, "That's OK. I've spent half my life making it possible for young musicians to be heard, so we'll bring him up at the beginning of the set and turn him loose." Lew Soloff had the trumpet chair and Clark asked him to let the kid sit in. "I kicked it off with a medium-tempo tune by Chris Woods," Clark continued. "A very simple tune, very easy to play on, nice changes."

Immediately, the kid started to solo, but Clark stopped the music. "It's when we get down to letter D is when you solo," he told the kid. "Before that, you play with the rest of us. At letter D, you can play along."

"I just wanted to express myself," the youngster said. Terry kicked the music off again, and the kid came in wrong again. "Express your ass off my stage," Clark told him.

"When we came off," Terry said, "I went straight up to the cats with the three guns and said, 'Now you see what you've done! You brought a dude up here and you stuck your necks out to represent this dude to do something that he's not qualified to do. He's not prepared. He didn't do his homework. He can't read music!'" One of the Black Muslims, in what Clark remembers as "a low grumbly voice," said: "Well, the son of a bitch didn't tell us that."

Terry didn't swear off working with kids, however. "Before the Jazzmobile started uptown, I gathered a lot of little kids out of Harlem and took them to a rehearsal studio on 125th Street," Clark said. "I bought some of these kids instruments and we rehearsed all the time. Then we got to use the facilities at Manhattan College, a real university atmosphere. When I couldn't be there, Ernie Wilkins or Kenny Dorham would take my place. We'd hire whoever was competent, black or white, to teach the kids.

"One time when I'd been away for a while, I came back and the attendance was down to almost nothing. One of the students had persuaded all the others not to respond to help from Caucasians. I confronted the kids, and finally one of them said: 'We don't want whitey trying to teach us about our music.'

"I said, 'You've got all the facilities of a college student here, and all the possibilities of learning anything you could learn in college—and you'd let bigotry come before that? OK, if that's what you cats are about, you got it. See you later.'

"And that was the end of that. I just walked away from all of it. We'd had to teach a lot of those kids how to read music, but attitude, bigotry, killed it."

But later Billy Taylor encouraged Terry to do clinics, and Clark obliged: "I became more and more involved, imparting knowledge, sometimes just relating my experiences."

Once, in Seattle, playing with Count Basie's small group, Clark was approached by a "little kid who came in, said he was learning to play trumpet and also wrote music, and asked if he could take some lessons from me. We worked it out so he could come in for a couple of hours—like 6 o'clock or so in the morning before he went to school—and before I went to bed.

"I couldn't dare to say no to this kid. I shudder to think what would have happened if I had said no. I never would have forgiven myself. I gave him all kinds of lessons I knew how to give him. I worked with him on his writing, theory and harmony. The kid stayed involved. Look at him now."

The kid was Quincy Jones. On the new Chiaroscuro CD *Clark Terry and the Young Titans of Jazz,* recorded at the Twenty-ninth International Jazz Festival Bern in Switzerland, the band is composed of musicians (aged seventeen to forty-four) from around the world, all of whom have been Clark's students. The drummer, Marcus Gilmore, is Roy Haynes's grandson. In the notes, Quincy Jones says: "Keep on keepin' on, Cee Tee. There will never, ever be another you."

2 | My Debt to Artie Shaw

If it hadn't been for Artie Shaw, I might not be writing about jazz here (or any other place). When I was eleven years old, walking down a street in Boston, I heard music coming out of a record store that made me shout aloud in excited pleasure. I rushed in, demanding, "What is that?" Artie Shaw's "Nightmare," I was told. Before then, the only music that had affected me so viscerally was the passionate, mesmerizing, often improvisatory singing of the hazan, the cantor in Orthodox synagogues on the High Holiday days. The hazan sounded at times as if he were arguing with God, and the depth of his witnessing to the human condition later connected me with black blues.

In the definitive Artie Shaw collection, *Self Portrait* (RCA Victor/Bluebird), Richard Sudhalter says that "Nightmare" is "a keening, almost cantorial melody in A minor, as different musically from the theme songs of his bandleading colleagues as Shaw was different from them personally and temperamentally." I think I remember Shaw himself saying that he based the piece on an actual cantorial theme. As he said in the *Self Portrait* set, "Certainly I can't deny the influence of my Russian-Jewish-Austrian ancestry."

Orrin Keepnews, the master orchestrater of reissues, is responsible for *Self Portrait,* for which Shaw made the selections from every band he ever led. He included airchecks, which he felt were truer to what he had in mind than studio recordings. Keepnews writes that when Shaw and Benny Goodman were rivals, "You had to make a choice. . . . You were either for Artie Shaw or [for] Benny Goodman." Back then, and even now, I get into arguments when I claim that while Goodman surely could swing and was a superb technician, Artie Shaw surpassed him in the range of his imagination and the exhilaration he conveyed of continually expecting more of himself and his horn.

As Matt Snyder once wrote of the clarinetist, "Shaw's playing was on a consistently higher level linearly and harmonically [than Goodman's]. . . . Of all the big band leaders, Shaw may have been the most musically gifted." I was pleased to see in the *New York Times* obituary, written and archived long ago by the late John S. Wilson, that clarinetist Barney Bigard, who brought a New Orleans sound to the Duke Ellington Orchestra, regarded Shaw as the greatest clarinetist ever, and that alto saxophonist Phil Woods models his clarinet playing on Shaw's.

At eleven, I was taking clarinet lessons assiduously from an alumnus of the Boston Symphony, but hearing what Shaw could say and sing on that instrument led me into the liberating sounds and rhythms of jazz. It was during the Depression, and working as an errand boy on a horse-drawn fruit wagon, I was able to buy 78s of Basie, Duke, Bessie Smith and Shaw at a cost of three for a dollar. Years later, when I was New York editor of *Down Beat,* Artie Shaw would call me from time to time to discuss not only my limitless deficiencies as a jazz critic but also all manner of things, from politics and literature to other things that came within his wide-ranging interests. As soon as he was on the line, I knew that for the next hour or so my role was to listen. It was hard to get a word or two in. (Interviewing Benny Goodman was different. Cautious, he would often deflect a question by asking, "What do you think?")

What I admired about Shaw was that he exemplified what Ben Webster once told me when I was still in Boston: "If the rhythm section isn't making it, go for yourself." Artie Shaw refused to let himself be limited, even by success. After he first quit the music scene in 1939, walking off the bandstand at the Café Rouge of the Hotel Pennsylvania in New York, he said: "I wanted to resign from the planet, not just music. It stopped being fun with success. Money got in the way. Everybody got greedy—including me. Fear set in. I got miserable when I became a commodity." In 1954, at forty-three, he left for good and never again performed.

He turned to writing and an array of other interests because his curiosity about how much one could learn about learning never flagged. As he said in the notes to *Self Portrait,* "I'm not comfortable with categories, and I distrust most definitions. The word definition is based on the word finite, which would seem to indicate that once we've defined something, we don't need to think about it anymore."

On January 7, 2005, the National Endowment for the Arts declared Artie Shaw a Jazz Master. I sure would have liked to hear his acceptance speech. It wouldn't have been humble. He knew his worth, and then some. In a 1978 *Washington Post* interview, he said: "I don't care if I'm forgotten. I became a specialist in nonspecialization a long time ago. For instance, I'm an expert fly fisherman. And in 1962, I ranked fourth nationally in precision riflery. My music? Well, no point in false modesty about that. I was the best."

Shaw died, at the age of ninety-four, on December 30, 2004, but his music will continue to reverberate. I can't forget him because he brought me into the music that has given me ceaseless reason to shout aloud in pleasure.

3 | The Family of Jazz

Years ago, I took my daughter, Miranda, to a rehearsal of Count Basie alumni the morning of a Carnegie Hall tribute to their former leader. Some of the musicians were in their sixties and seventies. As is usual in the jazz life, most had not seen each other for some time and greeted each other warmly, jocularly, and started riffing on the times, good and bad, they'd had together.

Among the musicians was drummer Gus Johnson, whose crisply elegant riding of "the rhythm wave," as Basie's guitarist Freddie Green used to call it, has never gotten the fullness of recognition he deserved. And Harry "Sweets"

Edison, who captured Miranda's attention when—as the band ran down one of the arrangements for the evening—he stopped the music and turned his score back to the arranger. "Too many notes," Sweets said. I later told Miranda what Dizzy Gillespie had said to me not long before: "It's taken me all my life to know what not to play."

My daughter, though young, was already working gigs as a pianist and singer of her own songs. But she'd never been in the company of some of jazz's vintage creators. After several hours we left, and Miranda said to me, "I've never seen such love among musicians before."

The family-like love happened again in January in New York at the International Association for Jazz Education's Annual Conference when Dana Gioia, chairman of the National Endowment for the Arts (NEA), hosted an NEA Jazz Masters Luncheon. Around the table were musicians I hadn't seen for a long time: Benny Golson, Chico Hamilton, George Russell, Dave Brubeck, Randy Weston and Roy Haynes. And some I'd only talked to briefly during the years: Clark Terry and Jimmy Heath.

It was reunion for most of them too. They swapped stories of illusory royalties from record dates and, more glowingly, shared vivid memories of their idols. Randy Weston spoke of being a young man in the imperial presence of Willie "The Lion" Smith. Dave Brubeck and I traded stories about Paul Desmond, who was one of the most lyrical, witty, ironic and luminous melodic improvisers in the history of the music.

I told Dave of the crush Paul and I had on Audrey Hepburn and how we once waited, without success, just to look at her at a stage door. I never met her, nor did Paul, but he wrote the song "Audrey" for her. After she died, someone close to her said she played that recording very often. Paul never knew that.

At that NEA luncheon Roy Haynes told me, "When I was a kid, I used to listen to your jazz program on the radio." Roy is three months older than I am, but I started in radio when I was in my teens.

I returned the favor and told him and the others at our table about the first time I heard Roy. At one of the Sunday jam sessions at the Savoy, a jazz room in Boston, this kid, who couldn't have been more than seventeen or eighteen, asked to sit in on drums. He was going to Roxbury Memorial High School, near where I lived. As I remember, clarinetist Edmond Hall as well as other jazz pros were on the stand, and this was the first time I'd seen a high school student dare to be in such company. The young Roy Haynes, with crackling confidence, riveted everyone's attention and finished to a roar of applause.

As a reporter, I've gotten to know political figures, criminal defense lawyers, some of their clients, judges, even a Supreme Court justice. But I'd rather be in the company of jazz musicians, especially at reunions when the past comes alive again. Toward the end of his book *Myself Among Others: My Life in Music,* George

Wein speaks of "the humanity" of jazz players, whose "feeling for communication transcends the music and becomes part of their personal life."

The strangest story I know about how jazz makes the most different people into a sort of family was told to me long ago in Paris by Charles Delaunay, the standard-setter for jazz discographers and the creator of *Jazz Hot* magazine (many of whose stories and interviews ought to be anthologized). During World War II, working under cover in Paris for the Free French, Charles was picked up by the Gestapo and taken in for interrogation. As the questioning was about to start, an SS officer looked hard at Delaunay and referred accusingly to a Fletcher Henderson record from the 1920s. "You didn't have all the right personnel on that date," he said to Charles. Delauney was not held for long.

However, if any jazz person ends up in a tough spot with the secret police in Zimbabwe, China or Cuba, he or she oughtn't count on the jazz family ties being that helpful again. But those ties can be powerful. Jo Jones told me of a legendary Kansas City drummer, Baby Lovett, who, when his wife died, grieved so hard that he stayed home and stopped functioning. Jo canceled all of his gigs for a month, flew back to Kansas City, moved in with Baby Lovett and brought him back to life.

The music becomes a deep, regenerating part of the lives of all of us who can't stop listening to this family.

4 | Beyond the Process

The only negative review I've seen so far of my book *American Music Is* (Da Capo, 2004) was by Don Heckman in the July 4, 2004, *Los Angeles Times Book Review*. He titled it "Grabbing Music by the Tale." I'm grateful because Heckman got exactly right why I have presumed, all of these years, to write about this music that never ceases to be a large part of my life.

"More often," Heckman wrote, summing up the book, "Hentoff's worthy perceptions are swallowed up in his emphasis on the personality of the artist rather than on the process. . . . Lost along the way are the musically knowledgeable insights that gave such credibility to his early influential writing about jazz."

Actually, from the beginning, my emphasis has been on the person rather than the process. I began a 1961 book, *The Jazz Life* (reprinted in 1975 by Da Capo), with what W. H. Auden said of music in "In Praise of Limestone": "It can be made anywhere, is invisible, and does not smell."

But, I wrote under that epigraph: "Music is made by men who are insistently visible, especially as in jazz, when the players are their music. . . . Through telling something of where they came from and how they live, I hope their music, too, has become less disembodied."

In truth, although I studied harmony briefly and clarinet much longer before I began writing about the music, I'm not at all qualified to analyze "the process" as, for example, Gunther Schuller does so impressively. Yet as Gunther reminded me recently, when Thelonious Monk first began to record, a number of critics very knowledgeable about "the process" largely regarded him as exotic, hard to label and difficult. But in *Down Beat,* where I wrote many of the record reviews, I kept trying to indicate how joyously and challengingly original he was as a pianist and composer.

I heard Monk in clubs but also got to know him—as well as his wife, Nellie, so essential to his life, and therefore his music—in his apartment. Monk, usually known for his silences, would speak to me at length about where he came from and where he wanted to go in his life and music. In writing about what he said, I think I may have helped listeners go more deeply into the music. And, as Gunther noted, I helped Monk's record sales.

Still, I sometimes felt fraudulent because I couldn't describe what chords or inversions someone was playing. This disquiet intensified one day when my younger daughter, beginning a professional career as a pianist and composer, said accusingly: "How can you dare affect the income of a musician when you give him bad reviews since you can't say technically what you think he's doing wrong?"

Brooding about this while walking on the street one day, I saw Gil Evans coming toward me. I'd known him since interviewing him when he was arranging for Claude Thornhill. I decided to make Gil my rabbi, and told him what my daughter had said.

"I've been reading you for years," Gil began, "so I know what you listen to and how you listen. I also know musicians who can tell technically everything that's going on in a performance, but they don't get into where this music is coming from inside the musician—the story he wants to tell. You can do that some of the time. Stop worrying."

I didn't stop worrying, but I felt better. And I remembered when I was not yet 20 and plunged into Beethoven's late quartets, I was also reading about the discords in his life. I couldn't tell you then, or now, about the "process" of that galvanizing music, but knowing something of the life that Beethoven was impelled to put into his music deepened what I got out of it for my life.

As I've written before, John Coltrane would ask me not to write the liner notes for his albums because, he'd say, "If the music can't speak for itself, what's the use?" But since he was a kind man and knew I had this gig, he'd talk at length with me for the notes. He never got into "the process." Instead, he spoke of his constant search for meaning, for connections between his life and the cosmos. And about how widely he listened to all kinds of music of other cultures to expand his horizons.

That's what I wrote about Coltrane—not about "the process."

Also, as a writer on this music, I'm indebted to Don Ayler for what he told me long ago: "Become part of the whole. Don't fix on the parts: the chords, the rhythms, the timbres." And Duke Ellington: "I don't want people listening to how my music is made. I want them to open themselves as they hear it."

I've written about Duke a lot, including what he told me about being a black man in America. All he'd tell me about "the process" was how he wrote the parts for each person in the orchestra. "I know their strengths," he'd say. I do not in the least undervalue those who write about "the process." Within my limited capacity in that regard, I learn from them. But if my work is to have any value, it comes from what Charlie Parker said: "Music is your own experience, your thoughts, your wisdom. If you don't live it, it won't come out of your horn."

What I keep trying to do is learn and write about those lives because they're in the music. Gary Giddins once accurately and generously characterized what I do. He said I'm "a chronicler." Critics who can authentically describe the structure of the music know more about "the process" than I do. I want to know the musicians, and my life is fuller for having known so many. Duke said in one of his songs, "What am I here for?" I can answer that.

5 | Playing Changes on Jazz Interviews

I expect that if anything I've written about this music lasts, it will be the interviews I've done with the musicians for more than fifty years. My books on jazz consist mainly of interviews, as do the liner notes I've written. My hope is that some of them become part of jazz histories. And I learn a great deal from interviews done by others—particularly by the actual makers of this music.

For example, the late Art Taylor, an extraordinary drummer, wrote a book, *Notes and Tones: Musician-to-Musician Interviews* (Da Capo, 2004). The late tenor saxophonist Don Byas (much underestimated, these days) told Taylor of advice from his friend Art Tatum. Tatum said to Byas: "Just remember there is no such thing as a wrong note; what makes it wrong is when you don't know where to go after that one."

I was reminded of that after a recording session I'd made with Coleman Hawkins and Pee Wee Russell. Hawkins, pointing to Pee Wee, said to me: "Way back, musicians used to say he played weird, funny notes. They weren't funny or weird then, and they're not now. He makes them the right notes."

And Dizzy Gillespie told Art Taylor that he once rebuked drummer Teddy Stewart, telling him: "You're supposed to inspire the soloist." Unintimidated, Stewart told Dizzy: "Have you ever thought that the soloist is supposed to inspire me?"

"It's true," Dizzy told interviewer Taylor.

Currently, some of the most extensive and durably illuminating interviews are by Eric Nemeyer, a vibist, marimba player, drummer, pianist and composer who has worked with Sonny Stitt, Jon Faddis, Jimmy Heath and many more. He also publishes the quarterly *Jazz Improv Magazine* and its valuable monthly, *Jazz Improv's New York Jazz Guide*. Among his interviews in both magazines was one with Wynton Marsalis in which Marsalis defined the rare essence of enduring teaching—not only teaching jazz. (I wish I'd had it in mind when I used to teach journalism.)

Marsalis, who has had private students and is a veteran of many clinics, told Nemeyer: "The most important thing you can do is to empower another person to be themselves—even if what they're going to do is going to be the opposite of what you do . . . you don't want to teach them a dogma . . . you're a part of their story. A lot of times you [as a teacher] look at them as if they're a part of your story. You [should] try to empower them with tools to do what they want to do."

And in *Jazz Improv Magazine,* there was a very long, absorbing interview with bassist Buster Williams, about whom Richard Cook says in his *Jazz Encyclopedia* (Penguin, 2007) that he tends to make every performance a matchless master class. Said Williams: "A piece of music is alive. It's a misnomer to limit yourself by saying it has a beginning and an end. . . .

"Benny Golson has rewritten 'I Remember Clifford' many times. I've played it with him over the years in all its different forms. And Wayne Shorter says a piece of music never ends."

Or, as Clark Terry told me about Duke Ellington: "He wants life and music to be always in a state of becoming. He doesn't even like definitive song endings to a piece. He'd often ask us to come up with the ideas for closings, but when he'd settled on one of them, he'd keep fooling with it. He always likes to make the end of a song sound as if it's still going somewhere."

The late Whitney Balliett, a writer on jazz, was known internationally for his ability to transmute seamlessly the sounds of music into words. (It's inexplicable that *New Yorker* editor David Remnick, a superior journalist, effectively banished Whitney from the magazine. The publication's legendary editor William Shawn knew better, but he played jazz piano.)

Balliett was an attentively skillful interviewer, as in his profile of Pee Wee Russell. There were nights when Russell was the most original improviser in jazz, so much so that his colleagues on the stand would wonder how he could possibly come up with anything like a logical ending to one of his solos. I knew Russell, but in our conversations I never found out what was in his mind during those perilous journeys. Whitney was able to do so.

"You take each solo," Russell told him, "like it was the last one you were going to play in your life. Sometimes I jump the right chord and use what seems wrong to the next guy, but I know is right for me. I usually think about four bars ahead what I'm going to play. Sometimes things go wrong and I have to scramble, but if I can make it to the bridge of the tune, I know everything will be all right." Then the clarinetist made a statement that was, for me, very illuminating: "In lots of cases, your solo depends on who you're following. The guy played a great chorus... [and you think,] how am I going to follow that? Not jealousy, mind you. A kind of competition. . . . What the hell? I'll try something new. All this goes through your mind in a split second. You start and if it sounds good to you, you keep it up and write a little tune of your own."

Of all the interviews with musicians that I've done, there is one with Duke Ellington that has been a guide for me, not only in writing about music but in everything else I write and do. Ellington taught me to avoid categorizing anything:

"The other night I heard a cat on the radio, and he was talking about 'modern' jazz. So he played a record to illustrate his point, and there were devices in that music I heard cats using in the 1920s. These large words like 'modern' don't mean anything. Everybody who's had anything to say in this music—all the way back— has been an individualist... I listen for those individualists. Like Sidney Bechet, Louis Armstrong, Coleman Hawkins and like Charlie Parker was."

As I've told my children, who are now no longer children, I've learned a lot from talking to jazz musicians about life, which is where their music came from.

PART TWO

In the Presence of Ellington

6 | Inside the Ellington Band

Ruby Braff used to say that when he was very young, he entered the Louis Armstrong University, an educational institution from which you could never graduate because there was so much to learn. Duke Ellington's sidemen—those who stayed and those who left—felt the same way. And now, in the Jazz Oral History Project of Mark Masters's American Jazz Institute (at Claremont McKenna College, Pasadena, California), a reunion of Ellington alumni provides further illumination of what it was like to be inside that band where, as I've written, Clark Terry told me the music was always in a state of becoming.

"I think," says trombonist Walter van de Leur about the arrangements of Duke and his alter ego, Billy Strayhorn, "what made the music sound so very special was that you could be the second trombone and have the evening of your life." Another trombonist, Art Baron, adds that in all the other bands he played in, "I felt like anybody could sit in that chair." But the way Duke and Strayhorn wrote, "it really mattered what your personality was. You had to have an individual sound in your horn."

In Stanley Crouch's book *Considering Genius: Writings on Jazz* (Basic Books, 2007)—which will have a permanent place in the canon of jazz criticism—Stanley recalls Ellington's saying that "when he heard a particular note, he always had to decide whose note it should be."

"A man's sound," Duke explained to me long ago, "is his total personality. I hear that sound as I prepare to write, and that's how I am able to write." Accordingly, as Stanley Crouch continues, "A given note in Ellington's three-trombone section could have at least as many different colors as players."

And during the American Jazz Institute reunion, Art Baron, citing Billy Strayhorn's arrangement of the standard "Laura," says that playing second trombone on that arrangement "feels amazing. You feel vibrations in your body. It wasn't just a note. I heard a story." And Art Baron was in that story.

For all the individualized care that Duke put into his writing, once the music came alive, adds drummer Dave Black, "[o]f all the bandleaders I have worked for, he was very free—letting you play your way, your style. I remember one night we were playing 'Rockin' in Rhythm' and I just got the bug. I played it as Latin 6/8, and he loved it. I felt like a million-dollar star. When the set finishes, he said, 'That's it. When you feel something, just go for it. That the way to do it.'"

Black's comments remind me of how the 1957 CBS television show *The Sound of Jazz*—on which Whitney Balliett and I worked—so rivetingly captured the immediacy of this music, such that being part of that show was the most important thing I've ever done. With Count Basie, Billie Holiday, Lester Young, Coleman Hawkins, Jo Jones, Thelonious Monk et al. in the studio, the producer, Robert Herridge—who insisted the hour be live television with no editing—told the cameramen essentially what Duke Ellington told Dave Black: "When you get a shot you want, pay no attention to the control room, go for it! And if that shot includes another camera, so what? The musicians are the set!" With the cameras improvising along with the musicians, Herridge let nothing interrupt the life stories of the musicians. And in the control room, when Billie Holiday and Lester Young looked into each other's eyes during "Fine and Mellow," there were tears in all our eyes at the wonder of being in the presence of such searching intimacy.

But conflict—interpersonal conflict—is also part of making this ·music. Ellington alumnus Herb Jeffries, during the reunion, tells of Ben Webster bursting into Duke Ellington's dressing room between shows "with the most violent language you can imagine" as he thrust a telegram at Duke, "who was powdering himself with a big powder puff." Ben, furious at not having gotten a raise when, he thought, everybody else had, roared at Duke: "Take a look at this telegram I just got from Benny Goodman. He wants me to join the band and pay me [more than he was getting from Duke]."

"So," Herb Jeffries remembers, "Ellington, still powdering himself, said, 'I don't want to see it. If it's that good, I'd advise you to take it.'" Ben Webster later left the band, much to his subsequent regret because there was no university—or rather, jazz universe—like it.

Louis Bellson tells of the unique allure of working with Ellington. Juan Tizol had left Ellington's band to join Harry James's group, with whom Bellson and Willie Smith were working. Bellson recalls, "One time Duke called Juan and said, 'I understand you got a young drummer there and Willie Smith. Why don't you three guys come and join the band? You're only working one or two nights [a week] with Harry James. Come and have some fun.' So all three of us went to Harry James and said, 'Harry, we got a chance to join Duke Ellington.' And he looked at all three of us, and said, 'Take me with you.' That's one of the joys of my whole life—to work with Duke Ellington."

Just knowing Duke was one of the joys of my life. One night, the band was on, but he hadn't come in yet. Standing at the door of the club, I felt a hand on my shoulder, then heard his magisterial voice. (Duke was also a master of the put-on.) "You don't know who I am, but I know who you are." I felt I had been knighted.

7 | Duke Ellington's Posthumous Revenge

Long ago, I worked part-time at a Boston radio station that mostly played what its announcers solemnly called "serious music"—Bach, Beethoven, Bartók and other such cats. That reverential term was common around the country on such stations. On the air, I refused to categorize only European-derived classical music as "serious"—as if Armstrong, Ellington, Basie and Billie Holiday were only transient forms of impermanent cult music.

In 1965, the three-man music jury of the Pulitzer Prizes decided, for the first time, to acknowledge Duke Ellington as a somewhat serious composer, awarding him a token award "for the vitality and originality for his total work product." But the governing board of the Pulitzer Prizes overturned this rather superficial deviation from the Pulitzer canons. Two members of the music jury resigned in protest, but Duke told the press with his customary public silken graciousness: "Fate is being kind to me. Fate doesn't want me to be too famous too young."

He was sixty-six years old.

I spoke with Duke the next night, and he was furious. "I'm hardly surprised," he said, "that my music is still without official honor at home. Most Americans still take it for granted that European-based—classical music, if you will—is the only really respectable kind. By and large, in this country, jazz has always been the kind of man you wouldn't want your daughter to associate with."

It wasn't until 1997 that a jazz composition achieved "respectability" and the Pulitzer board anointed Wynton Marsalis's "Blood on the Fields," a three-hour oratorio with a cast of fourteen musicians and three singers. With respect to Wynton—and I mean that because he keeps growing not only as a musician but also as an educator and composer—that composition does not measure up to Ellington, Mingus and Monk. But at least the Pulitzer door was partly opened.

In 1998, the Pulitzer arbiters of musical worth awarded the deceased Duke Ellington a special citation to commemorate the centennial of his birth. I knew Duke well enough to believe that he would not have been appeased for the slight in 1965 with this "special" citation. It was more like an act of noblesse oblige than anything.

On June 2, 2004, however, the Pulitzer governing board announced that it is revising the rules for its music awards to reflect "a broad view of serious music." From now on, not only chamber and symphonic compositions, operas and choral works from what the board calls "the contemporary classical tradition" will reap nearly all the music prizes. A completely notated score will no longer be essential for consideration. And a recording of an improvisational piece will suffice for the performance requirements. Moreover, in addition to jazz being included for judging, the expanded criteria will include movie music and musical theater.

It appears that the primary democratizer of the Pulitzer music prizes was board member Jay T. Harris, who is the director of the Center for the Study of Journalism and Democracy at the University of Southern California. He was in charge of a yearlong study of reinvigorating the breadth and impact of the Pulitzer music awards.

Harris told the *Boston Globe*, "The changes in the wording are intended to make sure that the full range of excellence can be considered. The prize should not be reserved essentially for music that comes out of the European classical tradition. The intent is to widen the prize without weakening it."

I'd like to know who was on the 1965 governing Pulitzer board that decided that even a passing recognition of Ellington would have weakened the stature of the Pulitzers. But the ancient, elitist, parochial view is not entirely gone. Pulitzer winner John Harbison described the widened standards as "a horrible development. If you were to impose a comparable standard on fiction you would be soliciting entries from the authors of airport novels."

I would say to Mr. Harbison what a jazz sideman once told me: "The classical guys have their scores, whether they have them on stand or have memorized them. But we have to be creating, or trying to, anticipating each other, transmuting our feelings to the music, taking chances every goddamned second."

And that spontaneity was also part of Ellington's orchestra. As Clark Terry explained to me about Duke: "He doesn't even like to write definitive endings to a piece."

And on the bandstand, Duke's musicians weren't just reading scores—even though their own names were on them. When a newcomer to the band asked Duke one night what he should play in a solo on a piece that night, Duke said: "Listen, sweetie. Listen!"

8 | Essentially Duke (and Wynton)

Last November I was in Boston to be designated the Distinguished Graduate of the Year at the alumni dinner of Boston Latin School (BLS), the oldest public school in the country, founded in 1635. Previous alumni—somewhat before my time—have included Samuel Adams, John Hancock and Ralph Waldo Emerson. For me, the highlight of the evening was the vivid presence of the Boston Latin School Jazz Band, brilliantly directed by faculty member Paul Pitts (BLS class of 1973).

The band was there because my award citation included my involvement in jazz, which began, at age eleven, the year I entered Boston Latin School. I first heard these players—integrated by gender, race and ethnicity—a few years ago when I visited the school. They were playing Duke Ellington's "Things Ain't What

They Used to Be," and I was surprised, and impressed, by how deeply they got into his music.

I told them then that Duke would have been pleased, and several asked me, "Did you actually, really, ever talk to Duke Ellington?" I told them that when I was in my early twenties in Boston, he was a mentor of mine when he came to town, and he continued to be one in the coming years.

On that November evening, the school band again played "Things Ain't What They Used to Be," as well as three other Ellington compositions. I thought of how Duke loved his brass section as these trumpets and trombones brought to mind Ellington's "Braggin' in Brass." And the other sections were also resounding, playing tributes to Ellington.

Wynton Marsalis deserves direct credit for the band's success that night. As Paul Pitts told me: "All of these charts are the real deal, and have been made available through Essentially Ellington, a competition for high school bands across the United States."

Every year, Pitts continued, Jazz at Lincoln Center sends out "six Duke Ellington original charts, transcribed by David Berger, with a recording of the Lincoln Center Jazz Orchestra playing them and the information to find the original recordings. We have all learned so much by studying this music, and I think Wynton has done a great service to music education to get this music out there to high school students."

Last year marked the tenth annual Essentially Ellington Competition, which has introduced more than 200,000 students to Duke since it started. And as Marsalis wrote in the accompanying material for band directors: "While the arrangements in their original form may be daunting to young musicians, the satisfaction they feel having tackled 'the real thing' and the sense of accomplishment . . . knowing they've played what the masters played is a great motivator."

I could see that satisfaction in the Latin School musicians that night—and in Headmaster Cornelia Kelley (BLS class of 1944). She is a tough-love educator, and like her predecessors, insists that no child dare be left behind. As the evening ended, the band, very much including the brass section, was on fire, and the headmaster, sitting next to me, said emphatically to the audience: "That's what it's all about, ladies and gentlemen!" The life force of Ellington's music had reached and lifted her.

Paul Pitts sent me Wynton Marsalis's performance notes on the compositions played that night, and they reminded me that Marsalis is the preeminent jazz educator of our time. It's not only the extensive Jazz at Lincoln Center educational projects, including the Jazz for Young People concerts; there are also his occasional television appearances on which he so clearly gets inside the music both verbally and with his horn.

Marsalis's informal yet precise style of communication is evident in his notes to young performers for Ellington's "Launching Pad," which the BLS Jazz Band played during that alumni night: "This is a blues. It's a good tune to open up for kids to solo on. And it's a tune to get the right feeling in the rhythm section. An important thing to stress is attacking the syncopation, all those little accents on the ends of the beats. It's important to attack those beats to propel the music forward.

"Be aware of the balances needed between the solo instruments and the trio of the trombone, flugelhorn and the tenor saxophone. *Make sure that not only do they play in balance, but that they also get the proper human and vocal quality to their sound.* . . . It's important to find the right tempo; if it's too slow, it could be murderously long, but if it's too fast, it will sound frantic." (Emphasis added.)

Two years ago, the BLS band almost made the cutoff score for the second round of the Essentially Ellington Competition. But to use an old Boston term, they have a lot of sticktoitiveness. And they learn, and play, from the entire jazz legacy. Last year, for instance, they performed Charles Mingus charts, and that's as challenging and ultimately satisfying as reading Caesar's *Gallic Wars* in the original Latin, which I used to have to do at BLS.

These young musicians are learning what I heard Coleman Hawkins say during a recent National Public Radio tribute: "I don't think about music as being new or modern. I just play." And because of bandmaster Paul Pitts, what these players are experiencing now will last them the rest of their lives. As Paul says, "At times, they get inside a chord, a wondrous chord, and enjoy it for the beautiful thing it is!"

9 | Ellington's Band Is Heavenly in These "Live" Forties Recordings

I now have a sense of what heaven could be like. For those of us for whom Duke Ellington is rejuvenatingly contemporary, Storyville—the legendary Danish label, a cornucopia of ageless jazz—has released *The Duke Box*. The 1940s Ellington Orchestra (his most exhilarating) is heard entirely in "live" performances—from dance halls (where, as Duke told me, the dancers became part of the music), nightclubs, concert halls, and radio remotes from around the country.

In the forty-page booklet—with photographs by Herman Leonard and William Gottlieb, masters of decisive jazz moments—Dan Morgenstern notes that the sound of Ellington "live" is more vividly realistic than "the dead (non-resonant) studios of that time." (Those studio recordings also do remain essential because Duke insisted on no more than two or three takes a song for maximum immediacy.) But, as I can attest from having been at some of the dance halls and concerts, Ellington and his wondrously distinctive sidemen were most memorably heard in person.

The sound quality of *The Duke Box* is somewhat variable, but all of it is more than acceptable, and some of it is glorious. These eight hours of Ellington on eight CDs are in chronological order; but I recommend you start with the 1940s band's second CD—the one I would want with me if I were stranded on the proverbial desert island.

As featured on that CD, on November 7, 1940, the band, after a typically grueling road trip, arrived at the Crystal Ballroom in Fargo, N.D. Fortunately, on hand with recording equipment were two young Ellington enthusiasts, Jack Towers and Dick Burris. (Mr. Towers later became an unexcelled sound restorer of timeworn classic jazz recordings.)

As some of the sidemen later recalled, the band suddenly took fire that night. Here, on sixteen Fargo tracks, from "Mood Indigo" to "Harlem Airshaft" and "The Flaming Sword," the heroes of my youth and beyond—Johnny Hodges, "Tricky Sam" Nanton, Rex Stewart, Ben Webster, Ray Nance (who had just joined the troupe), Barney Bigard and "the piano player in the band" (as Ellington described himself)—demonstrated why this, of all Duke's orchestras, is the most revered.

But on every one of the eight CDs, the nonpareil Ellington mosaic of moods, colors, incandescent ensembles ("Duke loves his brass," as one player told me) and instantly identifiable soloists makes this a set I ought to include in my will. A historic event, from the Hurricane in New York, is the first performance, in 1943, of "Tonight I Shall Sleep." Duke had recently composed the ballad.

He might have even written it on the road. One night, at the Raymor Ballroom in Boston, I heard an Ellington piece new to me. During a break, I asked baritone saxophonist Harry Carney, "What was that?" "I don't know what it's called," Carney said. "He just wrote it."

Off the stand, Duke was often writing—or hearing in his head what he'd later work out on the piano. Mr. Morgenstern's comprehensive and deeply knowledgeable notes to *The Duke Box* end with Ellington's death, at age seventy-five—on May 24, 1974—of pneumonia and lung cancer. In his hospital bed, he was still composing; and that spring, he sent out Christmas cards. (I was privileged to get one of them.) Duke was always planning ahead—as in his music.

The remarkable achievement of researching, assembling and remastering the historic contents of *The Duke Box* is Storyville's contribution to Ellington's legacy. The Copenhagen company is now owned by Musical Sales Group, headquartered in London, and distributed in the United States by MRI Associated Labels in New York.

Looking through Storyville's extensive catalog, I always find CDs I must add to those I already have—from two volumes of Bing Crosby with Louis Armstrong and Jack Teagarden *(Havin' Fun* and *Havin' More Fun)* to *George Lewis and His New Orleans Stompers* and *Thelonious Monk in Copenhagen.* In the blues division, there is the deeply flowing blues of pianist-singer Otis Spann.

Named for the red-light district of New Orleans—where many later jazz legends performed—the label was started in Copenhagen in 1952 by twenty-three-year-old Karl Emil Knudsen, who jubilantly identified himself as "Doctor of Jazz Archaeology." Along with arranging for the release of many out-of-print American classic jazz recordings, he also produced sets by jazz masters visiting Europe, including some—like the magisterial tenor saxophonist Ben Webster— who took up residence in Denmark.

After Knudsen's death in 2003, Music Sales Group acquired Storyville Records, wisely keeping on Knudsen's longtime Copenhagen associates Mona Granger and Andres Stefanson, who share the founder's passionate conviction that the music in the Storyville catalog will remain imperishable.

In view of the diminishing interest by American record conglomerates in searching their archives for jazz to reissue, the lively persistence of Storyville is particularly worth celebrating. I spoke recently to the London-based head of Musical Sales (and Storyville), Paul Lower. I found him widely versed in jazz history—with the sense of mission of the label's founder. Among future releases, he told me proudly, is a Ben Webster boxed set.

And in the mail a couple of weeks ago, I found a harvest of more Storyville "Masters of Jazz" sets—Sidney Bechet, Teddy Wilson, Johnny Griffin, Johnny Hodges, Billie Holliday and Earl Hines. With four children and six grandchildren to remember in my will, I may well include these CDs in my bequests along with *The Duke Box.*

At a 1963 press conference in Calcutta, India, Duke Ellington was asked: "How have you managed to keep a big band so long when so many others have broken up?"

"It's a matter," said Duke, "of whether you want to play music or make money, I guess. I like to keep a band so that I can write and hear the music the next day. The only way to do that is to pay the band and keep it on tap fifty-two weeks a year."

Asked whether the rise of rock 'n' roll had taken away the jazz audience, Duke answered: "There's still a Dixieland audience, a Swing audience, a Bop audience. . . . All the audiences are still there."

And, for them, so still is Storyville Records.

PART THREE

Jazz Credentials

10 | Is Jazz Black Music?

In January, I was on a panel at Jazz at Lincoln Center. The subject, "Is Jazz Black Music?" is still a lively and even combative one in some quarters. When I was invited, what first came to mind was Duke Ellington's telling me long ago that in the 1920s he went to Fletcher Henderson and said, "Why don't we drop the word 'jazz' and call what we're doing 'Negro music'? Then there won't be any confusion." Henderson took a pass. But years later, when Louie Bellson was in Ellington's band, Duke said he was the most extraordinary drummer he'd ever heard.

We wouldn't have been at Lincoln Center for that discussion had it not been for black field hollers, ring games, call-and-response church music and the blues. So it's indisputable that jazz began as black music. On the panel, I proposed a line—obviously debatable—between the originators of this music and those who were original musicians but hadn't very deeply shaped the directions of jazz. Duke used to tell me it's always been the individuals whom others followed, and he named Sidney Bechet as an example.

My partial list of originators—and I'm sure you have yours—includes Louis Armstrong, Mr. Ellington, Count Basie, Charlie Christian, Charlie Parker, Miles Davis, Thelonious Monk, John Coltrane, Ornette Coleman and Lester Young. All were black, and some were influenced by non-blacks.

Lester Young told me that Frank Trumbauer, mainly known for his association with Bix Beiderbecke, "was my idol. When I started to play, I bought all his records and I imagine I can still play those solos. I tried to get the sound of the C melody saxophone on the tenor. That's why I don't sound like other people. Trumbauer always told a little story." But Trumbauer, though an original, didn't affect, as Prez did, the stories of countless jazz musicians around the world.

The moderator that night at Lincoln Center was historian and jazz professor Lewis Porter. He made the salient point that although the roots of the originators were black, they had big ears and were open to an infinite diversity of influences. As Charles Hersch notes in his important book *Subversive Sounds: Race and the Birth of Jazz in New Orleans* (University of Chicago Press), the jazz culture there "included [transmutations of] quadrilles, mazurkas and schottisches."

On the panel, I mentioned that world traveler Duke Ellington absorbed into his music the colors, dynamics and stories of the regional and national sounds he heard.

Porter emphasized, "It's typical of African-American music that jazz players are open to influences." Eric Dolphy told me how hearing birds sing became part of his music. But again, the roots are black. Or, as Porter put it, being that open "doesn't make it non-black."

That's true of both originators and originals. A necessarily partial list of the originals who are influential but didn't profoundly change the course of jazz would encompass such non-black players as Bix Beiderbecke (at whom Louis Armstrong marveled during Chicago after-hours sessions), Pee Wee Russell, Jack Teagarden, Toshiko Akiyoshi, Bill Evans, Jim Hall, Phil Woods and bandleader Woody Herman.

The black roots of jazz of course quintessentially nourished all of these non-blacks and many others. And the next unexpected originator, like Ornette Coleman, swooping into New York, could come from any place in the world. Between sets one night, John Lewis and I were talking about who might become the new compelling shepherd—the individual others would follow, in Duke Ellington's phrase.

"Right now," John said, "in a club in Romania, it could be a bassist or a trumpet player in a combo there."

He or she hasn't broken through the jazz firmament yet. And it certainly could be a she. As of now, that female person isn't in the Jazz at Lincoln Center Orchestra because Wynton Marsalis hasn't yet found a woman musician, of whatever nationality, color or age, who meets his standards for being a regular member. Since Wynton does have big ears, I remain puzzled at this omission. As a challenge (one I've issued the trumpeter before): why doesn't he try a blind audition, for once?

What I forgot to add about jazz and blackness at that Jazz at Lincoln Center panel was a scene I once witnessed at a club in New York where Charles Mingus was working. When a set was over, Mingus came off the stand and we started talking. A man strode over—a very black man—and, pointing at Mingus, said accusingly, "You're not black enough to play the blues!" Neither Mingus nor I had ever seen this guy before.

Mingus drew back his arm, clenched a fist, thought better of it, rushed back on the stand, got his bass, brought it down to where the accuser still stood, and played a blues that, as I felt it, shook the room.

The very black man, without a word, slunk away.

Mingus was one of the closest friends I've ever had, and he believed, as Art Blakey said, that "anyone can play this music if they can feel it." Or listen to it.

I suppose these probes of how black this music is now or in the future—or any of the people who play it—will continue. But I prefer Thelonious Monk's approach to defining the essence of jazz. As the late Leslie Gourse reported in *Straight No Chaser: The Life and Genius of Thelonious Monk* (Schirmer Books),

Monk told a *New York Post* columnist in 1960, "I never tried to think of a defini-tion [of jazz]. You're supposed to know jazz when you hear it. What do you do when someone gives you something? You feel glad about it."

11 | No One Else Sounded Like "Pee Wee" Russell

When I was a teenage fledgling clarinetist studying with an alumnus of the Boston Symphony Orchestra, I was startled to hear on a 1929 jazz recording by the Mound City Blue Blowers sounds I had never imagined coming from a clarinet: vocal-like cries and intimate whispers, breaking into triumphant, glow-ing lyricism in solos building to the edge of a cliff. It was Charles Ellsworth "Pee Wee" Russell.

Also on that 1929 session was Coleman Hawkins, who invented the jazz tenor saxophone. But in the years after that record date, while Benny Goodman and Artie Shaw became major clarinet influences, it was as if Pee Wee had invented only himself. No one else sounded like him.

In 1961, while head of Candid Records, I brought Russell and Hawkins together again, in a recording called *Jazz Reunion*. A sideman, trombonist Bob Brookmeyer, said between takes that "Pee Wee's choruses are really way out."

"I know, I know," the magisterial Mr. Hawkins replied. "For more than thirty years I've been listening to him play those funny notes. He's always been way out, but they didn't have a name for it then."

There still is no category into which Pee Wee—who died at age sixty-two in 1969—fits. The release in 2006 of *Pee Wee Russell: Portrait of Pee Wee* (Empire Musicwerks) reveals that his passionate adventurousness continues to transcend all jazz styles.

I got to know Pee Wee from the 1940s until he died. Shy, wry, he said of his solos—during which his colleagues often thought he could never extricate himself—"The more you try, the luckier you are." Out of print for years, *Portrait of Pee Wee* was originally made in 1958 with such warmly compatible and unpre-dictable improvisers as Ruby Braff, Bud Freeman, Vic Dickenson and Nat Pierce (who arranged the numbers).

In "That Old Feeling," "Out of Nowhere" and "Pee Wee Blues" (one of the most personal, mellow and then fierce blues I've ever heard), the nonpareil clarinetist displays, as he does throughout the session, what annotator Charles Edward Smith perfectly describes as Pee Wee's signature: "Having set the scene with a 'straight' jazz rendering, he proceeds to the attack, making full use of various registers or voices, and with a unique, uninhibited and fresh approach to that quality of sound called timbre. As he approaches the final statement, he is often flying by luck and by instinct." (I must pay tribute to Mr. Smith, who in his 1939 book *Jazzmen*, which came out when I was fourteen, showed me—as Whitney Balliett later did—that jazz could be put into words.)

Pee Wee Russell grew up in Muskogee, Oklahoma, long before Merle Haggard and the Strangers rode through the town. As a boy, at the local Elks lodge, he played, on imaginary instruments, along with the band. Then, at age fourteen, the lure of jazz became so irresistible that—as William Howard Kenney describes it in *Jazz on the River* (University of Chicago Press)—he borrowed a pair of his father's long pants, put a ladder near his bedroom window, and sneaked out to his first gig, with an Arkansas riverboat combo, the Deep River Jazzband. Later, at the Arcadia Ballroom in St. Louis, Pee Wee found a musical soul mate in Bix Beiderbecke.

As Pee Wee later recalled (in *Bix*, by Jean Pierre Lion, Continuum International Publishing Group): "We would do little things once in a while so drastic, or rather so musically advanced, that when we had a damn nice thing going, the manager would come up and say, 'What in God's name are you doing?' Naturally, we couldn't explain it to him."

Pee Wee came to New York in 1927, worked with Red Nichols and Broadway pit bands, and later toured with Louis Prima. By 1937, he was in residence with Eddie Condon's merry troupes—first at Nick's in Greenwich Village and then at Condon's own club—and on many recordings with Condon associates: brilliantly on nineteen tracks in the boxed set *Classic Columbia Condon: Mob Sessions,* and on *Bud Freeman: Chicago/Austin High School Jazz in Hifi* (both on Mosaic Records).

To his annoyance, Pee Wee was long categorized as a "Dixieland" or "Chicago-style" jazzman; but just as Henry David Thoreau said of himself, Pee Wee always listened to his own drum.

In the late 1940s, he was playing in a small, nondescript Boston club near the New England Conservatory of Music. On his last night, a student at the conservatory went up to the bandstand and unrolled a sizable series of music manuscript pages. Sitting near the stand, I saw that the pages were densely covered with what looked like an intricately scored, complex classical-music composition.

"I brought this for you," the student told the clarinetist. "It's some of your solos these past nights. I transcribed them."

Peering quizzically at this sudden tribute, Pee Wee said, shaking his head, "This can't be me. I can't play this!" Assured by the student that it was as faithful a transcription as he could manage, Pee Wee said, sighing, "Even if this is what I played, I wouldn't play it again the same way—even if I could, which I can't."

At the 1961 *Jazz Reunion* Candid Record session with Pee Wee and Coleman Hawkins, pianist Nat Pierce, also someone who had arranged all these numbers, said to Hawkins—one of the first of the legendary swing-era players to welcome Dizzy Gillespie and Thelonious Monk into his recording sessions—"Did you notice that one of Pee Wee's tunes we did sounded like something Monk might have written?"

Hawkins agreed. And a few years later, at the Newport Jazz Festival, Pee Wee Russell appeared with Thelonious Monk (who used to be announced at Birdland as the "onliest Monk"). Neither got lost in their collaboration.

In his essential *Jazz Encyclopedia* (Penguin), Richard Cook noted that the precise Benny Goodman considered Pee Wee's playing "comical." Nonetheless, Cook added that "on a good night, when the phrases fell just where he wanted them," Pee Wee was "supreme."

Actually, on such nights, those phrases often fell in ways that surprised Pee Wee as much as they did the other musicians on the stand—and the listeners. And that is why Whitney Balliett called jazz "the sound of surprise"—for the players and the rest of us who can't get enough of it.

12 | Just Call Him Thelonious

The most frequent word used in relation to the personality—musical and otherwise—of Thelonious Sphere Monk has been "enigmatic."

Part of the reason for this supposed opaqueness about Monk lies in the man himself, for he seldom verbalizes about his music.

His conversation on most subjects is spare enough. But with regard to his own work, his feeling appears to be that whatever communication there is in his music can be obtained only by listening, and that words only obscure the issue. Monk, therefore, has written no articles about his credo and engaged in no public debates. When he has something to say, he says it in his music.

As a result of this disinclination to talk much about his work—coupled with a cryptic sense of humor—Monk has not been an easy interviewee. Several European critics who tried to discuss music with him during his 1954 appearance at the Paris Jazz Fair were baffled.

In this country, part of the fault for Monk-the-enigma is chargeable to the jazz writers. And for lack of words from the source, writing and talking about Monk by nonmusicians often has been unusually expressionistic.

There is, for example, this note on his melodies by German critic Joachim E. Berendt: "I like to think of them as 'al fresco melodies,' painted directly on 'a blank wall' with nothing under it but hard stone. You cannot take them with you as you can with paintings which are framed. You have to come back. You will if you ever get their message."

Then there is the view, expressed in a Chicago club: "Monk's playing is like a painter who stands across the room and throws paint at a canvas. You can't object too much to the way it turns out because he has chosen such beautiful colors to throw."

Musicians who have been influenced or deeply stimulated by Monk know better. Monk's melodies *can* be taken with you, and his harmonic colorations are hardly conceived in a Jackson Pollock manner. Monk knows what he's doing. Yet here again, because of his own lack of interest in self-exposition, there is no detailed analysis available of Monk's harmonic system.

Also to be mentioned are those listeners, critics and some musicians who used to put him down as an eccentric, deliberate or otherwise, who has made peripheral contributions to modern jazz but is far from being a key figure in its development. This writer disagrees with this latter view.

Thelonious Sphere Monk, named after his father, was born in North Carolina, not in New York, as the reference books say. Monk's answer concerning his birth date is: "When shall I be born? I'm just playing a game like everybody else." Leonard Feather gives his birth date as October 10, 1920.

His mother was Barbara Monk. He went to Public School 141 in New York City, where the family moved when Monk was four. He attended the prestigious Stuyvesant High School, where sources other than Monk say he excelled in math, physics and music and was expert in basketball.

The rest of his story, in what, as far as I know, is the first interview with Monk to have been written in many years, is told by the pianist, with occasional comments from other sources. We did it at his home.

"It's hard to go back. Like what happened eighty-two bars ago. At least it's hard to go back earlier than ten years ago. I remember fooling around a piano when I was five or six years old, picking out melodies.

"No, my parents weren't musical. I did have a few lessons when I was pretty young, around ten or eleven, but what I've learned since I've mostly taught myself. I never picked no special musicians to follow. I've liked something about nearly every musician I heard, but I never patterned myself after any particular one. Of course, you have to go through certain stages to learn how to play the piano, but that doesn't necessarily mean you're copying somebody's style. I've learned from numerous pianists.

"I had decided to go into music full time way back, when I first took lessons. While still in my teens, I went on the road with a group that played church music for an evangelist. Rock and roll or rhythm and blues. That's what we were doing. Only now they put different words to it. She preached and healed, and we played.

"We had trumpet, saxophone, piano and drums. And then the congregation would sing. We would play in some of the biggest churches in the towns we went through. We traveled around the country for about two years."

It was probably during this period that Mary Lou Williams heard Monk for the first time in Kansas City. As she describes it:

> Thelonious, still in his teens, came into town with either an evangelist or a medicine show—I forget which. While Monk was in Kaycee, he jammed every night, really used to blow on piano, employing a lot more technique than he does today. He felt that musicians should play something new and started doing it. Most of us admire him for this. He was one of the original modernists all right, playing much the same harmonies then that he's playing now.

Monk continued the interview: "Back in New York, I tried to find jobs. I worked all over town. Nonunion jobs, $20 a week, seven nights a week, and then the man might fire you anytime and you never got your money. I've been on millions of those kinds of jobs. I've been on every kind of job you can think of all over New York. I really found out how to get around this city. Dance halls. Every place. How long did this scuffling go on? It hasn't stopped.

"As for my style, I've always been told way back that I was unique, but I never lost a job on account of that. I first met Dizzy when I was in my early twenties. There were a lot of places all over Harlem that had three or four pieces (playing), and there the musicians felt like blowing. Charlie Parker? I met him in Vic Dickenson's room where he was visiting one day. Charlie wasn't well known uptown around this time.

"Really, I don't remember all these details. I met a whole gang of musicians, and I wasn't paying anything that much attention. I was playing a gig, tryin' to play music. While I was at Minton's, anybody sat in who would come up there if he could play. I never bothered anybody. It was just a job. I had no particular feeling that anything new was being built. It's true modern jazz probably began to get popular there. But as for me, my mind was like it was before I worked in Minton's.

"Some of those histories and articles put what happened in ten years in one year. They put people all together in one time in this place. Over a period of time, I've seen practically everybody at Minton's, but they were just in there playing. They weren't giving any lectures. It got a little glamorous maybe on Monday nights when Teddy Hill, the manager, would invite the guys who were at the Apollo that week. As a result, all the different bands that played at the Apollo got to hear the original music, and it got around and talk started going about the fellows at Minton's.

"Another story about that time is that Dizzy began to write down what Bird was doing. Why should Bird get Dizzy to write something down? He could write it down himself. I can't answer for what Bird thought of me, by the way, but I always went for his playing.

"Bud Powell? He wasn't on the scene at first. Nobody knew about Bud until I brought him along. I met him in a juice joint uptown. At first, at Minton's, Kenny

Clarke didn't want Bud to sit in at the piano. The way I would put those years at Minton's and other places uptown was that we were just fellows working, and all the musicians would come by and jam."

Other musicians have declared that matters were not so entirely unplanned at Minton's. Gillespie and Clarke agree that there were often afternoon sessions and also caucuses on the job when Monk, Dizzy, Clarke and Joe Guy would work out new chord progressions, both to discourage incompetent sitters-in that night and also because they became more and more intrigued with the possibilities of these changing approaches to jazz.

Feather's *Encyclopedia of Jazz* states accurately that, except for a brief date with Lucky Millinder's band in 1942—"a week or so at the Savoy," Monk remembers—and a 1944 engagement with Coleman Hawkins on 52nd Street, Monk largely worked on his own heading a small combo.

"The first records I ever made," Monk said, "were with Coleman Hawkins." (These were in 1944.) "Hawkins can play. Nobody can pick up a tenor without playing some of him. He's the first one who started playing tenor. He created a very good job for the tenor players."

In 1954, Monk made his European debut at the Paris Jazz Fair. His playing, according to most observers, could be characterized as inconsistent at the least. Monk's recollection: "I enjoyed the visit very much. The only drag was I didn't have my own band with me. I couldn't find anybody to play with me that could make it. All the good jazz seems to be in the United States. But I'd like to go back over with my own group."

Monk, talking with characteristic slowness and long pauses between carefully phrased statements, covered several areas concerned with Monk-the-legend as opposed to Monk-seen-by-Monk:

"Do I think I'm difficult to understand? Well, like what? Tell me a particular number. Some of my pieces have melodies a nitwit can understand. Like I've written one number staying on one note. A tone-deaf person could hum it.

"My system of composing? I compose as it comes, as I hear it. I have no formula for composing. For people who've never heard any of my work before, and would like to know where to start, I'd say just listen to the music in the order that I've recorded it. Get the records, sit down, and dig.

"Am I planning any long works? I'm not planning anything. I write as the idea hits me. What's supposed to happen will happen, so I've heard. As for writing for full orchestra, I've done that years back for all kinds of pieces. I haven't been doing it because I'm not the kind of person who likes to arrange, and they don't pay enough for arrangements anyway.

"I'd like to talk about the lies that have been told about me that I'm undependable on jobs and the like. I don't know how that kind of legend got around. Some fools talk a big lie, that's all. Those lies get started, and you just can't stop them.

Without even investigating, people go for them, and the lies get to the booking agencies. They believe it, too, so fast, and condemn you before investigating. I think the booking agents and the public should investigate if rumors are true about people before they believe them.

"I have never messed up; I have never goofed a job in my life. Sometimes my name has been used in places that I knew nothing about, and the promoters never tried to get in touch with me. So, when the public comes and I haven't shown up, the promoter blames me when he explains it to them. But I *do* have a sense of responsibility about work."

A reliable Chicago observer notes that during Monk's last date there some months ago, "he wasn't elusive or uncooperative.... On his two nights off, he played a veteran's hospital benefit one night and a college concert-jam session the next. He did well at the Beehive and was held over. Actually, the owner had an odd number of days left before the next booking, and Monk happened to be available, but this particular owner never would have kept Monk on unless Monk was doing good business for the place."

Monk's comments on the present scene: "I keep up. I know what's going on. I've heard some so-called progressive music that sounded weird intentionally. Some people have the idea that if it sounds real weird, it's modern progressive. When you sit there and the music comes out weird, that's different. You can tell the difference when something is composed weird intentionally and when it just flows out weird. I don't like the word 'weird' anyway, but people got accustomed to it.

About young musicians: "I haven't heard anything new in so long. I mean something that is really original, distinctive, an original style. They sound like they're copying from somebody. I do like, though, the tenor I worked with in Chicago, John Griffin. He's one of the best. Also the bass player I worked with there. Wilbur Ware.

"I hear some of my things once in a while in the work of a gang of piano players. I don't mean all the way through. I don't want to sound conceited. I mean the way they attack a note or make a riff.... I don't teach. Quite a few pianists have come by the house. But it's not a formal thing. I couldn't find a system probably.... What do I do between club dates? I try to find something for the wife and kids to eat and me, too. I have a girl who is two and a boy who is six. The boy likes music. How would I feel if the boy became a full-time musician? The important thing is how *he* feels. How I feel don't mean nothing. He'll be the way he wants to be, the way he's supposed to be."

Monk is assembling a quartet with which he'll travel. After rehearsals and before the first date, plans call for a "first-night" audition for the quartet for critics, magazine writers and perhaps club owners.

"About original writing in jazz today," Monk added, "what I've heard hasn't sounded too original. It all sounds the same almost. The same chords. The melody might change a little, but there's been nothing really original in the last six or seven years. What is an original? If it *sounds* original. The construction; the melody. It has to have its own sound.

"Some people say I haven't enough technique. Everybody has his own opinion. There is always something I can't express that I want to. It's always been that way and maybe always will be. I haven't reached perfection. Maybe those people with those opinions have reached perfection. I went through a whole gang of scales like other piano players did."

13 | Remembering Dizzy

Of the jazz Web sites I visit, the most far-ranging—and therefore, most often surprising—is Jerry Jazz Musician at Jerryjazz.com. The publisher, editor, interviewer and selector of the relevant music is Joe Maita, based in Portland, Oregon. He tells me the title comes from a Woody Allen stand-up routine in the early 1960s: "When riding the subway to his clarinet lessons, Woody described himself as being dressed 'Jerry Jazz Musician style.'"

The Web site encompasses what could be called American civilization with jazz as the centerpiece—ranging from such guests as Gary Giddins to Donzaleigh Abernathy, daughter of Reverend Ralph Abernathy, Martin Luther King's closest associate. There is also a discussion on the state of jazz, including its economics, with Joshua Redman, Bruce Lundvall and Ben Ratliff.

Recently, Maita asked me to join James Moody in a session, "Remembering Dizzy Gillespie." Moody knew Dizzy much longer and better than I did, having been in his big band and quintet. Dizzy once said of the multireedist and vocalist: "Playing with James Moody is like playing with a continuation of myself." And both were joyously witty, on and off the stand.

I knew Dizzy for more than forty years, talked with him often and was always lifted up not only by his music but also by his warmth and generosity. One of my biggest kicks in the jazz life was when, after I hadn't seen him for a couple of years, I was waiting outside a rehearsal room where he was due to work with an all-star big band for a concert in his honor. Dizzy, coming down the corridor with a friend, saw me, gave me a big hug and said to his friend, "It's like seeing an old broad after a long time."

I've never been referred to that way before or since, but I glowed for quite a while.

During my conversation with Moody, I remembered what Hank Jones said at the funeral service for Dizzy: "He showed me chord inversions I hadn't even thought of." "Dizzy was a teacher," Moody said. "If he played something, and you asked him what it was, he would bring you to the piano and explain it. He felt if a player knows the piano, then he will know what the trombones are doing, what the trumpets are doing, what the saxophones are doing, because every instrument is right there in the piano. Many of the great musicians know something about the piano because, as Diz said, that is where everything is." Charles Mingus felt the same way, and could play piano with his customary distinctiveness.

Moody talked about how fair-minded Dizzy was, but also how keenly self-protective he had to be in the music business. Said Moody: "I will never forget the time he told me, 'Moody, you are a wonderful person, and I would trust you anywhere. But I have a little bit of an orphan in my heart.' I knew what he meant by that. He wouldn't take any 'stuff' from anyone. He would try to grab them before they grabbed him, because he was taken advantage of in his work. Many of the pieces that Dizzy wrote have someone else's name on it with his."

Back in the 1950s, I was walking down Broadway in New York, and Dizzy, walking toward me, was smiling broadly. "I've just come from seeing Billy Shaw," he said. (Shaw was a major booker of jazz musicians.) "I'd been meaning to say this to him for a long time," Dizzy said with satisfaction. "'Billy,' I told him, 'you got to remember that I don't work for you. You work for me!'" Laughing, Dizzy moved on.

A lot of musicians were taken advantage of. Moody said, "I believe Oliver Nelson sold 'Stolen Moments' for less than one hundred dollars, and it was his most famous composition. Regarding Dizzy, I can only imagine how much money he would have made if he had been Caucasian. I am not prejudiced—hell, my wife has blonde hair and green eyes. But if he were Caucasian, he would have made some serious money."

As we were talking about how Dizzy's very presence, before he played a note, made people feel good, Moody said: "A day doesn't go by that I don't think about Diz. I have pictures of him plastered all over my house. He touched me very deeply. I am now seventy-nine years old, and I often will be doing something when I will stop and say to myself, 'Aah, that's what he meant!' I guess as long as I live, I will be saying that to myself because that is how deep the man touched me."

A member of the serene Baha'i faith, Dizzy once told me that his religion taught him that "eventually, mankind will become unified, when there is world government and everybody belongs to it, and you don't need a passport. There'll be an international language taught in all schools. This should take another thousand or 2,000 years. But on the way, we get little pinches of unification. Like the United Nations."

"And jazz?" I asked.

"Yeah, yeah," he said. "That really is a pinch of unification. It really makes me feel good to belong to jazz, to that part of society."

What a gift it was to know Dizzy.

14 | Oscar Peterson

A JAZZ "BEHEMOTH" MOVES ON

Only when it was absolutely necessary, Oscar Peterson wrote, would he go on stage before a concert to check out the piano, because doing so "might lead to preconditioned ideas, and they can in turn interfere with the creative process so essential to a creative jazz concert."

For Peterson, who died on December 23, 2007, at age eighty-two, his full mastery of the instrument enabled him to keep striving for what to him was his ultimate reason for being. In his equally masterful autobiography, *A Jazz Odyssey: The Life of Oscar Peterson* (Continuum, 2002), he said of the "dare-devil enterprise [the jazz experience]" in which he engaged for so many years that it "requires you to collect all your senses, emotions, physical strength and mental power, and focus them totally on the performance . . . every time you play. . . . Uniquely exciting, once it's bitten you, you never get rid of it. Nor do you want to; for you come to believe that if you get it all right, you will be capable of virtually anything. That is what drives me, and I know it always will do so."

He wrote that after a stroke in 1993 that, at first, limited the use of his left hand. But "the will to perfection," as he called it, kept driving him, and as a result he regained much of his customary skill, and with it the satisfaction of continuing to surprise himself.

Born in 1925, Peterson was mandated by his father to practice piano at a very early age; but it was hearing Nat "King" Cole that fired his enthusiasm, and he won a talent contest at age fourteen. By the 1940s, Peterson was already a presence on the radio in his native Canada and in Montreal clubs. But his audience began to greatly expand when jazz impresario Norman Granz heard him and brought him to New York's Carnegie Hall in 1949 for one of Granz's "Jazz at the Philharmonic" concerts, where the competition was so intense that many careers of the participants were enhanced.

Granz became Peterson's manager and close friend as they toured Europe and other continents. Also a producer of records on his Verve and Pablo labels, Granz extensively featured Peterson, not only as leader of his own trios but also as an accompanist for a wide range of other jazz masters whom Granz recorded. Among them were Louis Armstrong, Dizzy Gillespie, Lester Young, Coleman Hawkins, Ella Fitzgerald, Benny Carter, Ben Webster, Billie Holiday, Duke Ellington and Roy Eldridge.

As classic jazz players used to say of extraordinary peers, Peterson had "big ears." In all the varying contexts of these Granz recordings, he remained himself while also being completely consonant with the diverse stylists on those sessions.

A fascinating section in his autobiography describes what each soloist required of Peterson as an accompanist. For instance, Eldridge "would slide over to me and quietly ask, 'Can I get my strollers, please?' By this he meant that he intended to start simply with a mute aided by Ray Brown's bass in the lower register.

"He trusted the remaining members of the rhythm section not only to sit out and allow the excitement to build between him and Ray, but more importantly, to anticipate exactly where to re-enter and move him up a few notches emotionally."

Moreover, as a writer from the inside of the music, Peterson's profiles of other longtime associates prove him to be a master practitioner of jazz history and criticism. As he wrote: "To have played for these and other behemoths of the music world certainly served to educate me in areas in which that type of education just isn't available [and] served to deepen my true realization of the immensity of the music we know as jazz."

Because of the scores of albums Peterson recorded, it's difficult for me to select any as the best. So, subjectively, two that make me rise and shout are *The Oscar Peterson Trio at the Stratford Shakespearean Festival* (1956) and *Night Train* (1962). (Both are on the Verve label.)

Another autobiography that matches Peterson's in moving the reader into the life force of jazz is Sidney Bechet's *Treat It Gentle* (Da Capo Press, 2002). He writes of growing up in New Orleans: "That music, it was like waking up in the morning and eating . . . it was natural to the way you lived and the way you died."

And for Peterson, the pleasures of being inside that music recalled, he wrote, "the joyful exclamation [guitarist] Barney Kessel produced after [the] first evening in my trio. He came over to me after the last set, shook his head, and said with that Oklahoma accent, 'Oscar, that was better than sex!'"

Wherever he went around the world, Peterson's effect on audiences demonstrated the truth of Art Blakey's invitation to extreme pleasure: "You don't have to be a musician to understand jazz. All you have to do is be able to feel."

15 | A Great Night in Providence for Jazz and Snow

Once in a while, a jazz person has told me of an unexpected and exceptional listening experience at a jazz club somewhere. Eagerly I always ask, "Was there a tape recorder?" Almost invariably, the rueful answer is: "No." But a wondrous exception, finally released in February 2005 on the Hyena label, is *Joe Williams/Havin' a Good Time! Featuring Ben Webster.*

As Junior Mance, the pianist on the 1964 gig at Pio's, a club in Providence, Rhode Island, tells the story: "In the middle of the week we were there, the city got hit with a blizzard. Enough people showed up, so Joe had to perform. When Joe and the guys got there, to their surprise, they found Ben Webster, saxophone in hand, sitting in a corner. They didn't know he was in town. Ben asked if he could sit in."

What jazz leader would refuse? Mr. Webster, a large, imposing, sometimes bristling man, could swing a military band—as he proved in his years with the nonbelligerent Duke Ellington. But on ballads he could be as tender as the memory of a first love, as he also demonstrated with Duke.

Mr. Webster gave me a lifetime credo when I was quite young. Sitting with me between sets at a jazz club in Boston, he said—after vainly trying to get a local rhythm section into a swinging groove—"Remember, if the rhythm section ain't making it, go for yourself!" That advice has kept me going in many situations where I had to listen to my own drum to be myself.

Mr. Williams became internationally acclaimed as a celebrator of the blues with Count Basie's big band; but then, on his own with a small combo, he was even more warmly, intimately compelling in small clubs.

That winter in Providence, with a rhythm section that delighted Ben, both Mr. Webster and Mr. Williams showed, as Junior Mance described it, "what jazz is really about. It's what happens when world-class players get together and do what cats have been doing for decades—make magic on the spot. Thank God somebody was runnin' a tape."

From "Kansas City Blues" and Joe Williams's hit with Mr. Basie, "Alright, OK, You Win," to such luminous, sensuous ballads as "That's All" and "A Hundred Years from Today," Messrs. Williams and Webster indeed gave the hardy souls who braved the blizzard that night a quintessential sense of what jazz is all about as Mr. Mance, bassist Bob Cranshaw and drummer Mickey Roker kept the time flowing.

What Mr. Mance calls the "magic" here comes from jazz players' ability to listen, instantaneously and deeply, to each other. During an interview with Terry Gross on National Public Radio's "Fresh Air" long ago, Mr. Williams told of how he composed a performance like the one so memorably illuminated in this recording of that night: "As a soloist, you don't get in the way of the music itself. You give everybody a chance to contribute. You mustn't have anybody . . . back there feeling, 'My part is not important.' All the parts are important. . . . I have to make room so all the parts are heard the way they want it to be heard." As he also noted, "The music will swing if you try not to get in the way."

This time capsule of the recording in Providence that is the essence of jazz was opened by Monk Rowe, director of the Hamilton College Jazz Archive in Clinton, New York, an invaluable collection of more than 250 videotaped interviews of musicians and singers. These conversations are on VHS, DVD and audiocassette and have been transcribed.

There is an interview, made solely for the collection, with Joe Williams; and among the material donated by his estate is Mr. Williams's private collection of live open-reel recordings. This tape from the winter night in 1964 was among them. Monk Rowe brought the tape to Joel Dorn, a jazz record producer, broadcaster, raconteur and all-around jazz insider for nearly forty years. I keep urging him to write his memoirs.

In the notes for the Joe Williams–Ben Webster CD on the Hyena label, a Joel Dorn record company, Monk Rowe says: "I was sure I had found the right producer [for this session] when Joel Dorn leapt out of his seat, and exclaimed, 'Do you know what you got here?'"

When Mr. Dorn sent me the recording, I was brought back to a night in Mr. Williams's dressing room at a small club in New York where he had just finished a set. As usual, he had been totally involved with the music—and the audience. We were talking about musicians we had both known over the years who had permanently left the scene, some of them by burning the candle at both ends. Joe pointed at me, and said, "You and I are survivors!" I felt honored to be included as some kind of jazz peer, though I can't play anything but an electric typewriter.

In 1999, at eighty-one, Joe Williams died in Las Vegas. Many of his recordings survive, but whenever I want to hear Joe again, this is the one I'll put on first.

What Mr. Williams was all about was told the day after he died on National Public Radio's "Morning Edition" by its then, and now much missed, host, Bob Edwards. He recalled going to hear Joe in a small Maryland club on the night of a Muhammad Ali fight on television: "Williams performed in front of just three couples, but he sang as if it was a packed house in Vegas." Joe was later asked by Mr. Edwards, "With only three couples in the room, why didn't you come down with laryngitis?"

"No," Joe said, "the only real reward is when you've done the best you could. It isn't money all the time."

16 | The Perfect Jazz Club

There should be a book about those jazz clubs that have been a vital part of the evolution of the music—Lincoln Gardens in Chicago, Birdland and the Village Vanguard in New York City and the various clubs in Philadelphia, Detroit, Los Angeles et al.—with reminiscences by the musicians who played and hung out there.

Kenny Barron's *The Perfect Set: Live at Bradley's II* (Sunnyside, 2005) is a tribute to the New York club that, while owner Bradley Cunningham was alive, was a home away from home for musicians—and for me. The music is also a tribute to the continually original Kenny Barron. "Bradley's was a real listening room," Barron says, "and a great place to hang out, especially for the last set at two in the morning when musicians came in from their gigs at other clubs."

In his liner notes to Barron's previous *Live at Bradley's* (Sunnyside, 2002), Russ Musto notes that "Bradley's was a place where pianists often picked up compositions by the other pianists who played there, so it was not uncommon to hear Larry Willis playing a John Hicks song or John Hicks playing a Kenny Barron tune."

Among the regulars, Paul Desmond so enjoyed the ambience that in his will he left the club the Baldwin grand piano that has delighted so many subsequent pianists. (The last time I saw Paul, a longtime friend, he was sitting at Bradley's after Charles Mingus and I came over from the nearby Cookery where Joe Turner was riding the blues.) One Saturday afternoon, I found Cecil Taylor sitting at the bar. He'd just come in to talk to whatever musicians he found worth talking to. He settled for me.

Bradley Cunningham was an imposing, sometimes impatient presence, but he was essentially a romantic for whom jazz was an elixir. He played piano but self-deprecatingly considered himself a lifelong apprentice. However, I'd come in during late afternoons, when there were few customers, to hear Cunningham's softly impressionistic improvisations.

I mourned when the life force that was the jazz room at Bradley's died when he did. To cite Russ Musto again: "The demise of Bradley's [in the mid-1990s] signaled the end of an era in the history of jazz in New York City. The room was much more than just another jazz club. It was a social center where the music community came together [creating] an atmosphere of camaraderie." Being a nonplaying part of that camaraderie filled me with anticipation the many nights I walked there from my other home two streets away.

You can hear Bradley's life force on Kenny Barron's *The Perfect Set*—which was the second one, at midnight, on April 6, 1996. The trio, with Ray Drummond on bass and Ben Riley on drums, had been together for over seven years; and as you can hear, they exemplified what Duke Ellington once told me was his criterion for hiring a new member of the orchestra: "I need somebody who knows how to listen." Included in the midnight set are two compositions by Thelonious Monk, who actually sat in one night at Bradley's. (It might have been his last public appearance.)

On both "Shuffle Boil" and "Well You Needn't," the antic, sometimes ironic and often insistently searching spirit of Monk comes through with bracing immediacy, but very much in Barron's own voice. "Shuffle Boil" shows Barron's awareness of Monk's stride-piano roots—an exhilarating use of the entire keyboard, which Kenny clearly also enjoys. And Barron's own "Twilight Song" is both beguiling and haunting. I expect it intrigued many of the visiting pianists standing at the bar that night.

The book I envision about jazz clubs—which my day job, checking the pulse of the Constitution, precludes my having the resources and time I'd need to write—should include profiles of some of the club owners through the years whose enjoyment of the music, as well as the night's proceeds, contributed to the camaraderie that was transfused into the music.

Another club I'd suggest including in such a book is the still ongoing 55 Bar, located in a basement on New York City's Christopher Street in Greenwich Village. Its owner, Queva Lutz, accurately describes it as "an old-fashioned jazz club." On the wall are jazz-album covers from her own collection. She provides a showcase for lesser-known musicians on the early set, for which there is no music charge. Later in the evening, when such players as Chris Potter, Ben Allison and Mike Stern appear, the cover charge ranges—and this is not a typo—from $5 to $10.

Singer Kendra Shank, a frequent performer, told me for the *Wall Street Journal:* "The environment Queva provides there encourages the musicians to stretch and use the gig to explore new material, new approaches. There's a feeling there for us, the musicians, and for the listeners, of being part of the creative process. There's like a cycling of energy between the musicians and the audience. Sometimes, at the end of a set, when I thank them for listening, I also thank them for creating the music with us."

In the British weekly *The Economist,* reader Quint Barker once wrote in to say, "True artists are discovered in clubs and bars, not manufactured in a studio."

Amen!

17 | Anita O'Day

THE LIFE OF A MUSIC LEGEND

During the sixty years I've been reporting on—and participating in—the jazz scene, there has been a perennial debate among musicians, critics and aficionados about the definition of a jazz singer. The answer couldn't be more clear: Anita O'Day.

Richard Cook, in his essential *Jazz Encyclopedia* (Penguin, 2007), gets to the core of the joyful excitement of hearing, and remembering, Anita:

"At fast tempos, she was incomparable, lighter and more fluent than Ella (Fitzgerald). Less regal but more daring than Sarah Vaughan, she could scat with a dancing ease."

And she had a signature sound. From the first note, you knew who was telling the story, *her* story. To be a lasting presence in jazz, you also have to have something to say that comes from your own life. As Charlie Parker said: "Music is your own experience, your thoughts, your wisdom. If you don't live it, it won't come out of your horn [or your singing]."

As Annie Ross, herself a true jazz improviser, described the impact of Anita: "There's a whole life in that voice!"

In the documentary by Robbie Cavolina and Ian McFadden, *Anita O'Day: The Life of a Music Legend* (2008)—the most definitive ever made on the inner life, the soul, of a jazz musician—Anita O'Day can be seen and heard for the ages in the fullness of her life force. In this portrait, arranger Johnny Mandel says—as you will agree—"Nobody sounded like Anita O'Day ever. She didn't borrow from anyone. Others borrowed from her later. It's not about notes, effects or any of that. You get into the song and make it live."

As Anita once recalled, "In the early, early days in Chicago, they just used to call me 'Anita O'Day, the Personality Singer.' And that's all they could say. I sure wasn't a torch singer."

The first time that personality hit me full force was in a small Chicago club many years ago. It was electrifying. Every bit of her was swinging. And no other singer I've ever heard so jubilantly embodied the very pulse, the life force, of jazz. The always surprising Pee Wee Russell could have been talking about Anita when he once defined jazz for me:

"A certain group of people—I don't care where they come from—have a heart feeling and a rhythm in their systems that you couldn't take away from them, even if they were in a symphony organization."

And in front of a band, Anita, as Richard Cook wrote, was one of the musicians—"a hip, up front member of the band, rather than one of the sequined canaries which were the stereotypical band singers of the day."

What makes the documentary so valuable is not only Anita in full but the hip selections of other singular musicians who provide a chorus of astute perceptions.

For example, Gerald Wilson: "We had a lot of black female singers like Sarah Vaughan and, of course, Ella Fitzgerald, but Anita O'Day was right there with them in that class. It doesn't matter what color you are—if you don't have the feeling to play the jazz. Because feeling is one of the biggest things you've got to get in there."

And you need to have the fun of being as free a soul as Anita was that you can share those exuberant feelings with your listeners.

Among the revelations about the nonpareil Anita that were new to me in this production is James Gavin's contribution: "Everything that happened in the room and every sound she heard, she would somehow work into her performance. I remember vividly that she talked about the ceiling fan whirling above her with a chu-chit, chu-chit, chu-chit, so she threw that into the music, making it part of her rhythm. That's a jazz singer!"

That's a jazz singer who is a completely spontaneous improviser. Eric Dolphy once told me that, waking up one morning, he heard the birds singing outside his window. And they became part of his music.

A truly historic jazz triumph in this documentary is what Anita called "the biggest thing that happened to me in my life"—her 1958 Newport Jazz Festival performance thankfully caught for all time in Bert Stern's film *Jazz on a Summer's Day*.

As always, Anita was totally immersed in the moment! "I didn't even know they were filming," she says here. "There were 150 musicians . . . everybody you could name was in that show. And there was my picture in *Time* magazine. Nobody else was mentioned."

The only comparably glorious jazz vocal—also continually reverberating in videos around the world—was Billie Holiday's dialogue with Lester Young in CBS TV's 1957 *The Sound of Jazz,* produced by Robert Herridge with a cast that Whitney Balliett and I assembled.

Anita's magical ability to lift the spirits of the musicians accompanying her—and her invigorated listeners—was caught in the March 2007 *JazzTimes* by Cheryl Bentyne, herself a jazz singer who once led The New Deal Rhythm Band on the road:

"With Anita, [swinging] was in her genes. I loved how I could actually hear her smiling in her music. Anita had her demons, but when she opened her mouth—stand back. Her essence lit up everything around her. . . . The stage was on fire, to be sure."

Then Cheryl Bentyne adds a blue note: "She was an absolute jazz legend who, in my opinion, never got her full due. Anita was one of a kind. Thank God we have her recordings."

Thank God we have this documentary, *Anita O'Day: The Life of a Music Legend,* that will help ensure that Anita does get her due. As for her most memorable recordings, we owe a special thanks to Norman Granz, whom I was privileged to know as a friend, and who recorded only those musicians—whether or not they were on the sales charts at the time—he deeply admired and wanted to preserve for posterity.

And so we, and those who come after us, have such Granz Verve recordings as *Anita Sings the Most with the Oscar Peterson Quartet* and *Anita O'Day Swings Cole Porter with Billy May.*

In his continually illuminating autobiography, *A Jazz Odyssey* (Continuum), Oscar Peterson tells of playing for Anita on many occasions: "I learned that Anita would never gad away in fear of any musical challenge. Indeed, she thrives on it: whatever its outcome, challenges seem to resuscitate her musically—nourishing further her desire to be something more than just another jazz vocalist."

Anita was so much more than "just another jazz vocalist" that, as Joe Franklin says here: "Besides being a fantastic entertainer, she was a force of nature!"

18 | The Music of the 1930s Is Back in Full Swing

Having discovered jazz in the late 1930s, I was in time for the big bands I heard on the radio from ballrooms and nightclubs around the country. I was lifted out of the Depression by the soaring reeds and strutting brass; the romantic fantasies that were an obbligato of the ballads; the verve and wit of Count Basie, Duke Ellington, Tommy Dorsey; and even the playfulness of the "sweet bands" (Russ Morgan, Sammy Kaye, Kay Kyser).

There have been attempts to bring back the swing era, including touring "ghost bands" playing the scores of deceased leaders of the past, but I thought that only those of us who had actually been part of those swinging times would ever know what it felt like to ride those rhythm waves.

But now it is possible for those born after the swing era to be in the actual presence of a fifteen-piece band, the Sultans of Swing, that not only keeps the joy of that heritage alive but has also absorbed much of the spirit and language of the jazz that came after.

The band is the creation of David Berger, age fifty-seven, a widely experienced composer, arranger and teacher; recipient of seven National Endowment of the Arts fellowships in jazz composition; and transcriber of more than fifty works by Duke Ellington. (Knowing that Duke's compositions were in a constant state of becoming, I never thought that achievement was possible.)

The Sultans of Swing came into being in 1996 to fulfill a deeply felt mission of Mr. Berger: "Over the past seventy years most people have forgotten the feeling of swing, if they are old enough to have known it at all. Still this music infects those who are lucky enough to be exposed to it. In those moments we feel fully alive."

This is a hardworking band, having played many gigs in this country as well as three European tours, residencies in schools, and—like bands in the old glory days—weddings and private parties. As Ellington did, Mr. Berger writes for the individual musicians, who range in age from twenty to sixty. At least half have been students of his; he now teaches at Juilliard and has held posts at the Manhattan School of Music, William Paterson College, Long Island University and Montclair State College.

The Sultans' fourth CD, *Hindustan* (on the Such Sweet Thunder label), was released in 2006. From the first few bars, I was a kid again, marveling at how much fun it must be to be in a band that swings so naturally—the crisp soloists interweaving seamlessly with the sections.

Composer-arranger Berger is a master of dynamics; a subtle, continually surprising colorist; and he lets the music breathe. *Hindustan* was recorded during a 2005 tour of Sweden. "Every time we go on tour," Mr. Berger says in the notes, "the music improves daily. After a few days, we surpass the highest level we ever achieved as a band. By the end of the tour we are all on a high that doesn't require artificial stimulants. I've always wanted to capture our peak moments on a recording. Well, here it is!"

Sonically, what makes *Hindustan* historic is how close it really does get to the live sound of the band. As Mr. Berger told me, there were no headphones on members of the band, allowing the players to fully hear one another, and it was mixed, he adds, "with absolutely no compression, so that what you hear on this CD is as close to a live performance as ever captured on any CD." The absence of compression means that the full dynamic range of the music is heard—including the extreme highs and lows. (If only I had had such an engineer in my brief time as a jazz record producer.)

This band's musical range is captured on *Hindustan*—from "Monkey Business," a tribute to Thelonious Monk, to a revitalized "Poor Butterfly" in which, Mr. Berger notes, "Mark Hynes keeps the Coleman Hawkins tradition alive, Ryan Keberle tests the limits of the trombone, and there's the swinging lead trumpet of Bob Millikan, who has a way of putting every note in the slot so the whole band can play together as one."

On a previous CD, *The Harlem Nutcracker* (Such Sweet Thunder, 1999), Mr. Berger challenged himself by adding to how Duke Ellington and Billy Strayhorn had reimagined *The Nutcracker Suite*. "The challenge," says Mr. Berger, "was to remain myself and not be intimidated by either of them—or by Tchaikovsky." Also contagiously evident is how much fun the sidemen had in not being intimidated by any of the four composers. This *Nutcracker*, taking place on Christmas Eve in Harlem, has so much good cheer that the music can barely stay in these grooves without exploding.

When I feel very sad or very good, tears come to my eyes. Listening again, as I write this, to the Sultans' fusion of centuries and cultures in *The Harlem Nutcracker*, I've had to stop to wipe the tears of pleasure away. I am grateful to David Berger for enabling me to be thirteen years old again—hiding the radio in my room, where I was supposed to be asleep, and tuning in across the fruited plains to this wondrously indigenous American music.

The late jazz critic George Simon was already writing in the past tense in his 1967 book about his specialty, *The Big Bands:* "Do you remember what it was like? Maybe you do. Maybe you were there. Maybe you were there in New York two-thirds of the way through the 1930's, when there were so many great bands playing—so many of them at the same time. You could choose your spots—so many spots."

But in 2006, in New York, you could choose to hear the Sultans of Swing, who played a Tuesday night summer residency—beginning, appropriately, on July 4—at Birdland, 315 West 44th St., between Eighth and Ninth avenues. As Mr. Berger described the event, "You can hear swinging acoustic big-band jazz in an intimate club—the way the music was designed to be experienced—where the band and the audience can feel each other breathe to the rhythms and inflections of American life."

19 | The Expansive Jazz Journey of Marian McPartland

Pianist-composer Marian McPartland's ninetieth birthday celebration took place at Jazz at Lincoln Center in Dizzy's Club Coca-Cola on March 19, 2008. The guest performers—of diverse styles and jazz eras—included violinist Regina Carter, singer Karrin Allyson, trumpet player Jeremy Pelt and pianist Jason Moran.

Having heard and known Marian for nearly sixty years, I can attest to a tribute by another master pianist who was also there, Bill Charlap, who said: "Her singular musical voice encompasses the past, present and future of jazz."

It was her late husband, the exuberant cornetist Jimmy McPartland, who transported the young English music-hall pianist, then Margaret Marian Turner, right into the Chicago-New York jazz scene in 1947. He once told me why he and Marian so enjoyed being jazz musicians. His mentor, Bix Beiderbecke, whom Jimmy replaced in the Wolverines combo, had said to him: "One of the things I like about jazz, kid, is I don't know what's going to happen next. Do you?"

Still on the road, Marian keeps surprising herself and audiences around the world not only on piano but also as a composer, educator and, since 1979, radio personality as host of National Public Radio's "McPartland's Piano Jazz." She's already booked guests for two years from now. Although I play only the electric typewriter, I've been honored to be one of her guests.

Her 2008 Concord Jazz CD is dedicated to Jimmy McPartland and titled, after one of her originals, *Twilight World*. With her longtime colleagues (they are much more than accompanists), bassist Gary Mazzaroppi and drummer Glenn Davis, Marian's version of "twilight" is much more dynamic than the title connotes.

Characteristically, her repertory here is far-ranging—from Irving Berlin, Alec Wilder and Duke Ellington to Miles Davis, John Lewis of the Modern Jazz Quartet and the still startling modernist Ornette Coleman. Never daunted by new musical frontiers, she says of her choice of Ornette's "Lonely Woman" and "Turn Around" that "as you hear new things, you grow into them."

Also in the set are two more of her own signature songs, "In the Days of Our Love" and "Stranger in a Dream."

A longtime champion of women in jazz—not only as pianists and vocalists—Marian cites the quintessential source of all enduring jazz narratives: "Each of us is an individual—unique, different. The kind of life we have lived comes out in our music."

Her music throughout *Twilight World* portrays a fullness of piano mastery that gives her a secure scope for her improvising; and, as always, she shows that the jazz pulse and luminous beauty are not antithetical. And there is an energizing clarity of tonal range—and of fluid structure—that, however unexpected, feels inevitable.

Each song becomes a story, as if she were speaking directly to the listener about her lifetime of discovering herself—and the world—in her music. As I once told her, it is impossible for her not to swing, at whatever tempo.

In the 1950s, after coming to New York to cover the jazz scene for *Down Beat*, I often heard her at the Hickory House, a spacious restaurant in midtown where the musicians performed above a long, busy bar. She cut through the conversation to a considerable degree, but it took her a while to understand a gently delivered, cautionary lesson she received one night from Duke Ellington, sitting at a table near the bandstand.

It was one of his few nights off, and when the set was over, Marian descended, acutely anxious to hear the Ellington reaction. Warmly smiling, he said to her, "My dear, you play so many notes."

Weeks later, recalling that pivotal moment, she told me: "I was green as grass. It took me a while to understand that he was telling me that I was playing too many notes that were getting in the way of what I was trying to say."

Marian did not forget that postgraduate ducal lesson, which I also heard, years later, during an afternoon's conversation with Dizzy Gillespie. "It's taken me much of my life," he said, "to learn what notes not to play."

Another memory of Marian's time at the Hickory House is in her book *Marian McPartland's Jazz World: All in Good Time* (University of Illinois Press, 2002; paperback edition, 2005), an engaging contribution to not only her own jazz history. In the chapter "You've Come a Long Way, Baby," she recalls one of her first reviews at the New York club by Leonard Feather in *Down Beat*: "Marian McPartland has three strikes against her: She's English, white, and a woman." But after all that has happened since, she added, "I don't feel I have any strikes against me—in fact, life for me is really a ball!"

Among the tributes she receives at the continuous ball are such honors as her designation by the National Endowment for the Arts as a Jazz Master; a Kennedy Center Living Legends of Jazz award; and, in November 2006, an honorary music degree from the justly prestigious Eastman School of Music in Rochester, New York. Also in November 2006, environmentalist McPartland premiered her composition for orchestra and improvised piano, "Portrait of Rachel Carson," with the University of South Carolina Symphony Orchestra—her first "classical" work after all her jazz classics.

She's particularly pleased with her most recent jazz classic, *Twilight World*, explaining that "I'm so happy to have done this album. It's nice to have something you're this happy with at this stage of life."

Her attitude about retiring at age ninety is like that of Duke Ellington while he was still very much on the road. After one of his more than 200 wearying one-nighters a year—like from Toronto to Dallas—I saw him between trips. He looked as if he needed many more days off, and I said: "You don't have to keep going through this. With all the standards you've written, you can retire on your music publishing income at ASCAP."

Ellington looked at me in exasperated wonder. "Retire?" he snapped, "to what?"

I wouldn't dare suggest retirement to Marian McPartland.

In her book *All in Good Time*—to which I often refer for her portraits of jazz creators, from Mary Lou Williams to Bill Evans—she shows why she dedicated her Concord Jazz CD to Jimmy McPartland, thanks to whom "things I would never have imagined have happened. . . . Anything can happen if you work, plan, and keep dreaming. Jimmy did this for me."

Whenever she was in doubt about that, Jimmy—whose cornet would light up a gig anywhere—kept telling her, "Be yourself!" She's always been a good listener.

20 | Going Inside Jazz with Wynton

Of the many books on jazz I've read, much of the permanent illumination has come from those written by the musicians themselves. I can add to the list Wynton Marsalis's *Moving to Higher Ground: How Jazz Can Change Your Life* (Random House, 2009). I don't look for analysis of techniques. That's obviously not my bag. I want to know more of the musicians, and how they hear one another. Wynton gets into the jazz experience from the inside. (Geoffrey C. Ward helped in the structure of the book; Wynton wrote it.)

A perpetual student, "I'm always reading," Wynton has said. "And listening." Soon after he came to New York from New Orleans, he found how much he had to learn. One night, Harry "Sweets" Edison "called a slow blues. 'Man,' Sweets said when it was done, 'you just played more notes than I played in my entire career.' Implied in that was 'And you didn't say anything.'"

Young Wynton asked John Lewis how he defined jazz and was told, "It has to swing or seem to swing. It has to contain the element of surprise, and it has to embody the eternal search for the blues."

Adds Wynton about Lewis, "The way he presented himself didn't make you think about the blues." In my own first meeting with the creator of the Modern Jazz Quartet, John had a copy of England's sophisticated political publication, the *New Statesman*, jutting out of his suit pocket.

But, Wynton writes, Lewis "understood the blues above all else. At every moment, wherever he was, he was going to find the blues."

I rarely saw John Lewis overtly angry, but one day he was smarting. He'd heard of an imminent Atlantic Records session with Joe Turner, and Lewis hadn't been asked to be part of it. "I'm a blues player!" he said to me in sharp frustration.

I knew Billie Holiday, heard her often in clubs, and read a lot about her. But Wynton shows us how to penetrate more deeply into her continuing presence among us. When he was growing up, his father often played at home the last recording she made, *Lady in Satin*. Says Wynton, "Some people hated it because so little of her voice was left. But for me, it teaches that the message you are delivering can be more important than limitations in the method of delivery.

"Billie could evoke dark, dark feelings by applying swinging sweetness. If you put a little salt in something sweet, it gets sweeter; if you put some sugar in something bitter, it gets more bitter. She was like that."

I knew Duke Ellington in a number of contexts and have written a lot about him, but again, Wynton adds more to my appreciation and understanding of his music: "He was fascinated by intense interactions and unusual human foibles. Two guys in the band didn't like each other? Make them sit right next to each other. Give them back-to-back solos. See what happened. . . . He loves musicians. Not just their playing. Them. . . . [A]nd more than any other jazz musician, he addressed the rich internal lives of men and women in love.

"One touch of his hand on the piano and the moon enters the room. He loved ladies and they loved him."

A recent Winston Churchill quote I found brought Duke instantly to mind: "I am a man of simple tastes, easily satisfied with the best." With Duke, that also included women.

Charlie Parker has, of course, a wide international audience. I don't use the past sense referring to his immortality, but in *Moving to Higher Ground*, Wynton reveals the often stunning breadth of Bird's impact. I had a friend, a New York City homicide detective, Don Baezler, who was a Bird enthusiast. A police precinct would be a rather unusual place to discuss Charlie Parker recordings. Or so I thought before I met Don.

But Wynton shows how parochial I was: "John Lewis told me all kinds of people would be at Charlie Parker's gigs. It always shocked him: sailors, firemen, policemen, city officials, prostitutes, dope fiends, just regular working people. Whoever it was, when Bird started playing, his sound would arrest the room."

I once ran into Bird briefly on a railway station platform. At that time he was only interested in talking about country music. As Wynton writes, Bird's music "had so much in it because it had come such a long distance. It had all of American music in it: fiddlers' reels and Negro spirituals; levee tunes and camp-meeting songs; minstrel songs; vaudeville tunes, and American popular songs; the blues and ragtime . . . European classical music"—Bird once told me a Bartók concerto had long resonated in his head—"and the irresistible stomping, riffing style of blues playing that tells you Parker came from Kansas City."

I recently interviewed the internationally celebrated Jerry Douglas, the master Dobro player, winner of a number of Country Music Association awards. Bird came into the conversation, and Douglas spoke excitedly of what a kick it was for him to record with Ray Charles.

Songcatcher Alan Lomax used to call what we have here, and sent around the world, "the rainbow of American music." In his book Wynton says, "No one knows how another person experiences living. It's too deeply rooted, based on too many unique circumstances. Language cannot express these private, ever-changing states of being. Music is much clearer about subconscious and super-conscious matters. Music makes the internal external. What's in you comes out."

Wynton notes that he wrote the book to "explore the creative tension between self-expression and self-sacrifice in [the ultimate wholeness] of jazz, a tension that is at the heart of swinging, in music and in life."

And because jazz is so deeply rooted in the evolution of American music, it changes your life all the more by surprising you in the range and continuous surprises of your feelings.

PART FOUR

The Jazz Life On and Off the Road

21 | Memories Are Made of This

A CONVERSATION WITH CLARK TERRY

At the 2006 International Association of Jazz Educators conference, *JazzTimes* sponsored a panel featuring veteran journalist Nat Hentoff and legendary trumpeter Clark Terry. A masterful player and dedicated educator, Terry recalls a lifetime spent guiding young players—several of whom became major forces in jazz history.

NAT HENTOFF: For many years you've been working with young musicians—sometimes very young—who want to become jazz players. I want to go back some years now, to Seattle, when a young kid came up to you. He was playing trumpet; he was composing a little.

CLARK TERRY: Quincy Jones.

NH: You were with [the] Basie small combo, and you said, "I can fit you in at six in the morning." What did you hear in this kid that made you figure to take the time? You had worked all night.

CT: He was so sincere. He had been there two, three nights in a row, and I'd seen him. I'd seen his little stick figure, skinny cat—he was so thin—and he finally made his way up to us, and he looked very serious and very sincere.

NH: I remember you saying you were glad you made time for that kid.

CT: I'm sure glad I did; he gets by all by himself now! Suppose I had said, "Get out of my face, man!"

NH: Then sometime after that, around the St. Louis area, you heard a kid whose last name was Davis (Miles Davis). What did you hear in him?

CT: His teacher, Elwood Buchanan—who's a good buddy of mine, we used to drink beer together, and he taught over in East St. Louis, at Lincoln High School—said to me, "Man, you gotta come over to school and hear this little Dewey Davis. You're not going to believe it." Dewey was his middle name; I used to think he was named after Dewey Jackson, the top trumpeter in the city. But his dad's name was Dewey also, so maybe his dad was as old as Dewey. I used to say, "Well, OK, I'll come over one day," and one day I went over and I met this little kid, man, and he was so thin, thin enough to ride a rooster. He used to look down all the time; he never looked up at you. I'd ask him a question [and] he'd look up and answer, then drop his head back down again. So when I heard him play I said, "Wow, this kid!" He was a teen, maybe 11 or 12 years old. He had just gotten into high school.

NH: Now, I just heard that you discovered Nicholas Payton when he was 14 years old. How did that happen?

CT: Well, I was on a tour in Europe, and a guy had a bunch of little kids from New Orleans that he had taken over to Europe and they played on streetcars and so forth, and Nicholas was a trombone player. I got to know him, and he was a nice, beautiful little young kid. And then I had an occasion to go through New Orleans, and I just said, "Let's get all the kids together!" So we put together a thing like a clinic in New Orleans and here comes this little kid with a trumpet, and I said, "Man, you look like this [other kid]" and he said, "I'm the same one." We indulged him in the clinic and it was a beautiful thing, and all the kids enjoyed it. That's when I began to know him as a trumpet player. He's always been like family.

NH: Is this the way we're going to get more players? Because the territory bands aren't around anymore, there are very few big bands around anymore. Some of the guys told me that years ago, they'd be on the bus and they'd learn from the older musicians, but I guess education is the only way now.

CT: That's the only way. I was fortunate enough to be able to learn from the older musicians, because I was not fortunate enough to go to college and learn how to do all those things that college kids do. So I guess one's as good as the other, as long as you get the results from it.

NH: There's going to be a building at William Paterson University in New Jersey called the C.T. Building. Now, those are familiar initials; what's going to be in there?

CT: It's a performance building, it's a rehearsal practice room, and it'll be an archive for all of my gatherings—and there's lots of gatherings. I can hardly get in my little house sometimes for all the proclamations, and the fifteen doctorates, and the pictures, and the statues and so forth. I have to go in carefully, but luckily it's going to be a beautiful home for all these people.

NH: When is that going to open?

CT: We just had the first concert to raise the funds with Bill Cosby and his Dream Band. Bill always loved Jimmy Heath, who is from Philadelphia, where he was from. As Jimmy was taking his solos, it always happened to be just at the time he wanted to take his solos on the flugelhorn. I had given him a flugelhorn—a large, raggedy thing like this with a bent bell—but a new mouthpiece.

The way that started, on one of his shows on Twenty-third Street, there was a crowd of people on the streets and Jimmy was walking through with a big case and I said, "Hey, sir, where are you going?" and I'm sitting on the doorstep on one of those little houses of New York. And he said, "I'm going to my gig," and I said, "What do you play?" and he said, "I play the saxophone," and I said, "A big old case like that?" It was a bass clarinet, you know, so I said, "Let me hear you play something, come on up here with me," and he came up on the banister, on the steps with me, and he sat down and whipped out the big bass clarinet and played a few ugly notes. And I looked at him and said, "Man, you're playing the wrong instrument! You should be playing a brass instrument," and he said, "I don't have one, all I got is this," and I said, "Well, I just happen to have one for you," so I gave him an old beat-up large flugelhorn, it was horrible, with a new mouthpiece. And I gave it, put it in the case, and on the case I wrote, "Screech Jones," and nobody knows who the heck Screech Jones was, nor is.

He would do this occasionally, he would come into a club where I'm appearing, and he would make himself visible through here and I would say to the audience, "Ladies and gentlemen, if I'm not wrong, I could have sworn I saw Screech Jones back there," and they don't know who the hell Screech Jones is, they couldn't care less. But it must be something big, you know, because we're talking about Screech Jones! So all of a sudden he makes it possible for me to see that it is Screech Jones, he walks through to me, "Oh!" I said, "It is Screech Jones! Ladies and gentlemen, give a big hand for Screech Jones!" and they're all applauding like they're expecting something great, you know. So he comes up and we got it, we had it all figured out. He would start to get his chops together and blow something, and every time he'd do that, I'd play something, you know. So we made a big thing out of it, and we did one of his shows that way, when he came through with the bass clarinet and sat down. And I said, "Uh, you need this brass instrument so you can pucker your lips like this and make a buzz," so he turned around to do the buzz, right on the set; and I said, "Hey, that's great!" So we did the same thing on that set, I said, "Let's hear you play something," and so they take the camera off him, off me, and put it on him, and he'd buzz, but I would be playing, you know. And people say, "Wow, this cat can play!" So we got to be good buddies like that. It was an act that was really funny.

NH: I want to ask you about a group or a class, let's say, that was pretty much left out of jazz for a long time. Wynton Marsalis, for example, he's a very good educator—but he's never, to my knowledge, had in his Jazz at Lincoln Center Orchestra a fulltime woman musician. When I was a kid, the players would say, "Well, you know, the chicks ain't got the chops." What's your feeling about this other class of musicians?

CT: I think you can erase that. I just heard Maria Schneider's group last night, and they had a girl trumpet player by the name of Ingrid Jensen. She's got chops, baby, she's got chops. She was all over the place, and I've known her for years, and she's always had beautiful chops. And my drummer currently is Sylvia Cuenca, and she's hard to beat, man. You can't find anybody that can play good swing anymore like her. So that's just a few of them.

NH: I never heard—except on records, obviously—the Sweethearts of Rhythm. Now, the legend is that Vi Burnside, the tenor player, could cut almost anybody.

CT: She could, she really could, man. That was a great band, a fantastic band. The Harlem Playgirls, that particular band—they were some good players in that band. You have to listen with your eyes closed, and not listen with your eyes.

NH: Jim Hall, who played all over the world like you have, he says, "You know, I play with musicians who can't speak my language, but we get along beautifully when we play." And that's the liberating thing, among other things, about this music. In terms of what's going to be at William Paterson, what do you envision as the curriculum?

CT: We have the course which I'm doing right now, once a week I'm meeting with these kids—we got a drummer, a bass player, a pianist, a tenor player, a trumpet player and a trombone player—the trombone player's here tonight, he's my assistant, he's a great trombone player. I think that in time—already they've started asking, the rest of the group in the music department are asking why is it that they can't play with our group. Now it started out like this: I met a few of these kids and we became very close, and I love to hear young jazz involvement, and I love to be involved with them and hear them play and watch them learn. So I made my home an off-campus classroom, and it was going so successfully that kids are going back to the school and saying, "Man, this is what we are here for, to learn how to play!" So the school finally decided to make me an adjunct professor. Now, I was doing this because I loved doing it, I wanted to do it, but I ended up being on staff, getting paid for something that I enjoy doing. So I think that's great, and I think that eventually what is going to happen is that, already somebody has asked, two kids have asked, "Why can't we play with that band?" We don't want it to be too unnecessarily big and full, because we don't want to have to write charts after charts, you know. We want people to learn how to use the most vital possession: the ear. We want them to learn how to do that, to learn how to put pieces together in intervals, punctuations, and so forth. That's what jazz is all about.

NH: So it's going to be the Clark Terry Graduate School of Listening. One thing that, through the years I've known musicians—my friend Charles Mingus, for example—who were not very happy with what they read by so-called jazz critics. If you were teaching somebody who wanted to be a writer on jazz, what would you tell him to do aside from listening?

CT: What would I tell him? The first thing I would tell him was "Consult Nat Hentoff!"

NH: Oh, there are people who disagree!

CT: I know you're a fair enough person to not ostracize or criticize somebody who's trying to do something. I've got some students who—I've had my drummer tell me that I was the best drum teacher he ever had in his life. And all I do is try to fill in that which is happening right now, and that which happened 40, 50 years ago. And there's a whole lot of stuff that happened that kids are overlooking, things like the Charleston, all that kind of stuff, riverboat beats, beats that they never heard of, the [he scats an impromptu tune], now that's a swinging beat, man, in that tempo. But the kids overlook things like that, the primary things they should have known for years and years and years; but they skipped way over that, over to here, and I think it's important that they should know about that. I happened to have been through that period, and I can relate this to them. And I know a little about the drum, pedals and . . . you know. So it makes me come off to some of the kids like a great drum teacher—I'm not a great drum teacher, I just like to bring to their attention the things which happened before they came on the scene, and the type of things that they should know.

NH: To quote the song "What Am I Here For?" when did you know what you were here for? What did you hear, at how young an age, that made you who you are?

CT: My older sister was married to a tuba player, that's back in the days when they didn't use string bass. So I was a very young kid in school and I used to listen to Cy [MacField] practice, so I asked Cy to take me to the rehearsal. They rehearsed at the homes of various members of the ensemble, and the band that he played in was Dewey Jackson and his Musical Ambassadors. One of the trumpet players, Mr. Lattimore, was a big fat cat and he loved candy. He always had two pockets full of candy, both of which were my favorite types of candy—caramels and Mary Janes. When they would take a break, he would give me a couple of pieces of candy, "Here's some, watch my horn until I get back." I was happy to see him, and I was so happy that he wasn't a banjo player. He would inspire me by just giving me that opportunity. Mr. Lattimore had a lot to do with persuading me to play the trumpet, because on one of the breaks they returned from—I was so magically drawn to his instrument because he was such a nice person—I was back there, trying to huff and puff some notes out of it. They come back from the break—he was the first one back—just in time to catch me huffing and puffing on his horn. And he said to me, "Son, you're going to be a trumpet player." And I was stupid enough to believe him! I was thirteen, maybe twelve.

NH: Now you've done so much, are there any things you still want to do, but haven't had a chance to do?

CT: There's one chance I won't ever have again, as I come from a very poor family—I wanted to learn to play piano and write, but there were no pianos in the area. We lived in an area where there was nothing but a dump, so we were lucky to be able to afford food and clothing. As a matter of fact, the way I learned how to box was, I had more sisters who were older than me, and as time went, the sisters got older, the clothes got smaller, the clothes came down. When they came down to me, they came from a girl, so I had to wear bloomers to school, and high-heeled shoes. I was in school trying to keep up with the boys and one particular day they played a game called Follow the Leader. And we had to run and jump over the fences, iron gates, and over cement fences, and leap over holes and so forth. So I'm trying to climb over one of the iron fences one day; my pants get stuck on one of the pickets, you know, and ripped them off, and there I was with a pair of bloomers. So the cats started giving me, "Clarky's got on bloomers! Clarky wears bloomers!" And this kept on for a whole semester, and finally we had a champion boxer in the neighborhood named Kid Corner, and this was in south St. Louis. And Kid Corner would say, "All you kids come in here, I want to teach you all how to box!" And the first thing he would do when he would walk up to you was hit you right in the stomach, just like that, and then he would say to you, "Tighten up, kid, tighten up!"

So he taught us all how to box and I became a very good boxer. As a matter of fact, I was almost in the same class at one time with Archie Moore, and Archie used to tell me, "Man, you gonna be a champion someday." But I couldn't stomach all those licks upside the head.

NH: Milt Jackson used to say, "People say jazz isn't popular, but it's not on television." Now suppose Public Broadcasting System decided to say, "OK, Clark Terry, you're going to have a series." What would you put on television?

CT: I'd have to really do some serious thinking about that and concocting of ideas and formulas and so forth, and put on something—and they never gave Duke a chance to do it, and he had several ideas, you know. So I don't know what would be acceptable, and you have to think about what would be acceptable.

NH: Maybe you could start by your home being a classroom, just how you did at William Paterson before you became an adjunct professor. That might be worthwhile, and then you could expand from there. And then your alumni would come in, and that would take about 10 years. After all your time with the Ellington language, then you were with Basie. How much of an adjustment was that for you?

CT: Duke was of course far more intellectual in terms of musical knowledge than Basie, but Basie had something that was a little bit different. He had a great, inborn feeling for jazz. He knew tempos like nobody in the world. Neil Hefti brought in the tunes and Basie went out and played them. So [Hefti] said, "What do you think, Governor?"

And Basie looked at him and said, "What?"

"You don't like the arrangement?"

"Arrangement's OK."

"What's wrong?"

"Tempo."

Basie had an uncanny inner feeling for tempos, and for the utilization of space and time. 'Cause from his group in the beginning, back in Kansas—Walter Page, Papa Jo Jones and all the people that were in his first band—this came about from the habit of socializing with his friends in the clubs, the Cherry Blossom, a tiny little club as big as this room and it had little gingham tablecloths and everybody that came in that joint to hear the band knew what Basie drank. So they all had a little taste on the table for Basie, and he would play, and he'd say, "Hey Joe!" and he'd get up and go and greet Joe, and have a little taste while Papa Jo would [play] until he comes back. And when [Basie] comes back [he would play] and then he'd say, "Hey Tom!" [and] go over and have a little taste, 'cause Tom had his taste on the table. So this is the thing that taught us all about the utilization for space and time.

NH: Now, you mentioned space, and Dizzy Gillespie once said to me, "It took practically my whole life to learn what notes not to play." When you teach, how do you teach space?

CT: Well, I teach them the old joke they used to say to us kids when they gave you a quarter: Don't spend it all in one place. It's just as basic as that: Spread it out. Don't try to say everything you know how to say in one chorus, you know. Use the space and time is something we were fortunate enough to have learned from Basie, but Duke and Strayhorn, they knew how to put things together. For instance, they would put minor seconds together, and that was something kind of unheard of, as far as jazz was concerned. And they put it together and made notes; it made you learn how to listen and say, "Oh, he's out of tune . . . oh, no, he's not!" If you listen closely, you'll find he's very much in tune. But they knew how to do that, and they knew how to supply themselves with people who were aware and knew how to do it so it was a marvelous thing. They were both very, very instrumental in the perpetuation of jazz and the colorations of sound and so forth.

NH: Now I know how to define jazz education.

AUDIENCE MEMBER: Could you tell that story about playing with Count Basie and trying to find rooms in places where they wouldn't let you stay?

CT: We were somewhere in a little town in Pennsylvania, and the band had to find rooms, and you couldn't stay in the hotels, you had to stay at Ms. Green's, and Mrs. Jones's, and Ms. Brown's, you know. And so we hustled around, and got everybody—it was a small band, thank God it was small—but we got everybody a room, and we look up, and Basie and I don't have a room. So we went to this one place, this lady with a shade down here and a little sign that said "Rooms." She's peeking out at us from under the shade, and that's what they used to do with the restaurants, they saw you coming and tore up all the menus and make more and put higher prices on them. And she's looking at us, and all of a sudden we go into this room and she says, "Yes, yes, come in."

"Well, we're looking for rooms and we have no rooms for our band, and we need two more rooms."

"Well, I don't have two rooms, but I got an attic with a big bed in it and a little bed against the wall."

And she said, "You can look at it," and we went up and looked at it, and of course the price had been doubled on what you were ordinarily getting. So there's one big bed in the middle of the room, and there's a little slab on the side of the wall, so I know Basie's gonna get the big bed and I'm gonna get the slab, I knew that already. So, just as we ordinarily do when we travel, empty our pockets in the dresser. So I empty my pockets right there, and Basie puts all his stuff right there, and we decide to take the room, in spite of the fact that we knew we were being held up financially. So we took the room, and Basie got in the middle of the bed, and he's reading his favorite literature: comic books. So we're all sitting up, topless, and he's got his comic book out, and I'm up against the slab, up against the wall with the slab, and I have to sleep, and he had the lights on. And at that time, I couldn't sleep with the light on, you know, I had to have the light off. And he couldn't sleep with the light off! So I said, "I know what I'll do—wait till he goes to sleep, and I'll sneak over and turn the light off." So that's when he started reading: "Haha, look at that! Did you see that?" and all of a sudden he starts snoring, and I hear the magazine hit his belly, and I said, "Aah, now's my chance!" So I sneak over while the light is on and he's sleeping, and I reach up and I pull the chain—before I could release the chain to turn off the light, he sat straight up in bed and said, "Put it back!" The first thing he thought was that I stealing his belongings—"Put it back!"

NH: There's a phrase—I've used it a lot, a lot of people have used it—jazz is the life force. Well, we've been privileged to hear from the life force Clark Terry.

22 | Man, I'm So Lucky to Be a Jazz Musician

PHIL WOODS

Nat Hentoff interviewed Phil Woods at the 2007 conference of the International Association for Jazz Education.

An unstoppable carrier of the bop torch, saxophonist Phil Woods has watched jazz education transform from informal mentoring in the back of the tour bus into a series of world-class, big-dollar institutions with a highly refined pedagogy. Here, acclaimed journalist and *JazzTimes* columnist Nat Hentoff helps Woods reflect on a lifetime spent performing, teaching and learning—Woods's own development came from all angles: as a pupil of the unsung innovator Lennie Tristano, as a clarinet student in the classical program at Juilliard, as a disciple of Charlie Parker recordings and via bandleaders like Dizzy Gillespie.

NAT HENTOFF: I want to start with a story about Norman Granz because it reminded me of you. He was going on a tour of Japan with Oscar Peterson, Roy Eldridge and others, and a reporter asked him a question: "Can you name the one person who really exemplifies what jazz is all about?" Oscar was saying, "Tatum, Tatum, Tatum." Then Norman says, "No, Roy Eldridge because he always plays like it's his last solo." [That] reminds me of you. Or am I wrong?

PHIL WOODS: Thank you, Nat. I remember that great article you did on me, and it was very touching, called "The Irrepressible Spirit." I think when the fire keeps burning you've gotta use it, and so far it's still ignited.

NH: You did an interview with Eric Nemeyer, and you said, "I'm all for jazz education, but I don't see it paying off on the street."

PW: We need somebody who can say, "It's over there, guys." It's like when Dizzy was around and Louis was around.

Yeah, we had people to follow. I think jazz is a street music, and I've also said, as an exaggeration, "Let's get jazz out of the schools and put it back on the streets where it belongs." You know what I mean? There are no more buses; there are no more places to refine your craft. I'm all for the jazz education, but most of the teachers teaching wanted to be players, and there's just not enough gigs. So now they're teaching other kids that there aren't enough gigs, and that's not their fault. A university should reflect the needs of society. Too many lawyers is a drag, but they always get a gig, but too many tenor players is uncontainable. I mean, there're 3,000 tenor players a year for three gigs, and two of them are playing for the door at a Ramada Inn playing Britney Spears medleys.

NH: In that same interview you said, however, "Even without the next Louis or the next Phil Woods there are some very good players around, and they're not getting the attention that they deserve . . . " Can you name some?

PW: Jon Gordon. Bill Charlap, who is getting some attention. Grace Kelly, a little fourteen-year-old. Francesco Cafiso, out of [Italy]. I do believe something that's overlooked in what the kids are not getting when they're getting educated is that jazz is not a business. It started out as entertainment in the first place. It walked a precarious line between art and entertainment and I think still does to a certain extent. Because it's a group effort it's not a solo with a backup, but it doesn't require megabucks and it doesn't require that every record sells a million, you know? I don't have a record contract, and I haven't had one for years. But it's such a strong, vital art form. It's already changed the planet. Thank God, my work is mostly done in Europe and Japan. I couldn't keep a band together for thirty years on what I make in the States.

NH: One of my favorite stories Jon Faddis tells was when Louis Armstrong was booked as an ambassador, they sent him to the Belgian Congo, and there was this really fierce civil war going on at the time, as there often is. Both sides suspended the war. They wanted to hear Louis.

PW: When I was with Dizzy, Iran was their first port of call and then we went to East and West Pakistan. We went to Beirut, we went to Greece, we went to Syria, we went to Turkey. I think they should have sent Dizzy a few more times. I think it's better to send cats with instruments than send cats with AK-47s.

NH: You once said that when you were with Dizzy you were never out of school.

PW: Always! He would love to share. Dizzy and Art Blakey kidnapped me one time. True story. I was in Birdland, and it was kind of a down period. I was drinking too much, I wasn't doing any gigs, I was doing the studio scene and I was, you know, ugggghhh. Dizzy and Art Blakey threw me in the cab and took me out to Dizzy's house. Now this was early 1960s, and Dizzy said, "Well what's your problem?" And I said, "I'm not getting any gigs, I'm playing for strippers, I haven't seen a woman from the front for the past three years." And he said, "Yeah, but you're working. You could be somebody if you clean up your act." And I said, "Yeah, but you know Dizzy . . . I'm a white guy." And he said, "Whoa, hold it, time out, baby. You know Charlie Parker did not play this music for only black people, he played it for the world, he played it for everybody and if you can hear it, you can have it. But remember, you can't steal a gift." And I never forgot that. I told Gene Lees that story, and he used it as the title of his book. But Dizzy and Art Blakey and those cats never played that game. If you can swing, you're cool. Just do the gig and do right by the music. God bless him for that.

NH: I always have trouble figuring out whom, if anybody, to vote for president. One year I wrote in Dizzy Gillespie and I was serious 'cause I knew the guy, I knew his bio and faith. . . . He would have been a hell of a president. About learning, you said in another interview that you had one teacher, Harvey LaRose, who made the big difference in your life. Why was that?

PW: You never know what kind of fortune is going to come your way, and it all depends on the teacher, which I always tell kids when I'm doing master classes. I discovered my uncle's saxophone when I was twelve years old and I was involved in melting lead and making toy soldiers. When I opened up the sax I saw that it was all gold and shiny and I thought, Man, I could melt this sucker down and make a golden hoard of warriors. And somebody mistook my nefarious intent for an interest in music. When the guy died shortly after, I was given the saxophone, which I proceeded to put in the closet and went back to melting lead. Now, melting the saxophone was really out of the question, since it belonged to me. After a couple of weeks, my mother said, "You know you ought to at least take a lesson." So I went to the yellow pages and looked up Drum Shop at State and Main in Springfield, Massachusetts, because I knew where that was, and I made an appointment with Mr. Harvey LaRose. I said, "Should I bring the saxophone?" You see, I was a real natural talent. I could hear him gasp and he said, "Yeah, it would be a good idea to bring your saxophone to your first saxophone lesson." And that's when my life changed, with that first lesson, 'cause I was faking it. He would show me the Rubank elementary method, and I would "du dah, du dah," and I would copy what he did. Then I went home and put the horn away and never practiced. I went back the following week and I could play the lesson, which I thought nothing about.

Now, if I had gotten a more straitlaced teacher that said, "How dare you! You're faking it, you're playing by ear." You can teach everything else, but you can't teach cats how to hear. Harvey realized I had a good tone, a fair retentive ability and I could play the saxophone. Mr. LaRose played alto, clarinet, flute, guitar, violin, piano. Repaired all of the instruments and taught all of the instruments and arranged for all of the big bands in Western Massachusetts; not a jazz man, but he was a great musician. And within a year the first solos he gave me were Benny Carter transcribed solos, and that's the first jazz I ever played. And he played piano and then one week he gave me a song by Duke Ellington called "Mood to be Wooed," and I was working on that very kind of bluesy ballad, beautiful song and, wouldn't you know it, Duke Ellington's band came to Springfield that week. And all us young kids—Joe Morello and Sal Salvador—went to see Duke and the lights all went down to a nice romantic blue and Johnny Hodges, the great virtuoso, stepped forward and played "Mood to be Wooed." And there is nothing like hearing a master play something that you are working on for your lesson. Mr. LaRose was giving me the hit parade, four pop songs of the week. You had your B-flat part, your E-flat part, your bass-clef part, your concert part and he would play the piano, tell me what the chords were, urge me to improvise, redecorate, and I took to it like a duck to water.

NH: When you teach, how do you teach aside from what you learned from Mr. LaRose?

PW: I make them play the piano.... Dizzy first recognized my talents in the middle of a jam session in Pakistan, I think. Dizzy was jamming with somebody and they were playing "Just You, Just Me," and the piano player was not making it. I'd never met Dizzy 'cause Quincy [Jones] picked the band, but I was doing a good job with the alto, but I realized this cat was not playing the right changes, so I said, "Let me play this one." I aced them out, and I started comping for Dizzy, and he looked over at me and gave me a big [grin]. We always shared the keyboard when we went on the road together, and I traveled with him a lot for years and years.

NH: He was the most generous guy I've ever met. In terms of all this jazz education that's going on, let's assume that there won't be many players coming out of it. But will there be listeners?

PW: There'll be more cultured human beings. I think it's important. If a kid buys a saxophone or a trumpet or a trombone he's less likely to buy a gun and shoot me. Unless he wants my gig. Don't let this gentle demeanor fool you; you don't know what I keep in my [saxophone] case!

NH: Another Phil Woods quote: "Music is the journey. You never arrive in music; the work is never over." You never say, "I'm gonna retire."

PW: The more I play, the more I realize that I don't know anything about the magic of music. I think we all realize that life is a journey. It's not about arriving . . . arriving is the last thing you wanna do. It's going through and always developing. I get up in the morning and I brush my teeth, I look in the mirror and I give myself a round of applause and say, "Let's get on with it." I go to the keyboard or go to the computer and start writing some music. I enjoy every day, and I thank the powers that be for giving it to me. All the awards I love. It keeps you going, but it's a lot to be done. I'm working on four or five projects as we speak.

NH: I once saw Duke after one of those road trips like from Toronto to Dallas. He looked pretty beat, and I presumptuously said, "You know, you don't have to do this. . . . You could retire with your ASCAP income." He looked at me and he said, "Retire? To what?"

PW: I remember being with Duke, and my son was traveling with the band in Europe, especially in France for the "sacred" concerts. He was the boy that read the poem. And after the gig at the big Roman Amphitheater, there was a reception for Duke. I offered Duke a hand [in climbing the steps], and as we were going up the steps he says, "I'm getting too old for this shit." He was really exhausted, and when we got to the top of the stairs where all the people were waiting, all of a sudden forty years dropped off of him. He started schmoozing with the girls. Benny Carter had the same magic. They'd be totally exhausted, but when they hit that stage, baby, they were twenty-four again. That spirit, that fire.

NH: Clark Terry has cancer and he has other troubles, and he needs help to get on the stand, but when he's up there he plays like he's twenty-two. The National Endowment for the Arts was originally going to call this interview "The Old

Folks." There used to be this mythology that jazz is a young man's game and it ain't so anymore.

PW: No, it only takes forever to learn how to be a player. All those guys [honored by the National Endowment for the Arts] aren't saying, "I am a Jazz Master." That's the last thing we consider ourselves. We know the work is never finished, and sometimes the young folks don't realize that. Whoever invented smooth jazz, man, I wanna kill 'em. You're turning an art form into a hooker. With that kind of thinking you can make so much money before you're thirty that you don't ever have to play again. That's the kind of player I want to follow? If I wanna play, it's gonna take me on a lifetime voyage, like a great baseball player. Like Johnny Pesky or something. In jazz, Benny Carter is my role model. He played right up to his nineties. I once asked him, "Benny, how the hell do you put up with it? I mean, not the musical part, I understand something about that, but I mean when they say your hotel room's not ready, the plane is canceled, you're not gonna get paid tonight." Benny looked me in the eye and said, "Phil, always go first class." So I thought I'd be clever, and I said to him, "And play with economy." Benny didn't even crack a smile, and then he said, "Phil, you ought to get your own television show."

NH: Speaking about how long it takes and how you never know enough, Dizzy once told me, "It took me most of my life to learn what notes not to play."

PW: Emphysema's teaching me the same thing. Emphysema is nature's way of saying, "You're playing too many notes!" Now with my pulmonary problems I have to shape my solos. A lot of people say, "You're really playing better than ever." And I'm convinced that there's more space in my music. You deal with the ailments you've got and you continue playing. I'm just happy to play that way. But it's true: I can always play a million notes, but now I'm trying to find the one note that means something. I'm still looking.

NH: Speaking of notes, Art Tatum once said, "There is no such thing as wrong notes. It's what you do after."

PW: Dizzy had the same thing, and most major composers will tell you that. But Dizzy was a guest with the Phil Woods Quintet not too long before he died. We did a tour all through Europe. He came down to meet the band and we did our first gig and we got in the cab together and he said, "Man, I'm so lucky to be a jazz musician." Here he is doing a tour with me and my band, and it says "The Dizzy Gillespie/Phil Woods All-Stars," and he always said how lucky he was to be a jazz musician. A lot of people dismissed him and said that Charlie Parker was the guy. I once asked him, "Diz, how did you break into your own way? I know you came from Roy Eldridge and all them." He said that when he heard Parker, the vernacular was discovered, the vocabulary, the way to speak the language, and he always gave the most credit to Charlie Parker. Yet I've always thought that Mother Nature has the ways of supplying the yin and yang. What a combination: Charlie Parker, the comet who flew across the sky and exploded and changed the whole universe, not just our planet, but probably the whole Milky Way. And Dizzy, the professor, always studying, always teaching and always passing on the information. But together with Monk and Max and Roy and all of those cats they gave it such incredible music. It's a black gift, but it's not exclusively black when some of the greatest players are coming from Japan and Europe.

NH: That quote, "I'm so lucky to be a jazz musician," I hear that quote from another musician . . . a guy named Phil Woods.

PW: I consider myself very fortunate to make a living staying in decent hotels, except for the one I'm in at the moment.

When I was a young man I'd study with Lennie Tristano when he would come to New York. I would go out to Flushing, Long Island, take the lesson and come back to Manhattan. Go to Romeo's for spaghetti, go to the Mainstand Record Shop and buy the latest shellac records, and then if we still had a dollar left go to Fifty-second Street and the Three Deuces. One lesson Lennie asked us, "Are you going down to Fifty-second Street tonight?" And I said, "Why do you ask?" Lennie says, "I'm opening for Charlie Parker and I thought maybe you'd like to meet him." And I said to myself, "I always wanted to meet God," 'cause the only reason I was in New York is because I wanted to be where Charlie Parker was, and Springfield wasn't that far away. So, sure enough, you could get a Coca-Cola for a dollar at the Three Deuces and the waiter got to know me and my friend Hal, and sure enough we sat by the drums. Not the choicest acoustic spot, but the Tristano Trio opened up, and then somebody came and got me and took me backstage—and there was Charlie Parker. I wouldn't call it backstage, 'cause they were all speakeasies; they were just joints behind the paper curtain. And there's Charlie Parker sitting on the floor with a big cherry pie, and he said, "Hi kids, you want a piece of cherry pie?" And I said, "Oh, Mr. Parker, cherry is my favorite flavor." I had to say something. So he said, "Well, you sit down here and I'll cut you a big slab," and he whipped out his switchblade and he bam, bam, boom. But that accessibility, the accessibility of Fifty-second Street and the clubs and the music—and the relevance of the music—wasn't that far removed from what America was dancing to. We all knew who Gershwin and Cole Porter were, that's before the amateurs. When the amateurs took over, finito.

NH: Charlie Parker said something to me once, and he was talking about [some music] he'd heard and he said, "The first time it didn't make any sense to me, I didn't like it. Then, later on, a couple of months later, I was in a different frame of mind and the whole thing opened up."

PW: I tell my students [to] listen to all music. Listen to music you don't even like and see why you don't like it. The only way I could go to school, I went to Juilliard as a clarinet player. I pretended to be constipated for four years. I had to start from A to Z and learn the classical repertoire because I didn't know it. I knew Charlie Parker, but that was not a classical clarinet player. I had to learn the fugal technique and keyboard harmony. . . . Some of those violinists who I was so intimidated by couldn't play "Come to Jesus" in the key of C on the piano. I learned about music the old-fashioned way. We all have the same set of screwdrivers, but you have to find the way that you want to play. I mention Elis Regina and I get this blank look. You know Astor Piazzolla? You ever listen to Nueva Flamenca? You ever listen to the pygmies improvise? Do you know what John Cage was talking about? Did you ever read a book or paint a painting? Did you ever be a cultured human being, which is what Benny Carter taught me, speak a language. Try to understand women—which is impossible—but try. I speak Italian and French a little bit and a little Spanish. I can drink and eat in many countries. I listen to everything because you hear jazz in all musics and that's the flexibility of jazz. We've got to rebuild Louis Armstrong's birthplace. I was in New Orleans and it's so sad. What an embarrassment! We're rebuilding the whole world and we can't rebuild New Orleans. Let's do something about that.

NH: It's as important as, let's say, Thomas Jefferson's birthplace. One story about Charlie Parker that I much appreciated, I think it was at Charlie's Tavern, they used to have a jukebox and he'd come in and play country music. One of the guys finally said, "How can you listen to that?" And Bird said, "Listen to the stories, they're about people."

PW: The giants, the masters, were very worldly about their taste. They were not into this thing, "Oh, I'm into jazz." Charlie Parker [was] all about [listening to all different types of music and being open to arts]; that's when jazz was aware of world music. I'm not sure that kids are getting that; maybe in some of the better schools.

NH: All they care about [in the schools these days] is testing for reading and math and they cut out music and all that stuff. About jazz education, I talked to Benny Carter after he'd been to North Texas State. Benny said, "It was very impressive they could read anything, play anything, but there was one thing missing. They all sounded alike." How do you break through that if you're an educator?

PW: You don't. It's too late. We no longer have a regional sound. We don't have a Chicago sound, a New Orleans sound. We used to have a sound up in New England. There was a Boston sound. There used to be a Kansas City sound. You could tell where a guy was from. Now it's all homogenized 'cause they all got the same rulebook and the same licks and the same mouthpiece and the same codified way of going about this music. Instead of going and grabbing what interests you and transcribing it. Now you just buy the transcribed solos. I tell my students, "Don't just read the Omnibook of all Bird's solos—at least transcribe one by yourself. You'll get more of a picture of what the man's music is about by doing it yourself."

NH: How are we gonna break out of this codified music?

PW: I have other priorities, man. I'll leave it to the generation that's going to have to deal with it. . . . Now there's a lot of guys that can play and we've gotta find more gigs. If we find more gigs there'll be more interest. . . . The guys that are gonna get the gigs are gonna be the ones that have an individual sound. But it has nothing to do with the numbers that we're graduating. I don't wanna say that it's bad that kids are playing instruments—that's a good thing! That makes a strong society, but I always ask my students, "Are you entertaining notions of either being a brain surgeon or a tenorman? Be a brain surgeon." Music is only for those that have no choice, and sometimes they don't figure that out at that age. I say, don't be in a hurry after high school to go into a university. Take a year off, get on a tramp steamer, go to Europe and learn those things that I mentioned before. Learn a little bit about another language; play in the street, especially in Europe, which has a whole different viewpoint of the arts. Go to the museums and try to be a man or a woman—try to be a cultured person, and then see who you are.

23 | Conventional Unwisdom about Jazz

A doomsday statistic I hear often—and, I confess, have used myself—is that jazz record sales are only 3 percent of the total in this country, proving the very limited popularity of the music. I have now been disabused of that misleading factoid by a letter from Bill Kirchner in Gene Lee's invaluable *Jazzletter*. Said Kirchner: "As Dan Morgenstern has pointed out, the oft-cited figure applies to only major labels. It doesn't include independent labels, or imports, or bootlegs, or sales of used records." And, I would add, it doesn't include musicians' increasing use of the Internet to sell their self-produced recordings.

I called Dan Morgenstern, who made the tellingly visual point: "You go into Tower Records [which no longer exists], or others of the major record stores, and you see oceans of jazz releases. It would make no sense for these stores to give so much space to jazz to fit if it doesn't sell."

Another alleged fact is that "jazz books don't sell." As I can attest, this is an increasing reaction from book editors, including some of those who used to be more welcoming to jazz proposals but now go back to their in-house committees for approval and are told to offer minimal advances, if any. My response, out of my own frustrating experiences with some of my published books, is that jazz books indeed don't sell if they're not promoted with knowledgeable skill and determination as others of mine have proved.

An illuminating case history of how to promote a jazz book is the odyssey of *Tommy Dorsey: Livin' in a Great Big Way* by [the late] Peter Levinson (Da Capo Press, 2005), the first book on Dorsey in thirty-two years. (In the February *JazzTimes*, Christopher Loudon called it a "thoroughly enlightening and entertaining biography [which] will help push the deserving Dorsey back into the spotlight.")

I first knew Peter Levinson decades ago as a remarkably resourceful public relations professional. Over the past thirty years, his clients have included an abundance of jazz creators, from Count Basie to Benny Carter, Artie Shaw and Phil Woods. His previous books are *Trumpet Blues: The Life of Harry James* and *September in the Rain: The Life of Nelson Riddle,* both of which will be essential for researchers and surprised readers into the future.

In detailing how Peter Levinson planned and executed the promotion of his jazz book, I first have to note that some publishing houses have able publicity personnel, but they need the support of their employers to spend the time and effort to bring a book into the spotlight. But some of their bosses restrain them with the shopworn mantra "Let's first see what kind of word of mouth the book will get."

Levinson, knowing that his publication date was November 1, 2005—and that the date of Tommy Dorsey's 100th birthday was eighteen days later—began his campaign over a year before the book would hit the stores.

He called Jeff Jones, a senior vice president of Sony Music, and the result is a three-CD Tommy Dorsey, *The Sentimental Gentleman of Swing—The Tommy Dorsey Centennial Collection,* orchestrated by the legendary discographer-historian Michael Brooks. As a bonus, Jeff Jones added *The Essential Frank Sinatra with the Tommy Dorsey Orchestra.* Meanwhile, Lisa Warren, Da Capo Press's publicity director, was at work setting up an interview, with music, on National Public Radio's *Weekend Edition.* Levinson parlayed that into a spot on CBS TV's *Entertainment Tonight,* which designated the Dorsey book an essential Christmas gift.

Tuning in CBS's *Sunday Morning* on New Year's Day, I saw Peter, along with Tommy Dorsey clips, in an interview he had set up. Along with book signings around the country, many of which Levinson arranged, he also was responsible for a week of Tommy Dorsey's music at Jazz at Lincoln Center's Dizzy's Club Coca-Cola, with the Juilliard Jazz Orchestra; and Tommy Dorsey's 100th Birthday Cruise Line in November with the Tommy Dorsey Orchestra directed by Buddy Murrow. In addition, Levinson arranged for five Tommy Dorsey film musicals to be shown in March 2006 on Turner Classic Movies, in the course of which his book was prominently cited. There were also a range of radio interviews and, through Levinson's contacting many major newspapers, reviews of the book on those pages.

Obviously, Levinson's many contacts over many years in the music business have had a lot to do with this aurora borealis of publicity. But it's important to document what can be done with a book on jazz, including a book about a musician, however masterful and influential a trombonist and leader he was, whose music is otherwise exceedingly hard to find on the air these days and rarely mentioned in jazz publications.

The NPR interview with Levinson, which I heard, began with Linda Wertheimer: "You're listening to Tommy Dorsey and his orchestra . . . [who] influenced a generation of performers. With his brother, Jimmy, . . . he defined American popular music from the twenties all the way to the fifties. . . . Mr. Levinson, welcome."

Well, Dorsey surely helped define popular music all those years, but how many listeners—except those of a certain age—suddenly discovered these unexpected pleasures that Saturday morning? The book also brought back the surprises for me back then of the volcanic Bunny Berigan with Dorsey, and the band's *Milenberg Joys,* one of the hottest jazz records of all time.

Milt Jackson once told me jazz could be more popular if only more people knew about it, and that takes promotion!

PART FIVE

Who *Is* a Jazz Singer?

24 | Are Krall and Monheit Jazz Singers?

As long as I can remember, there have been bristling arguments among musicians, critics and aficionados about the qualities that define jazz singers. Was Bing Crosby among the elect? Yes, by my criteria, whenever he wanted. In any case, he was a natural swinger, even when he talked. Frank Sinatra? My suggestion to any aspiring singer, male or female, is to listen to *Frank Sinatra with the Red Norvo Quintet: Live in Australia* (Blue Note, 1959) and *Sinatra and Sextet: Live in Paris* (Reprise, 1994). Meeting Billie Holiday on the street and hearing her say "Hello" was jazz to me. Or, for a less fragmentary definition, Carmen McRae accompanying herself on piano—as she used to do long ago at Minton's in Harlem—brought it all together.

But now we come to the much publicized Diana Krall and Jane Monheit. I'm not suggesting that they be compared with Billie, Carmen, Anita O'Day, the later Ella Fitzgerald, Sarah Vaughan, Betty Carter or Lee Wiley. But listen to them along with Maxine Sullivan, Etta Jones or that remarkable minimalist Blossom Dearie. Pee Wee Russell's definition of jazz playing also includes jazz singing: "A certain group of guys—I don't care where they come from—that have a heart feeling and a rhythm in their systems that you couldn't take away from them, even if they were in a symphony organization." (Like Maxine, Etta and Blossom.)

Diana Krall's time is, at best, sluggish. If you wanted to tap your foot to her singing, it would fall asleep. In the July 5 *New York Times,* Neil Strauss was much kinder: "Sometimes the effect was something like that of stepping into a wading pool warmed by the sun. It's a safe, comfortable body of water, an easy place to relax and drift off without worrying about drowning, but it lacks a deep end." In reviewing her performance at Carnegie Hall during the JVC Jazz Festival, Strauss added that "she always erred on the side of caution." Even the most subtle jazz singer—Lee Wiley in "Down to Steamboat, Tennessee" being a prime example—couldn't be called cautious. On the contrary, they got so inside the lyrics as to make you remember desires, erotic and otherwise, in your own life that keeps the music in your head after it stopped. Jazz people get inside you. There can be no "sound of surprise," in Whitney Balliett's phrase, in a wading pool.

Jane Monheit's success is a triumph of savvy management and publicity—the right clubs and television spots aided by scribes who have temporarily suspended their jazz judgment. In the September 2001 issue of *JazzTimes,* Lara Pellegrinelli was not beguiled. Writing of Monheit's "predictable and narrow" lyric interpretations, she went on to note precisely that "Monheit's rehearsed, theatrical quality has less in common with jazz musicians than [with] torch singers, cabaret artists and those who sing musical theater." But even in that milieu, she is nowhere near the same league as Mabel Mercer (a key influence on Frank Sinatra) or, among male cabaret performers, Hugh Shannon or the nonpareil Charles Trenet, who sang and wrote as magically as Fred Astaire danced. And, by the way, if Krall and Monheit can find a copy of Norman Granz's album of Astaire singing—backed by top-of-the-line jazz players—they can learn a lot about inner jazz rhythms.

Another unsolicited suggestion for Monheit and Krall and other singers with jazz eyes, as Lester Young might have said, is to spend a good many hours listening to him. Lester told me once that he never played a ballad until he first became intimate with the lyrics, and his preferred way of doing that was to listen to Frank Sinatra recordings. In jazz, whether singing or playing, the basics are: swing (implicit or as pulsing as a heartbeat); feeling (which can't be taught as such because it comes out of your life and how deeply you understand who you are as you keep changing); and your own unmistakable sound, which comes out of the preceding elements.

Krall and Monheit have nothing that interesting to say about themselves in their music. As Jo Jones used to say, in jazz you can't fake who you are—or who you're not. Furthermore, Krall and Monheit don't have the chops to make it on bravura, which is sometimes impressive technically, though not for long. Can you imagine what would have happened to Krall and Monheit if they had been in a cutting session with—at their prime or near it—Anita O'Day or Betty Carter or Kay Starr? Years ago, in the small hours at Minton's, both Sarah Vaughan and Ella Fitzgerald were in the audience. The crowd—like an audience at the Colosseum—insisted they go at it. And they did, for an hour or so. It was an exhilaratingly close match. I had the nerve to give the edge to Sarah because of her astonishing instrument, but Ella also stayed in my head for days.

Jazz singing is much more than a craft. Like jazz playing, it is—as Valerie Wilmer put it—as serious as your life. And sure, there are gradations in capacities, but to merit being called a jazz singer you have to have something to say—your own story—as it moves you then and there. Arrangements tailored just for you—and, in Krall's case, a carefully constructed aura of taking yourself seriously—won't help if you don't know when and how to let yourself go.

25 | Billie Holiday, Live

A BIOGRAPHY IN MUSIC

"Billie must have come from another world," said Roy Eldridge, often heard accompanying her on trumpet, "because nobody had the effect on people she had. I've seen her make them cry and make them happy." Lady Day, as tenor saxophonist Lester Young named Billie Holiday, still has that effect through the many reissues of her recordings, including *Lady Day: The Master Takes and Singles* of the 1933–44 sessions (Columbia/Legacy, 2007) that established her in the jazz pantheon.

I grew up listening to those sides, which infectiously demonstrated—as Bobby Tucker, her longtime pianist, noted—that "she could swing the hardest in any tempo, even if it was like a dirge . . . wherever it was, she could float on top of it." But none of the previous reissues, as imperishable as they are, have as intense a presence of Lady as in the truly historical five-disc set *Billie Holiday: Rare Live Recordings 1934–1959* on Bernard Stollman's ESP-Disk label (2008).

This is a model for future retrospectives of classic jazz artists of any era because researcher and compiler Michael Anderson, in his extensive liner notes, provides a timeline of her jazz life—describing the circumstances of each performance in the context of her evolving career. One example: a live radio remote from Harlem's Savoy Ballroom in 1937 when the twenty-two-year-old singer "began a special association with her comrade, 'The Prez,' Lester Young"—grooving with the Count Basie band in "Swing Brother Swing."

Producer Anderson is a veteran radio broadcaster (including gigs at WBGO-FM in Newark, New Jersey, and with Sirius Satellite Radio) and former jazz drummer. He was in Sun Ra's fabled visionary Arkestra and led bands of his own. As Mr. Anderson was growing up, collecting jazz records, "In my early teens," he told me, "I would have a Billie Holiday day each week where I only played her music."

His devoted immersion in tracking down performances by her from around the country takes us, for example, from an after-hours Harlem club, Clark Monroe's Uptown House, in 1941, to the Eddie Condon radio show in 1949, where Holiday dedicates "Keep on Rainin'" to Bessie Smith, whom she heard on records back in her hometown, Baltimore.

There is a series of extraordinarily moving sets at George Wein's Boston club Storyville (from which I used to do jazz remotes), in 1951. Billie, backed by just a house rhythm section, is more deeply affecting in "I Cover the Waterfront," "Crazy He Calls Me" and other songs here than in any of her studio interpretations.

Six years later, she was on CBS TV's *The Sound of Jazz*, for which Whitney Balliett and I had selected the musicians. In a sequence still being played around the world, she sings her own blues, "Fine and Mellow," with Lester Young among the players.

Once close, Billie and The Prez had grown apart. But on this meeting Young, though in failing health, stood up and played one of the purest blues choruses I'd ever heard, and Billie—her eyes meeting his—joined him back in private time, smiling. In the control room, there were tears in my eyes and in those of the director and the sound engineer.

It was on that program that she said, "Anything I sing is part of my life." And her singing became part of many people's lives.

She sometimes performed just for friends. During a private recording in this collection, Billie sings "My Yiddishe Mama" and then her own autobiographical song of rebellious independence, "God Bless the Child," to a youngster in the room. I doubt that child fully understood the import of the lyrics then, but the child may well have later in life.

Especially revealing of Billie's evolving approaches to a song is a series of rehearsals with bassist Artie Shapiro and pianist Jimmy Rowles, the master accompanist to jazz vocalists. Between takes, she talks about her early jobs with bands and jokes with Rowles.

What should surprise some of the critics who have concluded that in Billie's last years her voice and spirits showed the wear and strain of her sometime discordant personal life are the final performances here at Storyville in April 1959. Her singing, three months before she died at the age of forty-four, swings with the verve, the wit and the essential quality that her admirer Ray Charles sums up at the end of the fifth disc: "To be any kind of a singer you have to have feeling, and the one thing you can't teach is feeling." As evidence, Holiday concludes her last 1959 set at Storyville with her own "Billie's Blues":

> I ain't good lookin'
> and my hair ain't curled,
> but my mother, she give me something,
> it's gonna carry me through this world.

A year before Billie died, I was talking with Miles Davis about the increasing lament, even among some musicians, that she was breaking down into a much lesser Lady Day.

"You know," Miles said in exasperation at those ears that had turned to tin, "she's not thinking now what she was in 1937. And she still has control, probably more control than then."

At the end of his liner notes for his remarkable achievement in discovering and assembling this "live" musical biography in *Billie Holiday: Rare Live Recordings 1934–1959*, Michael Anderson writes: "Later generations have an entire legacy to discover, and veteran enthusiasts can always recollect the times the music of Lady Day was vibrant and alive through everything she had gone through in her life."

Billie once spoke of what Louis Armstrong's trumpet meant to her as a young girl in Baltimore: "He didn't say any words but somehow it just moved me so. It sounded so sad and sweet, all at the same time. It sounded like he was making love to me. That's how I wanted to sing."

It wasn't that, as Roy Eldridge said, she'd come from another world. Rough as her own life had been between songs in this world, Billie became—and will continue to become—part of so many lives.

26 | This Daughter of Jazz Is One Cool Cat

After listening to a continuous stream of releases by purported rising jazz singers—who couldn't have lasted through a chorus in a contest with Ella Fitzgerald or Betty Carter—it's a delight to hear the real thing in Catherine Russell. After many years on the road with rock, blues, jazz, soul and gospel bands, Ms. Russell—who turned fifty in September 2006—finally has her own album as a leader: *Catherine Russell—Cat* (World Village, 2006).

Cat, as she is called by fellow musicians, hits a groove (or, as she calls it, "the pocket") from note one on whatever she sings. From blues to ballads—and in swingers that make me want to dance (if only I knew how)—she tells an unusual variety of stories as if she were living them, and she has.

Accompanied by acoustic ensembles—a blessed relief from electronically amplified distraction—Catherine Russell is, she tells me, "on a mission to find rhythms that make you feel good all over, and in your hips. In jazz, you feel like moving to that rhythm even if you're not dancing. There's a joy in it."

She also finds joy in country music because "I like anything that swings." Starting with early George Jones recordings and Patsy Cline—whose "Someday You'll Want Me to Want You" she turns into her own story in this set. Ms. Russell was also drawn to Hank Williams and Merle Haggard (whom she went to hear in his last New York gig).

"I love songs," she says, "that tell you about the lives of the people singing, as well as of the writers. That's why Frank Sinatra is one of my favorites. You really get what he's feeling when he sings."

I told her that Charlie Parker greatly puzzled many of his jazz associates with his abiding pleasure in listening to country music recordings—and that he'd explain to the doubters: "Listen, listen to the stories!" Cat was glad to find that Bird was her soul mate in that music, as well as in jazz.

Ms. Russell is part of a noble jazz lineage. Her father, Luis Russell (1902–63), was a pianist and leader of one of the most impressive big bands on the early New York jazz scene after leading a group in New Orleans and moving to Chicago, where he worked with King Oliver, who gave Louis Armstrong his first big break.

On *The Luis Russell Story (1929–1939)* from Retrieval Records you can discover the too long forgotten Luis Russell band that, as British musician and critic Humphrey Lyttelton wrote, "not only romped but roared"—with such sidemen as Henry "Red" Allen, J. C. Higginbotham and George "Pops" Foster. For a time, the band later became Louis Armstrong's backup unit.

Catherine Russell's mother, Carline Ray—a bassist, pianist and singer—is an alumna of the International Sweethearts of Rhythm, an all-female band that collectively and individually proved that women have "the chops" to swing as deeply as men. Now in her eighties, Ms. Ray is still performing and, says her daughter, recently bought a new bass and is also writing a musical.

Included in her daughter's debut CD is a song by Luis Russell that became one of the most requested numbers in Louis Armstrong's repertory, "Back o' Town Blues." That song resounds triumphantly in this set—as does a rollicking fusion of Louis Jordan's "Juneteenth Jamboree" with "Royal Garden Blues," the latter long associated with King Oliver. And, always searching for "melodies with beautiful stories in the lyrics," she brings back Jimmy Van Heusen's "Deep in a Dream."

For her next album, Ms. Russell has found "South to a Warmer Place," a song performed by Frank Sinatra that, she says proudly, "not even Michael Feinstein knew." The composers were Alec Wilder and Loonis McGlohon.

I asked her about her choice of a background of mandolin, violin, guitars, piano, organ, tambourine, drums and, on two numbers, pedal-steel guitar.

"With acoustic swing string bands," she said, "there's room for me to do anything I want to—without fighting with the electric guitar." And she and the musicians were so comfortable with one another that most of the songs were recorded in two or three takes.

Duke Ellington had told me that he also preferred staying with that number in a recording studio. His reason was the same as Ms. Russell's: "Without the spontaneity," she explains, "you lose the edge. You lose what naturally happens between musicians as they inspire each other. And that's how you find 'the pocket.'" Which is what? "A pocket means to me what the feeling was when people were on a dance floor, like at the Savoy Ballroom in Harlem. That's when the music reaches into you."

I brought Ellington back into the conversation, recalling his telling me that when alto saxophonist Johnny Hodges would play one of his sensuously intimate solos in a ballroom, a sigh would come from one or more of the dancers; and, said Duke, "that sigh became part of our music."

"That," Ms. Russell said happily, "is another way of saying what I mean by 'finding the pocket.'"

Her view of the music she listens to and chooses to sing could be called holistic: "When the music is right, it heals everybody. It's all one energy—the band, the audience, the melody, the lyric, the swing. If any one of those ingredients is missing, is not working together, you lose the totality of the experience, the groove. When I heard Duke, Basie, Sinatra, I always felt included in what they were saying in their music. And when I'm on stage for two hours, I feel like I'm sharing something that brings us all together."

With this first of what will be a series of CDs, her career as a headliner is just beginning.

Jazz, of course, has to keep moving on. But as venturesome and cutting edge as it becomes, at the center of gravity that has always kept the music alive and surprising is "the groove" that Cat Russell embodies.

Her recording, she says at the end of its liner notes, is "Dedicated to my parents: Luis Russell and Carline Ray." She has certainly honored their heritage.

27 | The Springtime of Frank Sinatra

In 1940, I was fifteen, and my jazz record collection included the popular big dance band of Tommy Dorsey because "The Sentimental Gentleman of Swing"— as the trombonist-leader was called—had such sidemen as Bunny Berigan, Buddy Rich and the silvery clarinetist Johnny Mince. On ballads, I was also drawn to Dorsey's twenty-five-year-old vocalist Frank Sinatra, who had just joined the band that year.

He was not yet a jazz singer, but his phrasing—which he later said had been influenced by Billie Holiday—and his rhythmic ease flowed into the pop-jazz mosaic that Tommy Dorsey nurtured. As Sinatra later matured musically, and gained life experience, his singing added another quality of Billie Holiday's, as Carmen McRae described it: "She could make you visualize a song in a way that was just so clear."

The evolution of Sinatra—who himself came to deeply influence both popular singers and jazz instrumentalists—is celebrated in a four-CD set, *Frank Sinatra: A Voice in Time (1939–1952)* (Sony, 2007).

Even as early as his 1940s recordings with Tommy Dorsey, Sinatra put me, then and now, in an autobiographical reverie ("I'll Never Smile Again")—and then, feeling like the first day of spring ("Oh, Look at Me Now").

In his appearances at New York's Paramount Theater in the 1940s, thousands of teenagers transformed him into America's first "Teen Idol." Years later, as reported in *The Penguin Encyclopedia of Popular Music*, Sinatra, with uncommon modesty, said: "It was the war years, and there was a great loneliness. And I was the boy in every corner drugstore who'd gone off, drafted in the war. That was all."

But until 1952, as Sinatra was focusing on the now largely ignored Great American Songbook—the core of America's popular music—his recordings continued to top the hit charts. The lyrics and music of George Gershwin, Cole Porter, Harold Arlen, Rodgers and Hart et al. were—as Frank McConnell wrote in *Commonweal* on Frank Sinatra's birthday in 1995—among "the supreme accomplishments of our culture," and Sinatra was "the voice of that great tradition."

Hearing that tradition come alive again in this set, as he is framed by such master arrangers as Sy Oliver and Axel Stordahl, it is also clear what an accomplished musician Sinatra had become. In his exemplary notes for *Frank Sinatra:*

A Voice in Time, Will Friedwald quotes the producers of this essential legacy, Didier C. Deutsch and Charles L. Granata: "Frank Sinatra was a musician who exerted extraordinary control over every facet of his music. From song selection and arrangements to his vocal approach and the color of his sound, Sinatra's discriminating taste guided the creation of every record he made."

In the late 1950s, I was a witness to Sinatra's demanding control of the music he made. At the Copacabana in New York, I was at his afternoon rehearsal of the orchestra for that night's gig. Conducting, he suddenly stopped a number, turned to the brass section and said to a trombonist: "You just played an E-flat. It should have been an E-natural."

I was surprised. His longtime guitarist had told me that Sinatra couldn't read music. "He must have perfect pitch," said another musician when I cited that rehearsal. In any case, as venerable jazz musicians used to say, Frank Sinatra had "big ears."

A number of jazz musicians have told me that too, and in a long-ago *Down Beat* interview, Miles Davis said he had studied how to play ballads by listening to Sinatra's phrasing.

These recordings of the springtime of Frank Sinatra are not only "a voice in time" but also—in his choice of songs—a demonstration of how much this nation has lost with the Great American Songbook's not being even a memory now to most of America's young—and, maybe to future generations.

When I was in my early twenties, Duke Ellington—my mentor in music and in life values—urged me never to be locked into categories of music or the swirl of fashion. "There are only two kinds of music," he said. "Good and bad."

At the time, I thought he was being far too simplistic. But Duke was right. Of course, times and cultures change—as do definitions among the young as to what is currently called "cool." But over decades and centuries, music is indeed essentially either good or bad. For me, Bach always swings; and when I'm immersed in Beethoven's late quartets, I'm also reliving scenes—some of them newly meaningful—from my life.

A reissue of Louis Armstrong's *Hot Five* and *Hot Seven* recordings of the 1920s will never rival in sales those of a "new star" rapper, nor will a legacy compilation of Bessie Smith, "the empress of the blues." But such recordings will always have a cluster of listeners here and around the world.

What is missing, however, from contemporary American popular music culture are the grace, the wit, the worldly wise honesty and irony and the expectations of romantic fulfillment in such songs in *Frank Sinatra: A Voice in Time* as "She's Funny That Way," "Dancing in the Dark," "All the Things You Are," "Autumn in New York," "I Get a Kick Out of You," "September Song," "As Time Goes By," "One for My Baby (And One More for the Road)" and "These Foolish Things (Remind Me of You)."

It's possible, I suppose, that such timeless life stories of dreams and loss will be created in music again. After all, neither rock nor rap have euthanized jazz, and a new generation may yet create its own extension of the Great American Songbook.

28 | Sinatra Sings in Vegas, and You Are There

Years ago, I wrote in *Holiday* magazine that Tony Bennett was the true heir of Frank Sinatra. Soon after, to my surprise, I received a note—from Frank Sinatra: "You're right about Tony Bennett," he said. I greatly admire Tony Bennett's continually self-surprising singing, and I've gotten to know him, impressed by his knowledgeable interest in national and international affairs. But there is no heir to Frank Sinatra—any more than there is an heir to Fred Astaire or Billie Holiday.

One afternoon, at the home of Lester Young, the "president" of the jazz tenor saxophone, my host told me that he never played a ballad until he had learned the lyrics. "How do you do that?" I asked. He pointed to a stack of Sinatra recordings on a table near his chair. Long after, Jeremy Pelt, the rising young trumpet player, told me he used the same method of getting inside a song—and the same source for the lyrics.

But Sinatra not only made ballads move into listeners' own lives and memories. He was also—in both romantic reveries and jubilantly swinging performances—an authentic jazzman. In whatever he sang, he was in the groove with the other musicians in the band—and he was often improvising.

Sinatra attracted exceptional arrangers (notably Nelson Riddle), but especially in "live" performances those scores became fluid—flowing with the play of his emotions and the vibrations from the audience.

Although his studio recordings will be played as long as this civilization and its music survive, Sinatra is most rivetingly heard on "live" recordings—and now there is a historic boxed set of previously unreleased onstage Sinatra shows in Las Vegas, where he felt more at home than in any other venue. *Frank Sinatra: Vegas* contains eighty-eight tracks on four CDs and one DVD (Reprise, 2006).

It's 1961 to 1987, at the Sands (which Sinatra partially owned), Caesar's Palace and the Golden Nugget. And "You Are There!"—as a long-ago CBS docudrama series used to promise. The numbers are classics from the Great American Songbook (imperishable, except on commercial radio these days). Many are what Sinatra called "saloon songs"—"The Second Time Around," "I've Got a Crush on You," "The Lady Is a Tramp."

"I have a great reverence toward saloon songs," Sinatra says during a break on the recordings. "I've been singing in saloons longer than any other singer I know. They include torch songs, and I've had torches so high I've burned down buildings." On an especially tender, regretful, two-in-the-morning homage to Cole Porter's "Just One of Those Things," Sinatra is accompanied solely by his peerlessly attentive longtime pianist Bill Miller.

The "hot jazz" Sinatra joins the Count Basie Orchestra—conducted by a young Quincy Jones, mindful of the Count's insistence on letting the music breathe—in such swinging celebrations as "My Kind of Town" and "Come Fly With Me."

In one of the other conversational asides in the omnibus set, Sinatra says of working with Count Basie: "It was probably the most exciting engagement I've ever done in my life. That band comes at you like a juggernaut. You become part of it—or you get lost. We did things that were really jumping!"

The most revealing of the Sinatra comments begins: "When I found out that Ella and all the black performers and composers were living on the other side of this town—and that those I was working with couldn't stay in the same hotel as I did—I didn't understand it.

"Somebody said to me, 'Well, that's the life here in this state.' I began to make noise, and I made a few threats about how they'd better get another boy to work here. But it changed. I had made some demands on some people: 'If they're on the other side of town, you don't need me!' I think a few other entertainers picked up on that too, but I was the biggest mouth in town. I loathe bigotry of any kind."

The single DVD, a recording of part of a May 1978 CBS TV special, *Cinderella at the [Caesar's] Palace,* has a beginning—backstage palaver and an aimless comic—that should have been edited out, but the rest is worth the wait. Seeing as well as hearing Sinatra's spontaneous mastery of dynamics in his rhythms, and of phrasing—in direct contact with the audience—one can also see, in his very movements, the inherent drama of his storytelling. Now I know why he became so multidimensional a nonsinging actor in films.

On the DVD, you see what Whitney Balliett described in *Goodbyes and Other Messages: A Journal of Jazz, 1981–1990* (Oxford University Press, 1991): "The searchlight blue eyes that give the impression they are looking into every pair of eyes in the hall; the ineffable cool and skill that make his singing appear effortless; the flashing smiles that dispel the emotion of the last song and prepare the way for the next one."

Also on the DVD, you seem to see, in his eyes, what the lyrics mean to him, in the past and the immediate present.

Throughout all the performances—a boon not only to us but to future historians of a time when a Frank Sinatra could become a central part of American popular culture—the sound quality brings you right into those Las Vegas nightclubs. (You just have to pour your own drinks.) Great credit is due engineer and mixer Larry Walsh.

In the set's handsome sixty-page book, another legend, film director Billy Wilder, says: "When Sinatra is in Las Vegas, there is a certain electricity permeating the air." Until this set, I hadn't fully realized Sinatra's electric energy in live performance—the resilient strength as well as the subtleties of his voice, and the personality from which it came. Three years before Sinatra died in 1998, at age eighty-two, Frank McConnell wrote of him in *Commonweal* magazine: "As surely as Twain's or Hemingway's, or Basie's, his is the American voice."

Toward the end of a set in the DVD that closes *Frank Sinatra: Vegas,* the performer lifts a glass, toasting the audience: "May you live to be 150 years old—and the last voice you hear is mine!"

We're still listening, Frank.

29 | She's on the Road to Renown

Years ago, working at a Boston radio station, I was often at ringside, covering boxing bouts. I regularly saw exceptionally skilled local fighters who never broke through to become headliners. In the trade, they were called "club fighters." Similarly, in jazz, there have always been regional players, respected by their peers, who never became widely known. Coming off a road trip, Coleman Hawkins, the inventor of the jazz tenor saxophone, would tell me about some of those "club jazzmen."

Amanda Carr, a true jazz singer in a time of wannabes—after playing gigs around New England for years—is now getting national and international recognition, especially after the release of her CD *Amanda Carr: Soon* (OMS Records, 2007).

Also a pianist and composer, she sings and swings with the unaffected confidence of a genuine jazz improviser. Unlike some of the present alleged jazz vocalists, Ms. Carr does not try to imitate a horn. She is an authentic musician in the front line with her longtime colleagues on *Soon*—guitarist John Wilkins, bassist Bronek Suchanek and drummer Kenny Hadley (who produced the album). Also present is exuberant tenor saxophonist Arnie Krakowsky.

I've rarely heard a jazz singer fuse so naturally and pleasurably with what are ordinarily called "sidemen." In this group sound there is a lilting, often soaring, confluence of jazz time in a repertory that ranges from George and Ira Gershwin's "Soon" and A. C. Jobim's Brazilian ballad "If You Never Come to Me" to Fats Waller's "Squeeze Me."

Amanda Carr is both a daughter and granddaughter of jazz. In the 1920s, her grandmother played stride piano for vaudeville acts. And her mother, Nancy Carr, sang regularly at the Totem Pole Ballroom in Newton, Massachusetts, where, as I remember, there was a huge chandelier adding multiple colors to the romantic ambience on the dance floor.

Trumpet player Nick Capezuto, Amanda's father, is a veteran of the big-band era, having played with Glenn Miller, Larry Clinton, Louis Prima, Elliot Lawrence, Woody Herman—and Herb Pomeroy, who for years was a prime regenerator of the Boston jazz scene.

As Amanda proudly tells me, "There are a handful of us in the Boston area who are sons and daughters of the working jazz players of the forties, fifties and sixties. We have an unofficial obligation to carry on a musical legacy."

Now forty-five, she continues: "We are the younger set with the 'old-school' attitude: The ones that dress just a little bit better and show up a little bit earlier. We're the ones who work sick because you 'don't sub-out unless you're dead.' We drive 100 miles for a hundred bucks."

Amanda's first steady gig, when she was fourteen, was at a restaurant/bar in her hometown of Hingham, Massachusetts, for $45 a night. A pianist as well as a singer, she furthered her apprenticeship in dance nightclubs in the Boston area.

After filling in for her mother on some big-band gigs, she began, as she puts it, to feel an affinity for that genre—of which jazz was then an integral force. In 1996, she recorded her first album, *Carr Toons,* on which she felt honored to have Herb Pomeroy play. She told him defensively, "I'm not really a jazz singer"; but an Italian producer, upon hearing the CD, thought otherwise. He invited her to be a headliner at the 1998 EuroJazz Festival in Turin. With her on stage were famed tenor saxophonist James Moody and bassist George Mraz.

Having been a hit in Turin, Amanda was invited back the next year to record a live concert with an Italian trio that had accompanied her at her international debut.

In recent years, Amanda has toured this country as a featured vocalist with "ghost" bands—revivals of bands originally led by Artie Shaw, Harry James and Glenn Miller. Amanda has also occasionally starred in a traveling *Tribute to Peggy Lee and Benny Goodman* with the Everett Longstreth fifteen-piece band. The show starts a nationwide tour in September of next year.

Like all the durable jazz musicians I've known, Amanda keeps surprising and delighting herself with how much she has to keep learning. "Like," she tells me, "there's so much more room between notes than when I began; more subtle play and less need to break out every tool in the box to showcase good singing. It's having the sense of restraint—and especially the concept of the group sound, and homage to the element of space that shapes phrasing as much as the notes. You never see the end of the journey."

Hearing Amanda tell of what she's learned on her journey through jazz, I remember Dizzy Gillespie's saying to me: "It's taken me most of my life to know which notes not to play."

Since the music on *Soon* is so satisfyingly a group creation, the other players' credits should be cited. Guitarist John Wilkins has performed with Clark Terry, the Kenny Hadley Big Band and the Artie Shaw Orchestra. Mr. Hadley, one of New England's first-call drummers, has worked with master teacher Dizzy Gillespie.

Exemplifying jazz as an international language, bassist Bronek Suchanek was trained at a Polish conservatory but took the risk, at the time, of listening intently to jazz. He left his native land for Sweden, where he worked with such American originals as Thad Jones, Mel Lewis and Don Cherry. He now lives in the land where jazz began.

Tenor saxophonist Arnie Krakowsky, whose room-filling presence would have delighted Coleman Hawkins, has worked with Ray Charles, Mel Tormé and a variety of jazz and Latin combos. Of his association with Amanda, he says: "We're playing for each other and relating to what went down in the past. When you die and get to where you're going, all the masters are going to be there. Today everybody's sound is predicated on being famous, and much of it sounds the same. It's completely opposite of what this craft is supposed to be."

On a previous Amanda Carr CD, *Tender Trap,* there's one of my favorite, and seldom played, Duke Ellington songs: "What Am I Here For?" All the players on *Soon* know the answer to that question.

30 | Bing and Guests Swing on the Air

As a child, I'd listen in my room for my mother's favorite song as, in the kitchen, she'd wait for Bing Crosby's first network radio program and his theme "When the Blue of the Night Meets the Gold of the Day." Soon, he had gentled me to sleep.

Years later, after being immersed in jazz, I learned of the jazz credentials of the "crooner" (as he was called). He was one of Paul Whiteman's Rhythm Boys from 1926 to 1930, and his roommate on the road had been the precisely lyrical cornetist Bix Beiderbecke, with whom he had gone to after-hours jam sessions in Chicago and other cities.

In a 1976 interview, a year before he died at age seventy-four, Bing Crosby, reminiscing, told me: "Back then, there was a color line almost anywhere else, but at those sessions you could hear Bix, Louis Armstrong and Willie 'The Lion' Smith, all mixed together. The jazz scene was way ahead of the rest of the country."

We also talked about what, starting in the 1940s, had been my favorite radio show, Bing Crosby's *Kraft Music Hall.* He often had jazz guests, with whom he joined, like another swinging horn, in duets. I also greatly enjoyed his ad-libbing—with an urbane wit more sophisticated than I heard elsewhere on the air.

I asked him about his evident pleasure in playing with words. "Well," he said, "I read a lot. I'm no intellectual, you understand, but I like Graham Greene, Evelyn Waugh, Hemingway, John P. Marquand, Louis Auchincloss and Georges

Simenon. He really understands character." (I had found a fellow enthusiast for that prolific and penetrating mystery writer.)

Those wondrously relaxed, and relaxing, Bing Crosby radio shows are available again on a three-CD boxed set, *Swingin' with Bing! Bing Crosby's Lost Radio Performances* (Shout! Factory, 2004). Producer Ken Barnes and Peter Reynolds, a true master at remastering, have chosen seventy-five musical numbers, introductions and conversations from 1946 to 1953, fifty-seven of which have never been previously released. (Along with *Kraft Music Hall* sessions, there are takes from his Philco, Chesterfield and General Electric broadcasts.)

On the first CD, in addition to performances with Nat "King" Cole and the Andrews Sisters (a trio who could swing in Yiddish as well as English, but are not singing in Yiddish here), there are Crosby solos. He was so easeful a swinger that even on ballads, his phrasing grooved. And because he was so comfortable with the microphone, sounding as if he were singing directly to the listener, radio made him an international star.

As Mr. Barnes says in the extensive notes to this set: "It wasn't just the public that admired him. He had the respect of the nation's greatest musicians, Louis Armstrong, Bix Beiderbecke, the Dorsey Brothers. . . . He influenced every singer who followed him, including Frank Sinatra."

Jazz performers were eager to be on his radio shows because of the size of the audiences, but also because Bing was one of them. The second and third CDs include all the Crosby radio duets with Armstrong and Ella Fitzgerald. And for good jazz measure, there are appearances by the luminous trombonist Jack Teagarden, trumpet players Red Nichols and Ziggy Elman, guitarist Les Paul and the jubilant jazz violinist Joe Venuti. Most of the orchestral accompaniment was conducted by John Scott Trotter, who never got in Bing's way.

The flowing counterpoint between Crosby and Armstrong or Crosby and Fitzgerald in their duets defines jazz singing; and so do the brief appearances of Bing with the Mills Brothers. In the final number of this bonanza of classic performances—timeless beyond nostalgia—Ella, Louis and Bing celebrate themselves and their musical heritage in "Memphis Blues."

Among the other bountiful joys are Louis and Bing in "Blueberry Hill" and "Lazy Bones"; Bing, Louis and Jack Teagarden in "Gone Fishin'"; and Bing and Ella exulting in the New Orleans tailgating anthem "That's A-Plenty."

At the core of all these performances is Crosby. Reading a May 2, 2004, column in the *Washington Times,* I unexpectedly came upon a tribute to Crosby titled "Singer of a Century" that got to the heart of the abiding pleasure of his singing. The writer was economist, historian and controversialist Thomas Sowell, not previously known—by me, anyway—as a music critic: "Part of the greatness of his art [was] that it looked like it wasn't art. He didn't make a fuss about it, but he made history with it. It was a little like the way Joe DiMaggio played center-field, making it look easy even when it was superb."

I had never met Bing Crosby before the interview in 1976, and I was initially somewhat awed; but he was as natural and unaffected as his singing. He did surprise me at one point. We were talking about performers who took strong public political positions, a practice that has increased since then.

Crosby frowned. "I never thought it was proper," he said, "for a performer to use his influence to get anyone to vote one way or another."

He was considered to be a conservative, but he had not leapt on anyone's political bandwagon. However, he did tell me that he had been very much against the war in Vietnam. That was the first I'd heard of it, I said.

He frowned again. "I didn't know what to do about it," Crosby said. "So I didn't say anything."

As I was leaving, I asked if there was anything he'd wanted to do that he hadn't yet accomplished. He smiled. "No, I really have accomplished just everything I wanted to. It's been a good life, pleasing people over so many years."

He still does, all the way through *Swingin' with Bing*. And though it was so long ago when I first heard him (I was about seven), I can still hear and be moved by "When the Blue of the Night Meets the Gold of the Day."

PART SIX

The Life Force of the Music

31 | The Joyous Power of Black Gospel Music

Many years ago, as an announcer at a Boston radio station, WMEX, I became immersed in multiculturalism. There were regular Italian, Swedish, country music and Jewish hours—the last featuring renowned cantors who, I told Charles Mingus at the time, were the Jewish version of deeply resilient blues singers.

Saturday nights were a celebration, in one of our studios, of live black gospel music, with performers from churches in the Boston area. The disciplined, often virtuosic fervor of this witnessing has often regenerated me from then on. I collected gospel recordings; and one Sunday morning, during a Newport Jazz Festival, hearing Mahalia Jackson in a church in town, made this nonbeliever able to imagine the rewards if I could ever make that leap into faith.

Thomas Dorsey, the celebrated gospel composer and impresario who also played blues piano, said of Mahalia Jackson: "She enjoyed her religion—that was the key, the core of her singing." He had been her coach.

A stunning CD, *Gospel Music* (Hyena Records, 2006) is a bonanza of that joyous, pulsating power, exemplified by a range of classic black gospel soul stirrers: among them, the Swan Silvertones, the Harmonizing Four, the Staple Singers, the Original Five Blind Boys of Alabama, the Reverend James Cleveland and—of course—Mahalia Jackson.

For years, searching in second-hand record stores, I particularly looked for what David Stowe, a historian of American culture (*How Sweet the Sound*, Harvard University Press, 2004), describes as "the communal experience," in an urban setting, "of the antebellum 'hush harbor,' where a 'caller' would evoke responses among participants as co-worshippers rather than as a subservient flock responding to an authoritative leader." In the rising climaxes of "Get Right Church" and "Be Decided to Die" in this set, James Cleveland and his congregation communally leap out of these grooves.

The other performers in *Gospel Music* are also in the tradition of "callers" who are reverberatingly skilled, as Mr. Stowe notes, in "inspiring a response without dictating it, eliciting and evoking through example rather than through prescription." Being moved out of my chair by the Golden Gate Jubilee Quartet's "Go Where I Send Thee," I was brought back to years ago, hearing such compelling sounds on a street in Harlem that led me into a Daddy Grace assembly where I almost became part of the congregation.

This glorious revival of mainstays of the gospel circuit, mostly in the 1950s and 1960s—who worked many nights a year in churches and small auditoriums around the country—is the lasting work of Joel Dorn and Lee Friedlander. Mr.

Dorn, a radio veteran, has also produced scores of albums, from Max Roach and Charles Mingus to Roberta Flack and Lou Rawls. Mr. Friedlander, the world-renowned photographer, had a retrospective of his work, including famous portraits of jazz players, at the Museum of Modern Art, in 2006.

These two gospel music enthusiasts listened to 1,500 recorded performances, selecting the eighteen in this collection. Mr. Dorn, who has composed a good many notable liner notes, chose only this sparse comment for "Gospel Music": "If there's one thing this album doesn't need, it's any words of explanation. This music comes from the epicenter of the core of what Black American Music is about. When you listen to Gospel Music, I guarantee you that without even knowing it's doing it, your brain will write its own liner notes. That's how powerful this music is. The only thing this album needs is your ears and your heart."

Nonetheless, I asked Mr. Dorn for more background. "While all the artists on this album," he said, "flourished in the gospel circuit, only four crossed over at any point into the mainstream music market. But many of the others did sell large amounts of records, though not enough to be on the Billboard Charts because the bulk of their sales were in small independent stores in the inner city or the Deep South. Still, the Reverend James Cleveland could sell as many as 100,000 albums, as did the Swan Silvertones and the Dixie Hummingbirds."

The four who crossed over were Mahalia Jackson, the Staple Singers, the Five Blind Boys of Alabama and Sam Cooke, lead singer of the Soul Stirrers.

There still is a gospel circuit, often in megachurches. As the February 17 *Washington Post* reported: "Black gospel music stars sold about $140 million worth of CDs last year." Significantly, the story continued, "According to the Barna Group Ltd., a religious research group, about 53 percent of blacks in the country regularly attend church—many of them in houses of worship with memberships of more than 2,000."

At Reid Temple African Methodist Episcopal Church in Glenn Dale, notes reporter Hamil Harris, as Bishop Paul S. Morton was preaching about the ravages of Hurricane Katrina, "There were shouts of amens. People stood and lifted their hands. Then he began to sing his award-winning song, 'Let It Rain': 'Open the flood gates of Heaven, and let it rain. Let it rain.'" The singing bishop was also the keynote speaker at the Gospel Heritage Foundation 2006 Praise and Worship Conference.

The continuing soul-lifting spirit of this music has its roots in antebellum field hollers and ring shouts and, later, in the permanent treasures of the Dorn-Friedlander *Gospel Music* CD. It also characterizes the recorded work of such jazz creators as Art Blakey's Jazz Messengers, Julian "Cannonball" Adderley, Horace Silver and Charles Mingus.

In a conversation about his musical roots, Mingus got to the core of where he and the Swan Silvertones, the Soul Stirrers and the Dixie Hummingbirds came from: "All the music I heard when I was a very young child," Mingus told me, "was church music. Especially in the Holiness Church where my stepmother took me. There the congregation confess their sins and sing and shout and do a little Holy Rolling. The blues was in the Holiness churches—moaning, riffs and that sort of thing between the audience and the preacher."

So Mingus was prepared when, he recalls, "I was eight or nine years old before I heard a Duke Ellington record on the radio. And when I first heard Duke Ellington in person, I almost jumped out of the balcony"—eager to become part of the music.

32 | The Healing Power of Jazz

In 1969, Louis Armstrong told his longtime friend and associate, Phoebe Jacobs, the grande dame of the New York jazz scene, that he wanted to start a foundation "to give back to people some of the goodness I've had from them all these years." Thus began the Louis Armstrong Educational Fund, of which Ms. Jacobs is vice president.

Among its projects, including the Louis Armstrong Public School Jazz Outreach Program in New Orleans, the nonprofit foundation has added to Armstrong's huge role in the shaping of jazz history a significant contribution to the history of medical music therapy in hospitals and other care centers.

Several times, Armstrong had been a patient at Beth Israel Hospital in New York, where he became very impressed with the medical staff, and decided to provide funds that would be devoted to music therapy for children—a field in which he'd had some experience, having years before, for instance, provided recordings of a wide range of music to help create a more relaxed ambience for children being born in a New Orleans hospital.

For more than ten years, at Beth Israel, the Louis and Lucille Armstrong Music Therapy Program—directed by Dr. Joanne Loewy, internationally known for this work—has supported research and clinical music therapy for infants, children and families at the hospital, and for outpatients and patients with HIV.

The program has been enlarged to include the hospital's nationally recognized Department of Pain Medicine and Palliative Care, its intensive care units and the neonatal intensive care unit—an addition that would have greatly pleased the large-hearted funder of these advances in the healing power of music.

In November 2005 a ribbon-cutting at Beth Israel took place to further expand the founding program by Armstrong and his wife by adding the new Louis Armstrong Center for Music and Medicine. Its focus will be on medical treatment for children and adults with asthma and chronic obstructive pulmonary disease (COPD).

"Asthma," said Dr. Joanne Loewy—who radiates her enthusiasm for the palpable results of her work—"is the No. 1 admitting diagnosis for children in hospitals. So we are currently studying the effects of wind playing—such as playing a flute or a horn—in lung volume capacity and quality of life in children and teenagers."

On the morning of the ribbon-cutting—before the speeches and a tribute to hospital trustee Richard Netter, whose $1.25-million gift helped make possible the full Music and Medicine Center—all conversation stopped as a joyous thunderclap of jazz resounded from a balcony near the ceiling.

There, standing alone, Jon Faddis, a trumpet player of prodigious lyrical force, was playing "West End Blues," a Louis Armstrong recorded solo in the 1920s that electrified the burgeoning jazz community then, and has done ever since.

The program guide had accurately described Mr. Faddis as a "herald" of this life-enhancing event. And there, next to him, in a wheelchair, was the other "herald" of the morning, the ceaselessly inventive octogenarian Clark Terry, who played another song long associated with Louis Armstrong, "What a Wonderful World."

Sitting below, I was lifted by the two glowing trumpeters into a memory of Louis Armstrong's exuberant pleasure in giving pleasure to his listeners, including other musicians. Mr. Terry once recalled that when he and Dizzy Gillespie (a mentor of Mr. Faddis) were living in Corona, Queens, they'd walk over to Louis Armstrong's home. Welcoming them, Armstrong would say, "Sit down, I'm gonna give you the history of jazz." On this morning, they were witnessing Louis's legacy of expanding the history of jazz to illuminate its healing powers.

Ms. Jacobs, in her remarks when we came down to earth, said: "You might think Louis Armstrong is dead. He's not. His spirit keeps on infecting us all."

Then, looking around the room, Ms. Jacobs paused and said to the doctors and the past and potential patients present: "Music is more important now that we have all these troubles in the world, and here in this country. You don't have to be in a hospital to benefit from music therapy."

Later, I told Ms. Jacobs what Merle Haggard, whose roots are in jazz as well as country, had said to me: "When I get really way down, and nothing lifts me up, only music can."

Dr. Loewy and her staff at Beth Israel, sharing their research with medical centers in this and other countries, are lifting up many bodies and spirits.

In an article in the March *Medical Herald* about her work at Beth Israel, she says: "Rhythm is the first area that helps us understand the logic of medical music therapy, because the heartbeat is the first thing that a doctor looks at to assess the physical parameters of the body. If we can look into the rhythm and look at the effect of rhythm in terms of healing, that kind of work is very important, especially in diseases such as Parkinson's where you're looking to improve gait control. . . .

"Once I begin to use music," she continues, "people see results. . . . Parents see their children start to sing when they can't talk. The same thing with stroke. We know that music combines right brain and left brain. So, we just see the results of music therapy."

When a Music Therapy Wellness Center for Musicians was planned at Beth Israel, a summary sent to me by Dr. Loewy explained that the center would care for "musicians who suffer from, among other things, depression, anxiety and overuse syndrome. An interesting phenomenon among musicians is that women musicians are at significantly greater risk for playing-related injury, as are players of string instruments. Typically, people don't think musicians are injured and this is clearly an under-recognized health problem."

Wind and brass players, Dr. Loewy notes, have problems affecting facial muscles, hands, wrists and arms. "The role of the Wellness Center would be to implement musical visualization techniques and provide intervallic synthesis breathing and physical exercises to implement breathing, thus preventing such injuries."

"Of all people," she emphasizes, "the power of music to bring people together was enhanced by Louis Armstrong. We would like to hallow the Armstrong name in a tangible, living way."

There are many more choruses to come as the rhythms of Louis Armstrong keep reverberating.

33 | Old Country Jewish Blues and Ornette Coleman

There's a country music song, "Will the Circle Be Unbroken?" of which I never tire, and it jumped to mind when I read Ben Ratliff's characteristically illuminating new book, *The Jazz Ear: Conversations Over Music* (Times Books, 2008). You may have seen some of them in Ratliff's "Listening With" series in the *New York Times*. He not only has a deep, far-ranging knowledge of jazz but, like Count Basie comping his band, Ratliff leaves breathing and feeling space for the musician with whom he's talking.

He asked fifteen musicians for a list of five or six pieces of music he or she would like to listen to with him, among them Wayne Shorter, Sonny Rollins, Paul Motian and Maria Schneider.

Ornette Coleman's first request startled me into freshly realizing—like that country music song—how central jazz has been to the unbroken circle of my life for more than seventy years. Ornette's choice was a recording by Josef Rosenblatt, a Jewish cantor (chazan) in a 1916 (that's not a typo) recording from the Sabbath services in an Orthodox Jewish synagogue (a shul). Ornette's selection jolted me back to when I was a boy, sitting next to my father, in a shul in Boston's Jewish ghetto.

The first music that went all the way through me was the soul music of the chazan, both in that shul and others I kept going to just to hear what I described in another column I wrote, titled "Jazz and Deep Jewish Blues" (*JazzTimes*, February 2002): "The cry, the krechts (a catch in the voice), a cry summoning centuries of hosts of Jews . . . a thunderstorm of fierce yearnings that reverberated throughout the shul and then, as if the universe had lost a beat, there is sudden silence, and from deep inside the chazan, a soaring falsetto."

This was during the so-called Great Depression, and by the time I was eleven, working as a delivery boy on a horse-drawn wagon, I had enough money to buy three-for-a-dollar records by Louis Armstrong, Peetie Wheatstraw ("the devil's son-in-law") and Josef Rosenblatt.

Ornette told Ratliff he first heard a Rosenblatt recording some twenty-two years ago when, in Chicago, a young man asked him to come by and listen to what he thought would interest Ornette.

The reaction by Ornette: "I started crying like a baby. The record he had was crying, singing, and praying, all in the same breath. And none of it was crossing each other. I said, 'Wait a minute. You can't find those "notes." They don't exist.'"

That's what early listeners of Ornette's used to say. I first heard him at one of his first recording sessions in Los Angeles for Lester Koenig's Contemporary label. The penetrating human sound as he sang through his horn made me feel I'd found a soul brother. I didn't know then that Josef Rosenblatt was part of our troika.

Also in Ratliff's book is a listening session with Roy Haynes. I first heard Roy live during a Sunday afternoon jam session at Boston's Savoy Café, which was my second home. My parents thought it was where I really lived. A kid in his teens walked into the club and asked if he could sit in. He was a student, I later found out, at Roxbury Memorial High School, near where I lived.

That kid lit up the room with a propulsive beat that lifted everybody up, including the bartender. His name was Roy Haynes. Many years later, Roy and I were in the same class of National Endowment for the Arts Jazz Masters (all I could play was the electric typewriter), and I told him of that session at the Savoy. He laughed and said, "You know, when I was in school in Boston, I used to listen to you on the radio."

On the air, while a staff announcer at WMEX, I got a jazz show in a time slot management couldn't sell. And during a series on jazz history, I played Louis Armstrong recordings with Baby Dodds on drums, including a ten-inch "instructional" recording Dodds made (I think for Moe Asch's Folkways label) on topics including "Playing for the Benefit of the Band."

There was Baby Dodds, brought back to life during Ben Ratliff's interview with Roy, who said, "I used to travel with that [Baby Dodds] record." And Ratliff included in the excerpt from the record: "You must study . . . a guy's human nature. Study what he will take or what he will go for . . . that's why all guys is not drummers that's drumming . . . You can't holler at a man, you can't dog him. Not in music. It's up to me to keep all that lively. That's my job."

Livelier than ever—that's still Roy's job.

Roy spoke of his idol, "Papa" Jo Jones, who, as Ratliff notes, "was proud of his 'kiddies,' the musicians whom he influenced." When I was still on Boston radio, doing remotes from the Savoy, Jo Jones stunned me when he decided I was to be one of his "kiddies." I couldn't play anything, but I had a radio show and was writing about the music, so I had to be instructed in the calling I'd become marginally involved in.

One night, Papa Jo sat me down at the Savoy and, until the club closed, told me where the music had come from, where he had come from, and how to listen to this music by paying attention to what's really inside the players, because that's what the music was all about.

In his introduction to *The Jazz Ear*, Ratliff explains what he learned by listening to musicians as they were listening to other players: "What are the things they notice? What are their criteria for excellence? What makes them react involuntarily? The answers indicate what a musician values in music, which comes to connect with what a musician believes music is for in the first place. And that is the big thing, the big question, from which all small questions descend."

That's why *The Jazz Ear* will be a permanent part of learning how to listen inside the musicians playing. Jo Jones never stopped keeping an eye on his "kiddies." From time to time, he'd let me know if he felt I needed more instruction. Papa Jo would be proud of "kiddie" Ben Ratliff.

Clearly, jazz has also been at the center of the unbroken circle of Ben Ratliff's life all these years—and we're all fortunate that the *New York Times* recognizes his value.

34 | The Jewish Soul of Willie "The Lion" Smith

In the morning, the first thing I see in my office is a photo of Willie "The Lion" Smith at the piano, wearing his derby, with a cigar jutting challengingly from his mouth. Soon after I became part of the New York jazz scene in the early 1950s, one of my great pleasures was to pick up the phone at home and find the Lion calling just to chat. That other grandmaster of stride piano, James P. Johnson, once said, "When Willie Smith moved into a place, his every move was a picture." So were his stories on the piano, in his compositions and on the phone.

In March of 1958 the head of Contemporary Records, Les Koenig, asked if there was anyone I wanted to record for his label. I quickly made my way to Nola Studios on West 54th Street, where Mat Domber of Arbors Records now does a lot of his recordings, with Willie and the equally formidable—and, like Willie, endlessly melodic—pianist Luckey Roberts. The resulting album, *Luckey and the Lion: Harlem Piano,* has been reissued on CD by the Concord Music Group.

"He was a myth you saw come alive," Duke Ellington said of Willie, whom he considered his main mentor. But I thought I knew a lot about the man until Michael "Spike" Wilner—a jazz pianist, a scholar of stride piano, and the owner and manager of the now-legendary Smalls Jazz Club on West 10th Street in Manhattan—sent me his book of revelations: *The Lion of the Piano: 8 Piano Compositions by Willie "The Lion" Smith,* with transcriptions and an essay by Michael "Spike" Wilner.

Most startling to me was something about which I had a clue in the 1950s but stupidly never followed up on. Willie and I had the same internist, and among the displays on this doctor's wall was Willie's business card, written in English and Hebrew. I figured this was Willie's antic wit at play—perhaps a nod to the Jewish managers, bookers, and record executives in the jazz business. Was I wrong!

Willie's mother, Spike Wilner writes, was a laundress, and her son delivered the clean clothes to her customers, including "a prosperous Jewish family that treated Smith as one of their own," much like the Jewish family in New Orleans that bought young Louis Armstrong his first horn. Every Saturday, when a rabbi came to the family home to teach Hebrew classes, Willie was welcome to join in.

What fascinated young Willie, Wilner writers, was "the chanting of the rabbi." Reading this, I was a boy again in an Orthodox synagogue in the Roxbury neighborhood of Boston, in mandatory attendance during the High Holidays. My guess is that the chanting rabbi Willie heard was also a cantor, or *chazan,* who sang, often with improvisations, the Jewish prayers.

As I wrote in my memoir *Boston Boy,* the voice of my temple's *chazan* penetrated so deeply into my very being that I almost shouted aloud, as I did on a Boston street when I first heard jazz. I didn't shout in the *shul* (synagogue), so not to embarrass my father. But it was this same *krechts*—the soul cry of human promise, transcendence and vulnerability—that I later found in the blues of Billie Holiday, Charles Mingus and John Coltrane, just to name a few of the jazz *chazans* I have known.

The rabbi who reached Willie as I had been reached, Spike Wilner continues, "took special pains to teach him alone." At thirteen—and I had to stop reading to fully grasp this—Willie Smith "had his bar mitzvah in a Newark synagogue."

Wilner quotes the Lion himself: "A lot of people are unable to understand my wanting to be Jewish. One said to me, "Lion, you stepped up to the plate with one strike against you—and now you take a second one right down the middle! They can't seem to realize I have a Jewish soul and belong to that faith."*

The Lion of Judah actually later became a *chazan* himself at a Harlem synagogue of Black Jews!

What I would have given to have heard him there! Although I've been a Jewish atheist since I was twelve, I would have become a member of that congregation. Had there been any objections, I'm certain Rabbi Smith, with the vibrant force of his stride piano, would have told the objectors to learn the interconnectedness of us all—in music.

He knew—as he once said—"music doesn't stem from any single race, creed or locality. It comes from a mixture of all these things. As does the Lion."

Spike Wilner includes in his book Duke Ellington's recollection of the first time he heard the Lion play piano: "Actually everything and everybody seemed to be doing whatever they were doing in the tempo the Lion's group was laying down. The walls and furniture seemed to lean understandingly—one of the strangest and greatest sensations I ever had. The waiters served in that tempo; everybody who had to walk in, out or around the place walked with a beat."

In my youth, a Yiddish soul brother was called a "landsman." I always thought of Willie as a soul brother. If I'd listened intently enough, I would have known he was also a landsman and caught in his often jubilant stride rhythms an ageless touch of Jewish klezmer swinging.

Why was he called the Lion? During World War I, Willie served in an all-black battalion, the 350th Field Artillery. One time, while fighting in the trenches for 49 days without a break, he volunteered to man the "Glorious 75"—the big, ungainly and deadly French 75-millimeter cannon. Having been cited for bravery, Willie was called "the Lion" by his colonel.

Back in the States, the Lion wore a derby "because the rabbis did." Underneath, on the Holy Days, was his yarmulke. In my anti-Semitic Boston boyhood, wearing a yarmulke could have gotten you bashed in the teeth as "a Christ killer." But Lord help anyone who would have tried to mess with the Lion.

---

*Tim Wilkins of Jazz.com notes that in Smith's 1965 autobiography, *Music on My Mind*, the Lion also asserts that his birth father, Frank Bertholoff, was Jewish.

PART SEVEN

Finding the First Amendment Groove

35 | Satchmo's Rap Sheet

The FBI is proposing a new computer-profiling system, STAR (the System to Assess Risk), which, as National Public Radio reported on July 17, 2007, will be sifting through some six billion pieces of data by 2012, "about twenty records for every man, woman and child in America." Many of those "persons of interest" suspected of terrorism links will be databased for additional scrutiny by the CIA and other intelligence agencies. They won't know they have FBI files.

Back in J. Edgar Hoover's reign, even without databasing, the FBI amassed files on great numbers of Americans with purported ties to Communism and other subversive activities. Later, through the Freedom of Information Act, I was able to get my FBI reports—including an extensive file of articles I'd written, petitions I'd signed and people I'd known—with no mention anywhere that, as I've written, I'd been a fierce anti-Communist since reading Arthur Koestler's *Darkness at Noon* (about Stalinism from the inside) when I was fifteen.

Hoover had a special interest in black Americans, so I was not surprised to find recently—thanks to Louis Armstrong archivist Michael Cogswell and Louis's longtime friend and associate Phoebe Jacobs of the Louis Armstrong Educational Foundation—an FBI file stamped "This Summary Had Been Prepared for Use at the Seat of Government and Is Not Suitable for Dissemination." This secret Armstrong summary was dated August 8, 1962.

Then, as now, the FBI specialized in imaginary conspiracies based on its suspects' associations. In Louis's file: "A letter from Embassy Paris, dated 5/8/56 . . . revealed that a 'Congress of Scholars of the Negro World,' sponsored by the leftist 'Presence Africaine' . . . was scheduled to take place in Paris, September 19–22, 1956 . . . Louis Armstrong [was among] the American delegates who were invited."

Whether or not Louis ever came, the suspected association was duly noted. After all, as the FBI added the next year, this Armstrong person was extremely critical of President Eisenhower: "A newspaper clipping from the 9/19/57 issue of the *Southeast Missourian* . . . reported that Armstrong [who had been picked to serve as a cultural ambassador], while in Grand Forks for a concert, declared that he was dropping plans for a government-backed trip to Russia [saying that] 'because of the way they are treating my people in the South, the government can go to hell.'"

This musician-agitator, said the file, also called Eisenhower "two-faced" and accused him of having "no guts" for letting Arkansas governor Orville Faubus, who had forbidden black students to enter Little Rock schools, "allow cursing white mobs [to] stop the brave kids."

As an indication that FBI sources of information on subversives included patriotic citizens, directly under the entry of Armstrong's denunciation of the war-hero president was "[a]n anonymous letter, dated 9/21/57, with the envelope postmarked Boston, Mass., revealed that the writer was concerned about 'various well known Negroes,' who, according to the writer, were associated with CP members.

"The writer stated: 'Louis "Satchmo" Armstrong is a communist, why does the State Dept. give him a passport?'"

(Maybe the passport had been issued by one of those Communists who Joe McCarthy told us had infested the State Department.)

When the Supreme Court unanimously ordered Governor Faubus to let those Negro children into the Little Rock schools and Eisenhower reluctantly agreed (saying, "there were extreme myths on both sides"), Louis's FBI files ran clips from the *New York Herald Tribune* and the *Washington Post* reporting that Louis might change his mind about a government-sponsored tour of Russia.

The FBI's unblinking eye, however, stayed on Louis: "A letter from Embassy, Lome, Togoland, Africa, to the State Department dated 12/9/60 [focused on the] distribution in Togo of Communist Propaganda . . . which presented a vicious attack on US racial policy [and] 'made its appearance at approximately the dates on which Louis Armstrong performed in Lome.'" (The FBI must have surmised that wasn't a coincidence.)

At least Louis was in Africa on that date. My own FBI file reported that I had been at a meeting of "radicals" in North Africa around the same time. I have never been to Africa, North or South.

Hardly any possible unlawful activity of Louis was ignored by the FBI. An 11/30/50 entry "indicated that Louis Armstrong and his orchestra were playing at the Flamingo Hotel and Armstrong was dissatisfied with the situation." A person whose name was redacted said "he would take care of Armstrong by calling him on the telephone and by sending him a bottle of Scotch or a couple of reefers." Possession of reefers could get you busted.

Almost entirely blacked out was a 7/13/48 report that someone's [name redacted] address book contained the name of Louis Armstrong, 9200 Wilshire Boulevard, Beverly Hills, Calif." If Congress funds the FBI's new STAR profiling operation, capable of harvesting billions of names, some Americans may decide to look carefully in their address books, whether in print or electronic form.

In my own FBI file, a particularly damning report involving jazz was that I had given a course on jazz in the 1940s in Boston at the Samuel Adams School, which was on the list of Communist-front institutions. Actually, it was, and I knew about some pinkos on the faculty, but no other school had ever asked me to teach a course on jazz, and I couldn't resist.

Of course, I often mentioned Louis Armstrong during my lectures, and that might have heightened the FBI's subsequent sustained interest in me. I prize any association with Louis, even thanks to the FBI files.

36 | The Constitution of a Jazzman

Early one morning years ago, I was at the Blues Alley Jazz Club in Washington, D.C., to do a television interview with Max Roach. As always, I was early. There was no one in the club except Max, alone at the drums, practicing for the night's gig. He played with as much intensity—and as many surprises—as if he were before hundreds of listeners.

Like Roy Eldridge and Phil Woods, Max always played as if it were his last gig on earth. With Charlie Parker, Dizzy Gillespie, Thelonious Monk and another drummer—Kenny "Klook" Clarke—Max changed the direction of jazz as Louis Armstrong had decades before.

Washington Post jazz critic Matt Schudel distills how Max liberated jazz drumming: "By playing the beat-by-beat pulse of standard 4/4 time on the 'ride' cymbal instead of on the thudding bass drum, [he] developed a flexible, flowing rhythmic pattern that allowed soloists to play freely, [and] by matching his rhythmic attack with a tune's melody, Mr. Roach brought a newfound subtlety of expression to his instrument."

Off the stand, however, Max was one of the few musicians to publicly speak out, with no subtlety, about Jim Crow in and out of the music business: "We invented, we created the music. . . . Hell, man this is black classical music. [Compared to the money we get] so much of that European classical stuff is on relief, subsidized by foundations."

Max once instructed me on the correlation between jazz as free expression and the Constitution: "Ours are individual voices," he said, "listening intently to all the other voices, and creating a whole from all of these personal voices."

Since then, when I hear a debate on whether ours is a "living Constitution," Max comes to mind.

Also a composer, the drummer created a work titled *We Insist! Max Roach's Freedom Now Suite* in 1960, as the civil-rights movement was gathering momentum and controversy. It helped spur other jazz musicians to bring those national polyphonic protest rhythms into their music.

I was privileged, to say the least, to produce the incandescent *Freedom Now Suite* performances for the Candid Records label. By "produce," I mean only that

I wrote down the length of each section and made sure Max was present to decide on the final cut. It was his byline, not mine.

Everyone on the session, including the engineer, was swept up in the cascade of emotions that Max and lyricist Oscar Brown Jr. propelled into motion. The magisterial tenor saxophonist Coleman Hawkins—with a sound that never needed a microphone—actually seemed to fill the building. And that very afternoon, Abbey Lincoln was being transformed, because of Max, from a supper-club singer into the utterly singular and penetrating storyteller who has since resounded around the world.

Ranging from slavery (the bitterly sardonic "Driva Man") to the beating of black students going on at Southern lunch counters, "Freedom Day" to "Tears for Johannesburg," the *Freedom Now Suite* created such a surge of rebellion that it was soon banned in South Africa, to the pleasure of everyone who had been in the studio that day.

As he continued to lead influential groups—nurturing such hard-swinging and also lyrically searching young musicians as the late, great trumpet player Clifford Brown—Max himself was so deepening his mastery that, as Michael Bourne of jazz radio station WGBO said to *Daily News*'s David Hinckley the day after Max died: "He could play a whole concert on just the drums."

That's what I was hearing on that afternoon long ago at the Blues Alley in Washington, D.C.

In his extraordinarily illuminating memoir *Jazz Odyssey* (Continuum, 2002), the prodigious pianist Oscar Peterson speaks of Max not only as a drummer who could rivet an audience all by himself but also as a virtuoso accompanist:

"Max . . . has a flair for 'floating'—playing patterns between the soloist's phrases without interfering or disrupting them. This kind of 'sensitive intrusion' is a very special gift. Only a handful of percussionists can separate themselves bodily from the time in order to add another separate linear, yet rhythmic, string of improvisational phrases—without altogether shredding the musical fiber of the performance."

Max didn't like the term "jazz," regarding it as too limiting because *he* could not be limited. With his music certain to endure as long as there is civilization (itself not an entirely safe bet), Max exemplified what Duke Ellington told me long ago about not heeding such transient definitions as "modern," "postmodern" or "cutting edge."

During a break in the recording of the *Freedom Now Suite,* Coleman Hawkins—himself an imposing individualist—was marveling at Max's strong, bold, often towering melodies. He kept asking Max, "Did you really write this, Max?" Max just smiled. "My, my," was all Hawkins could say.

And in the erupting protest section, Abbey Lincoln startled us with fierce yet musical roars and screams of rage that, in Max's composition, told of the centuries-old black roots that led to what A. Philip Randolph, architect of the 1963 March on Washington with Martin Luther King, called "America's unfinished revolution."

"I've learned a lot from Max Roach in recent months," Abbey told me that afternoon, "about being *me* when I sing."

Max had what Oscar Peterson calls the "will to perfection" in continuing to find out through his music who *he* was. Oscar says that will is a prevailing force among jazz musicians, explaining that "it requires you to collect all your senses, emotions, physical strength, and mental power, and focus them entirely onto the performance with utter dedication, every time you play.

"And if that is scary. It is also uniquely exciting . . . you never get rid of it. Nor do you want to, for you come to believe that if you get it *all* right, you will be capable of virtually anything."

But Max also knew, as did Coleman Hawkins, that it's essentially the *striving* that keeps musicians and the rest of us going. During one of Hawkins's best solos in the *Freedom Now Suite,* there was a squeak. "Don't splice that!" Hawkins told me. "When it's all perfect in a piece like this, there's something very wrong."

What Max had created was in real, raw time—for all time.

37 | How Jazz Helped Hasten the Civil Rights Movement

On January 19, Martin Luther King's Birthday, Jazz at Lincoln Center and the Rockefeller Foundation, also focusing on the next day's presidential inauguration, presented at Kennedy Center *A Celebration of America.* Headlining the cast were Sandra Day O'Connor and Wynton Marsalis. As Jazz at Lincoln Center declared, Dr. King called jazz "America's triumphant music," and the presence of Mr. Marsalis is to "illustrate that American democracy and America's music share the same tenets and embody the same potential for change, hope and renewal."

This focus on jazz as well as on then President-elect Barack Obama (who, I was told, has John Coltrane on his iPod) should help make Americans, including our historians, aware of the largely untold story of the key role of jazz in helping to shape and quicken the arrival of the civil rights movement.

For a long time, black and white jazz musicians were not allowed to perform together publicly. It was only at after-hours sessions that they jammed together, as Louis Armstrong and Bix Beiderbecke did in Chicago in the 1920s.

In the early 1940s, before I could vote, I often lied my way into Boston's Savoy Café, where I first came to know jazz musicians. It was the only place in town where blacks and whites were regularly on the stand and in the audience. This led police occasionally to go into the men's room, confiscate the soap, and hand the manager a ticket for unsanitary conditions. There was no law in Boston against mixing the races, but it was frowned on in some official circles.

I had heard, however, of a New York jazz club, Café Society, where there was open, unquestioned integration. In *Café Society: The Wrong Place for the Right People,* a book by Barney Josephson, with Terry Trilling-Josephson (University of Illinois Press, 2009), Mr. Josephson, Café Society's founder, is quoted as having said: "I wanted a club where blacks and whites worked together behind the footlights and sat together out front. There wasn't, so far as I knew, a place like it in New York or in the country." He hadn't ever been to imperiled Savoy Café in Boston.

But Jim Crow was so accepted in the land that when Benny Goodman, during the 1930s, brought Teddy Wilson, and then Lionel Hampton, into his trio and quartets, it was briefly big national news. And Artie Shaw later hired Billie Holiday and Roy Eldridge, both of whom often met Mr. Crow when having to find accommodations separate from the white musicians when on the road.

When booked especially—but not only—in the South, members of black jazz bands had to be put up in homes or other places in black neighborhoods. Nor were they seated in restaurants outside of those neighborhoods. In a 1944 *New Yorker* profile of Duke Ellington, Richard Boyer told of a white St. Louis policeman enthusiastically greeting Duke Ellington after a performance, saying: "If you'd been a white man, Duke, you'd have been a great musician."

With his customary regal manner, Duke, smiling coolly, answered, "I guess things would have been different if I'd been a white man." Later, Duke told me how, when he was touring the deep South from 1934 to 1936, he sidelined Jim Crow.

"Without the benefit of federal judges," he said, "we commanded respect. We had two Pullman cars and a seventy-foot baggage car. We parked them in each station, and lived in them. We had our own water, food, electricity and sanitary facilities. The natives would come by and say, 'What's that?' 'Well,' we'd say, 'that's the way the president travels.' We made our point. What else could we have done at that time?"

A stronger point was later made throughout the South and anywhere else blacks were, at best, seated in the balcony. In his touring all-star tournament, Jazz at the Philharmonic, Norman Granz by the 1950s was conducting a war against segregated seating. Capitalizing on the large audiences JATP attracted, Granz insisted on a guarantee from promoters that there would be no COLORED signs in the auditoriums. "The whole reason for Jazz at the Philharmonic," he said, "was to take it to places where I could break down segregation."

Here's an example of Granz in action: After renting an auditorium in Houston in the 1950s, he hired the ticket seller and laid down the terms. Then Granz, personally, before the concert, removed the signs that said WHITE TOILETS and NEGRO TOILETS. When the musicians—Dizzy Gillespie, Ella Fitzgerald, Buddy Rich, Lester Young—arrived, Granz watched as some white Texans objected to sitting alongside black Texans. Said the impresario: "You sit where I sit you. You don't want to sit next to a black, here's your money back."

As this music reached deeply into more white Americans, their sensitivity to segregation, affecting not only jazz musicians, increased. A dramatic illustration is the story told by Charles Black, a valuable member of Thurgood Marshall's team of lawyers during the long journey to *Brown v. Board of Education*. In 1931, growing up white in racist Austin, Texas, Black at age sixteen heard Louis Armstrong in a hotel there. "He was the first genius I had ever seen," Black wrote long after in the *Yale Law Journal*. "It is impossible," he added, "to overstate the significance of a sixteen-year-old southern boy's seeing genius, for the first time, in a black. We literally never saw a black then in any but a servant's capacity. It was just then that I started toward the Brown case where I belonged."

Armstrong himself, in a September 1941 letter to jazz critic Leonard Feather, wrote: "I'd like to recall one of my most inspiring moments. I was playing a concert date in a Miami auditorium. I walked on stage and there I saw something I'd never seen. I saw thousands of people, colored and white, on the main floor. Not segregated in one row of whites and another row of Negroes. Just all together—naturally. I thought I was in the wrong state. When you see things like that, you know you're going forward."

As Stanley Crouch, a keenly perceptive jazz historian and critic, wrote in the *New York Daily News*: "Once the whites who played it and the listeners who loved it began to balk at the limitations imposed by segregation, jazz became a futuristic social force in which one was finally judged purely on the basis of one's individual ability. Jazz predicted the civil rights movement more than any other art in America."

Also providing momentum were the roots of jazz—going back to the field hollers of slaves reaching each other across plantations; gospel songs and prayers connecting slavery here with Old Testament stories of deliverance of Jews from slavery; and the blues, the common language of jazz, echoing in Armstrong's singing "What did I do to be so black and blue?"

In his *The Triumph of Music* (Harvard University Press, 2008), spanning four centuries and diverse nations, Tim Blanning, of Cambridge University, tells how black musicians have helped prepare and participated in the civil rights movement. As when opera singer Marian Anderson, denied permission to sing at Constitution Hall by the Daughters of the American Revolution in 1939, sparked the start of the 1963 March on Washington by rousing the huge crowd with "I've Been 'Buked and I've Been Scorned."

I was there, at the back of the stage, covering this typhoon of protest for West-inghouse Radio; and during Martin Luther King's world-resounding speech, Tim Blanning writes, "Mahalia Jackson called out to him: 'Tell them about your dream, Martin!'"

The black tribunes of soul music also energized what A. Philip Randolph, the primary organizer of the March on Washington, called "the unfinished revolu-tion"—among them James Brown, "Say It Loud—I'm Black and I'm Proud."

During the 1950s and early 1960s, when my day and night jobs were all about jazz, I wrote of the civil rights surge among jazz creators: Sonny Rollins's "Freedom Suite"; "Alabama" recorded by John Coltrane; and an album I pro-duced for Candid Records that was soon banned in South Africa—Max Roach's "Freedom Now Suite."

It was Max who first taught me the connection between jazz and my other passion, the Bill of Rights. "Like the Constitution, we are individual voices," he said, "listening intently to all the other voices and creating a whole from all these personal voices."

My involvement in his "Freedom Now Suite"—whose album cover carried a wire-service photo of black students at a whites-only lunch counter in the South—was to work with the engineer on the sound checks and the timing of the tracks. I wouldn't have dared interfere with the incandescent fusion of anger and triumph in the studio, with Max propelling the black American experience from "Driva Man" to "Freedom Day."

One of the griots was the magisterial Coleman Hawkins, who invented the jazz tenor saxophone, and whose signature sound was so huge he didn't need a microphone in a club. He filled the room that day. And Abbey Lincoln, the former subtly sensual supper-club singer, was transformed before my eyes into a blazing Sojourner Truth.

After Rosa Parks was arrested on December 1, 1955, for refusing to leave her seat in the front of a bus in Montgomery, Alabama, Dr. King spoke before some 15,000 black citizens in, and on the sidewalks around, Holy Street Baptist Church. Dr. King, as recalled by his close friend and adviser Clarence B. Jones in his book *What Would Martin Say?* (HarperCollins, 2008), energized the transportation boycott that followed the arrest: "We are determined here in Montgomery to work and fight until justice runs down like water and righteousness in a mighty stream."

Not long after, when some black civil rights activists rebuked Ellington for not having been publicly enough involved in the movement, he said to me: "People who think that of me have not been listening to our music. For a long time, social protest and pride in the Negro have been our most significant themes in talking about what it is to be a Negro in this country—with jazz being like the kind of man you wouldn't want your daughter to be associated with."

Suddenly he brightened: "When Franklin Roosevelt died, practically no American music was played on the air in tribute to him. We, our band, were given a dispensation, however. We did one radio program, during the period of mourning, dedicated to him."

On January 20, Barack Obama joined Franklin Roosevelt in the lineage of American presidents. If I'd been asked about the music to be played in Washington the night before, I'd have suggested to Wynton Marsalis that he and the orchestra swing into a song I often heard during an Ellington set, "Things Ain't What They Used to Be."

Not that Jim Crow has finally been interred, but jazz has been a force to hasten that day. Clark Terry, long an Ellington sideman, told me: "Duke wants life and music to be always in a state of becoming. He doesn't even like to write definitive endings of a piece. He always likes to make the end of a song sound like it's still going somewhere."

That's how we, too, felt on that Martin Luther King's Birthday and Inauguration Day.

38 | The Congressman from the Land of Jazz

Since 1964, seventy-five-year-old John Conyers—a long-serving Democrat in his nineteenth term, a founder of the Congressional Black Caucus and a leading critic of the U.S. Patriot Act—has represented the Fourteenth Congressional District of Michigan, which includes Detroit. His legislative record includes the passage of a 1987 resolution declaring "the sense of Congress that jazz is [a] rare and valuable American national treasure."

Mr. Conyers told me once that he often communicates with his "spiritual musical ancestors" by playing recordings in his office of John Coltrane, Miles Davis and Charlie Parker. He adds, "This really helps me in my work here." When he's asked about the pressure of that work, Mr. Conyers says, "It really isn't that hard for me because I always have my music with me."

Jazz has been an integral part of his life from the ninth grade, when he started playing cornet and became a regular visitor to Detroit's Paradise Theater to be in the presence, over the years, of Duke Ellington, Sarah Vaughan and Dizzy Gillespie. While histories of jazz focus on such vital centers as New Orleans, Chicago, New York and the West Coast, Detroit has been a bountiful source of a long list of singular and influential masters of the music.

Fellow students at Northwestern High School were such subsequently renowned jazz figures as Betty Carter, later in life a startlingly inventive jazz singer; and the deeply swinging tenor saxophonist Billy Mitchell. At Cass Technical High School, the congressman told me, "there were bassist Paul Chambers, trumpet players Howard McGhee and Donald Byrd." Also from Detroit, he enthusi-astically added, were guitarist Kenny Burrell, vibraphonist Milt Jackson and the formidable Jones brothers—Elvin (drums), Hank (piano) and Thad (trumpet).

As a teenager, "putting my age up and deathly afraid of being found out," Mr. Conyers frequented the city's most significant jazz clubs—Baker's Keyboard Lounge, the Blue Bird Inn, El Sino and the Frolic Show Bar. The challenge was that, to act his alleged age, he had to order a beer—but he couldn't drink it because it would make him sleepy. Still, it was in plain sight on his table.

While in high school, he heard a recording that, he says, "changed my whole cultural approach to music—Charlie Parker's 'Now's the Time' with Miles Davis, and Dizzy Gillespie playing piano. I became an instant bebopper. I've played that record at least 10,000 times."

Having interrupted his glowing memories to go to the House floor for a vote, the congressman returned to the phone interview with a story of a trip some twenty years ago to Ghana, where he attended a meeting of the Organization of African States: "There were about fifty women singing and shouting, and they had these huge conga drums. There was this little guy with a horn, blowing a riff at everybody. I realized that this was the precise background music I'd heard in John Coltrane that I thought he had created. But I knew these Africans hadn't heard Coltrane on any recording, so it was very clear who got what from whom. Coltrane had brought this over, creating this African song as part of his music. It was the same song! I thought, 'Oh, God, this is tremendous!' Like I said, jazz for me is like recontacting my spiritual ancestors.

"But," he continued, "although this is an African-American-created music, it's available to everybody if you want to get it. I've always argued that white guys can learn to play jazz." Citing baritone saxophonist Pepper Adams, the congressman said, "He was the greatest on that instrument there ever was—and he came out of Detroit! There are African Americans that can't play jazz. But if you've got it, you can play it. You're never too old. It's never too late."

After another interruption, Mr. Conyers came back excited: "Hey, guess what happened, Nat! I ran into Neil Abercrombie [Democrat congressman, Hawaii] in the hall. We've been working on getting an appropriation for a Billy Strayhorn Chair at the Duke Ellington School of the Arts in Washington." (Pianist-composer Billy Strayhorn was Duke Ellington's alter ego in writing for the orchestra.)

"With Rodney Frelinghuysen of New Jersey, chair of the Appropriations Committee," Mr. Conyers went on, "and Tom Davis of Virginia, the Number 2 Republican in the House, they're going to write a line in the Appropriations Bill for the Billy Strayhorn Chair." That legislative accomplishment didn't make the news wires, but it made Representative Conyers's day.

I asked him if he still played the cornet. "You know what," he said buoyantly,

"I just told my sons this weekend before I left Detroit that I'm buying two cornets, two trumpets and a clarinet, and we're going to all start playing again." John is in junior high, and Carl is in elementary school.

While he was reminiscing again, about Detroit's jazz clubs, the congressman noted that Baker's Keyboard Lounge is still going strong. Indeed, a release on the Warner Brothers Records label is saxophonist James Carter's *Live at Baker's Keyboard Lounge*. And the extensive, definitive, illustrated history of Detroit jazz, *Before Motown*, by Lars Bjorn with Jim Gallert, is available from the University of Michigan Press in Ann Arbor. The introduction states: "Jazz historians have usually passed by Detroit when discussing the development of jazz."

However, the congressman from the land of jazz remains one of its best informed chroniclers, and emphasized: "There's a lot of jazz still going on there. And there's a lot more Congress can do for jazz once we're over Iraq. There'll come a time when we'll be able to look back at our domestic program and get an effective national infrastructure to support, preserve and celebrate this national treasure." The National Endowment for the Arts (NEA) Jazz Masters Program and the efforts of the Smithsonian Institution are important. But the congressman believes more can be done to increase the audience for jazz in this nation.

39 | Jazz Musicians in the Public Square

In 1955, when the late Nat Shapiro and I put together *Hear Me Talkin' to Ya: The Story of Jazz Told by the Men Who Made It*—in which only musicians spoke—a primary reason was to counter the notion at the time that jazz players were only articulate on their instruments but otherwise had little to say of interest about public issues.

Since then, of course, Max Roach, Charles Mingus and others have spoken vigorously and publicly about controversies outside of music. Particularly notable was Louis Armstrong's reaction to Arkansas governor Orville Faubus's blocking the integration of public schools in Little Rock. "The way they are treating my people in the South, the government can go to hell," said Armstrong. And when President Eisenhower spoke of extremists "on both sides" of that conflict, Armstrong trumpeted: "The president has no guts."

These days, continuing that legacy of public citizenship, Wynton Marsalis, writing in the November 7, 2006, edition of *New Republic* about Hurricane Katrina's devastation of New Orleans, placed the blame not only on clueless politicians but on the citizenry of that city, and on the country.

"It was also we who watched as money to fix the levees was removed from the federal budget in spite of the warnings of dire consequences from the U.S.

Army Corps of Engineers," wrote Marsalis. "As we look at what happened in the Crescent City, we are brought closer to this simple truth: The ingredients for social disaster are present in cities all over the United States. . . . We are too busy to worry about poverty, public education, homelessness, drug addiction, the arts, even the political process."

Marsalis has already shown that as a music educator—on television, and in his young people's concerts at Jazz at Lincoln Center—he is the Leonard Bernstein of our time. But he also controversially expanded his educational views during a celebration in New York of the sponsorship of the Eagle Academy in the Bronx by the 100 Black Men of America organization. As Stanley Crouch wrote in his November 14, 2006, New York *Daily News* column, this school provides mentors for the all-male student body "to make sure that the boys become accustomed to seeing and knowing successful [black] men who are not corrupt and corrupting and with whom they can talk and from whom they can get advice." Present at the event, Wynton Marsalis not only cited the value of mentoring programs but also—as Crouch reported—emphasized that "black American culture, which once produced so many musicians of worldwide importance, is being debased and now pumps out trash that pollutes and weakens the community.

"Marsalis said that it was important to salvage the greatness of black American culture because of its human importance beyond all lines of color, sex, religion or nationality. Jazz, he said, represented not just the triumph of a single ethnic community; *it represented the triumph of the human spirit.*" (Emphasis added.)

The blues, from the beginning, were open and often ironic about sexual relationships, but did not—unlike much of the rap lyrics Marsalis indicted—debase women and glamorize preening violence.

In his *New Republic* article, Marsalis probed deeper than rap music into the continuing racial dissonances in this land: "The race issue has always been used to polarize the lower classes. Many of the calls I receive from New Orleanians decry an increase in racism. Friends of mine from high school tell me that they have never seen such vitriol, and these are white comrades talking about their friends and family, not victims of the rap game." Marsalis ended by making the historic point that "the development of jazz showed what Americans can do when we come together. . . . Swing is a philosophy of steadfastness. . . . Anyone can swing for a few measures—but swinging is a matter of endurance. It tests the limit of your ability to work with another person to create a mutual feeling. . . . Will we now recognize that we are in this land together?"

He didn't answer the question because he couldn't. This nation hadn't been so bitterly divided—on the war in Iraq, on the abuse of the Bill of Rights at home, and on the gaping inequalities in health care, etc.—for many decades. Jazz can't cure any of this; but as Wynton notes, he—as a product of this legacy of the American experience—can speak out in its name "to work . . . to create a mutual feeling" in the public and political square. Jazz shows it can be done. That's why it's encouraging to see its growth in schools.

Another outspoken jazzman, Charles Mingus, prophetically spoke of much of our current condition years ago: "It's not only about color any more. It's getting deeper than that. . . . People are getting so fragmented, and part of that is that fewer and fewer people are making a real effort any more to find exactly who they are and to build on that knowledge. Most people are forced to do things they don't want to most of the time. And so they get to the point where they feel they no longer have any choice about anything. . . . We create our own slavery."

Through the years, I've learned a lot from many jazz musicians, and not only about music. They don't have the solutions to what divides us, but their music continues to show the world what Wynton Marsalis calls "the wisdom in the enduring jazz principle of swing." Because of what they've learned about themselves in the mutuality of growth in this music, jazz men and women do have something of worth to say in the public square.

40 | Quincy Jones—Past, Present and Future

When I left Boston in 1953 to become New York editor of *Down Beat,* the first musician I came to know well was Quincy Jones. He was twenty and already writing crisply uncluttered arrangements for a variety of jazz record dates, and soon was contributing some of them to Count Basie, who had no patience for excess notes.

Quincy was so guileless that at first he appeared naive; but as he became a key part of the jazz scene, it became clear that he was interested in, and quickly knowledgeable about, all of music, and uninterested in the stiff categories set up by critics and even some musicians.

By 1956, he had been musical director for Dizzy Gillespie's big band, and the next year, he studied with Nadia Boulanger in Paris. In the early 1960s, Quincy was conductor and arranger for Frank Sinatra, who nicknamed him Q, which his closest friends—who seem to be in the hundreds—have since called him.

Continually challenging himself, Quincy wanted to write for films, and as he learned the craft, his scores included *In the Heat of the Night* and *In Cold Blood* (which won him an Oscar in 1967). He was also in the recording studios, not only as a leader-arranger but also as a producer at Mercury Records in 1961. Three years later, he became a vice president of the label, the first black person to head a jazz division of a major record company.

Widely traveled, Quincy did more than absorb the music of various countries. He saw how music was able to ease tensions among people of otherwise different cultures, and he began to figure out how to use music to make a difference in the lives of children in grave need. In 1985, he produced and conducted a recording, *We Are the World,* with international artists across the musical spectrum, that raised $60 million to deal with famine in Africa.

Wherever Q went, he created ways to change the attitudes and lives of kids. Once, in New Orleans, he persuaded a television station—as Scott Smith reported in *Hemisphere Magazine*—to run frequent stories about a different student who had achieved A's. He wanted, he said, "to redefine in that community what it meant to be cool."

In 1991, he told me he had founded the Listen Up Foundation to get youngsters involved in other people's problems. One program, From South Central to South Africa, involved bringing Los Angeles inner-city kids at risk of being recruited by gangs to South Africa, where five of them helped Habitat for Humanity build homes for poor citizens. Since then, Listen Up has given $400,000 to build homes for the homeless in South African townships.

In recent years, Quincy has been working on his most ambitious project, We Are the Future, to provide training and health services to "children who struggle in the face of hunger, violence and disease" (wearethefuture.com).

Among his partners in this insistent expansion of the Listen Up Foundation are the World Bank and its former president, James Wolfensohn, and the Rome-based Glocal Forum, founded in 2001 to be of use wherever youngsters are in areas of conflict. Also involved are United Nations agencies.

In early May 2004, a four-hour *We Are the Future* concert at the Colosseum in Rome was shown live on Italian television and taped for later, edited broadcasts on other MTV networks around the world. In the United States, the concert was heard live on XM Radio, a satellite network; the two-hour TV version of the concert aired May 28, 2004. Among those present were Norah Jones, Alicia Keys, Herbie Hancock, LL Cool J, Cirque du Soleil, Oprah Winfrey and Muhammad Ali. Helping Quincy coordinate the event were then U.S. United Nations Ambassador John D. Negroponte; Glocal's Uri Savir, former Israeli negotiator at the Oslo peace talks; and Palestinian-American businessman Rani Masri.

At the event were 2,000 children, ages five to eight, embodying the scope of We Are the Future: Palestinians and Israelis, Tutsis and Hutus, Serbs and Croats. Quincy, though he never wastes notes in his musical arrangements, never thinks small when it comes to kids under fire, whether from weapons or disease.

The concert was just the start. In its March 2004 progress report, We Are the Future emphasized that it "goes beyond awareness raising and fund raising. WAF is about building youth centers for children living in conflict cities and across the developing world; and building global city-to-city networks to support these centers." Already, six centers have been established in Africa and the Middle East.

Back in the 1950s, Quincy and I talked about all kinds of festering conflicts, in and out of jazz. But as dangerous dissonances have grown around the world, Q realized, he says, "that in the last decade alone, two million children were killed as a result of conflict, six million were injured, and twelve million have become homeless.

"These children," seventy-one-year-old Quincy Jones adds, "are not the victims of natural disasters—but of mankind."

PART EIGHT

Roots

41 | King Oliver in the Groove(s)

When I was in my teens, reading about the storied sites of early jazz, I envied the Chicagoans of the 1920s who were hip enough to spend nights at the Lincoln Gardens café where King Oliver's Creole Jazz Band was in residence, shortly joined by Oliver's young New Orleans protégé, Louis Armstrong. But the few recordings I could find sounded as if time had worn the music down and dim, including the clicks and scratches of those used early discs.

Now, however, in a remarkable feat of sound restoration, *King Oliver/Off the Record: The Complete 1923 Jazz Band Re-Recordings* (Archeophone Records, 2007) makes it very clear to me why among the regulars in the audience back then were the young white jazz apprentices who thronged to hear King Oliver's Creole Jazz Band whenever they played in Chicago. According to Lil Hardin, the pianist in the band, as reported by me and Nat Shapiro for *Hear Me Talkin' to Ya*, a book we coedited in 1955: "They'd line up ten deep in front of the stand—Muggsy Spanier, Dave Tough, George Wettling—listening intently. Then they'd talk to Joe Oliver and Louis." (Also among them were Eddie Condon and fourteen-year-old Benny Goodman.) Drummer George Wettling described the excitement in the club: "Joe would stand there, fingering his horn with his right hand and working his mute with his left, and how they would rock the place! Unless you were lucky enough [to be there], you can't imagine what swing they got."

Now we can. David Sager (a recorded sound technician at the Library of Congress) and Doug Benson (a teacher and recording engineer at Montgomery College in Rockville, Maryland) created their Off the Record label last year to bring King Oliver's Creole Band back to life. Working on rare original recordings supplied by collectors, Mr. Benson, writes his partner, "began to capture onto the digital domain clean, smooth transfers of the discs, using a wide array of styli." The actual music was deep in the original grooves—though until now poorly reissued and reproduced. The 1923 sounds had to be excavated.

While there were distinctive soloists in the band—clarinetist Johnny Dodds, trombonist Honore Dutrey and, of course, the leader and newcomer from New Orleans who would eventually swing the world—this was essentially a dance band.

In his exceptionally instructive notes, Mr. Sager explains: "That the Oliver band's sound was replete with marvelous invention, and a superior 'hot' sound, was the added premium. The principle, however, was rhythm."

Joe Oliver never had to announce the next number. As trombonist Preston

Jackson recalled, "He would play two or three bars, stomp twice, and everybody would start playing, sharing with the dancers the good time they were having."

"After they would knock everybody out with about forty minutes of 'High Society,'" Wettling said, "Joe would look down at me, wink, and then say, 'Hotter than a forty-five.'"

Years later, I would hear from musicians who had been at Lincoln Gardens about the always startling, simultaneous "hot breaks" Armstrong and Oliver played. (A "break" is when the rhythm section stops and one or more horns electrify the audience for a couple of measures.)

Among the thirty-seven numbers in the two-disc set, these legendary "breaks" can be heard on "Snake Rag," "Weatherbird Rags," "The Southern Stomps" and "I Ain't Gonna Tell Nobody."

Energized by joining the players and dancers at Lincoln Gardens, I remembered a night long ago at Preservation Hall in New Orleans where, in another "hot" dance band, trombonist Jim Robinson lifted me into joy. What Oliver and Armstrong brought from New Orleans to Chicago, and then to the rest of the planet, exemplified how Robinson also felt about his New Orleans birthright: "I enjoy playing for people that are happy. If everyone is in a frisky spirit, the spirit gets into me and I can make my trombone sing. If my music makes people happy, I will try to do more. It gives me a warm heart and that gets into my music." Oliver and Armstrong felt the same way.

Since the members of King Oliver's Creole Jazz Band were driven by the desire to keep the dancers and themselves happy, hearing them as they were at Lincoln Gardens provides a keener understanding that this music began in the intersecting rhythms of the musicians and the dancers' pleasure.

And in all the different forms jazz has taken since, when it ain't got that makes-you-want-to-move swing somewhere, it may impress some critics with its cutting-edge adventurousness, but it's not likely to make anyone shout—as King Oliver's banjoist, Bill Johnson, did one night at Lincoln Gardens—"Oh play that thing!"

In his deeply researched article on King Oliver in the Summer 2007 issue of the invaluable *American Legacy: The Magazine of African-American Life and Culture,* Peter Gerler notes that after Lincoln Gardens was destroyed in a fire on Christmas Eve, 1924, Joe Oliver brought a new band, the Dixieland Syncopaters, into the Plantation Café, which like Lincoln Gardens "was a 'black-and-tan' club, where crowds of blacks and whites mingled, danced, and enjoyed the music of top black bands." A *Variety* review of the new King Oliver band exclaimed: "If you haven't heard Oliver and his boys, you haven't heard real jazz. . . . You dance calmly for a while, trying to fight it, and then you succumb completely."

Now that Messrs. Sager and Benson have brought us inside the Lincoln Gardens, their other attractions on their Off the Record label include 1922 recordings by Kid Ory, the New Orleans king of the "tailgate trombone"; long unavailable sessions by Clarence Williams's Blue Five (with Louis Armstrong and Sidney Bechet); and the classic Bix Beiderbecke sides on the Gennett label. There are more to come.

Messrs. Benson and Sager have been friends since junior high school, where both played in the trombone section of the school band. Mr. Benson also plays bass and piano and is a composer and arranger. They have now parlayed their lifelong enthusiasm for this music into a permanent sound library of historic jazz performances freshly retrieved from inside the original grooves.

With regard to what's ahead on their label, Mr. Sager says eagerly: "It will be interesting to see what technology enables us to do in the coming years." I yearn to listen to Bix Beiderbecke directly, so I can hear what Louis Armstrong said (quoted in *Hear Me Talkin' to Ya*): "You take a man with a pure tone like Bix's and no matter how loud the other fellows may be blowing, that pure tone will cut through it all."

42 | Giants at Play

During television's early years, jazz was infrequently seen, except when its few popular "names," such as Benny Goodman and Louis Armstrong, appeared on variety shows like Ed Sullivan's. But on December 8, 1957, live on Sunday afternoon, many members of the jazz pantheon appeared on CBS TV's *The Sound of Jazz*, among them Billie Holiday, Count Basie, Thelonious Monk, Lester Young, Coleman Hawkins, Red Allen, Gerry Mulligan, Pee Wee Russell and Roy Eldridge.

Because nearly all the legendary originals on the program are dead, videos of this historic (and never to be equaled) event have been played and replayed around the world. Along with the late Whitney Balliett of the *New Yorker*, I selected the musicians. For me, it was a jazz fan's fantasy come true.

Making it all possible was the producer, Robert Herridge, the most creative, and stubbornly independent, force I've known in my various television forays. (Among the works he transmuted to the screen were Dostoevsky's *Notes from the Underground, All the King's Men*, and *The Trial and Death of Socrates*.) His only instruction to Whitney Balliett and me was, "Make it pure!" He didn't care if most of the players were unknown to a general audience as long as they exemplified what Whitney had described as "the sound of surprise" of this music.

Only one of our choices caused trouble. During a sound check, Herridge received a note from a representative of the sponsor, read it and tore it up. He paraphrased the message for me and Whitney: "We must not put into America's homes, especially on Sunday, someone who's been imprisoned for drug use."

Herridge told the bearer of the note that if Billie Holiday could not go on, he, Whitney, and I would leave.

The show went on.

Because of his extensive experience at CBS, and having worked with many cameramen, Herridge selected those he knew could improvise. "When you see a shot you want, take it," he told them. "We'll handle it in the control room." Director Jack Smight, himself an extraordinary improviser, enthusiastically agreed.

The set for *The Sound of Jazz* was simply the studio, with viewers seeing the cameramen, and some of the musicians in informal attire, wearing hats—as jazz players habitually did at rehearsals. I had neglected to tell Billie Holiday that this would not be the usual television setting, and when she found out, she told me angrily: "I just bought a goddamn $500 dress for this show!"

But once in the musical company of her peers, Billie happily swung into the groove. Aware that there would be no splicing out of clinkers in this entirely "live" hour, the unfettered musicians, as at an after-hours jam session, played to impress their peers as well as themselves. As a viewer wrote to CBS: "One so seldom has the chance to see real people doing something that really matters to them."

I had heard all the players often in clubs, concerts and recording studios. But that afternoon, there was a special exhilaration in their interaction—in part because they knew they were on "live," going for broke, and also because many had not played together for a long time, adding to the thrust of being challenged, which is the essence of the jazz experience.

Only one of the musicians arrived for the session looking as if he were not up to the challenge: Lester Young—"Prez," the president of the tenor saxophone—was waiting, alone and weak, in an empty room next to the studio. I told him that he didn't have to be, as scheduled, in the reed section of the Count Basie/All-Star Orchestra—alongside such powerful, equally famed and formidable tenor saxophonists as Coleman Hawkins and Ben Webster. He nodded but told me he was up to the small group session, later in the show, featuring Billie Holiday.

That sequence turned out to be the climax of *The Sound of Jazz*, and has been continually shown around the world. Billie and Lester had been very close—musically, as in her early recordings, and personally as well. But, as several musicians told me, that was no longer true.

Billie was to be accompanied in this quieter session by Lester, seated in a semicircle with Coleman Hawkins and Ben Webster, trumpeters Roy Eldridge and Doc Cheatham, trombonist Vic Dickenson, Gerry Mulligan on baritone saxophone, and a rhythm section of drummer Osie Johnson, bassist Milt Hinton ("the Judge," musicians called him), and guitarist Danny Barker. Her number was her own composition, a blues number, "Fine and Mellow."

In the control room we expectantly leaned forward. Billie was her usual knowing, tender, subtly sensual, and swinging self. When it was time for his solo, Lester did not remain seated, as I'd suggested to him he could be; Prez played a spare, pure, transcendent blues chorus that brought tears to my eyes and, as I looked around, to the eyes of Robert Herridge, Jack Smight and the sound engineer. Billie, her eyes meeting Lester's, was nodding, smiling, and seemed to me to be with him, back in time, in a very private place.

Both Billie and Lester died two years after *The Sound of Jazz*. Lester went first, on March 15, 1959. Until reading Gary Giddins's perceptive notes for the new Columbia/Legacy Billie Holiday set, *Lady Day: The Master Takes and Singles*, I hadn't known that Lester's widow, Mary, prohibited Billie from singing at his funeral. But I've since learned, from Dave Gelly's masterful new biography *Being Prez: The Life and Music of Lester Young* that Mary's decision was because of the state Billie was in.

Billie died four months later, on July 17, 1959. But the last mutual chorus, across time, between Prez and Lady Day has been preserved in *The Sound of Jazz*.

I have another lasting memory from immediately after the program ended on December 8, 1957. I had come down into the studio from the control room, and Billie was coming swiftly toward me. She didn't say anything about the $500 dress she hadn't been allowed to wear on the show: Still glowing from the music, Billie kissed me. That award excels any others I've received.

Years later, after a showing of *The Sound of Jazz* at the Museum of Television and Radio in New York, a young man asked me, "How were you able to get so many great players in one place at the same time?"

"They could all use the gig," I said. And it was a gig they all remembered.

43 ǀ Barrelhouse Chuck Goering Keeps the Blues Alive

For two weeks, the children at the Braeside Elementary School in Highland Park, Illinois, near Chicago, had been listening to Barrelhouse Chuck Goering play the piano, sing and tell stories about historic blues masters he'd known. He'd come, a teacher explained to the *Chicago Tribune*, "because we wanted to show the kids the roots of American music." At one point, a nine-year-old said: "I didn't know any of those famous names he talked about. It was like they were keeping a secret from us." And another youngster, brand-new to the blues, added, "I really like the songs."

Those lively teaching moments took place three years ago, but Barrelhouse Chuck—still keeping the blues alive every way he can—told me in December 2006 that earlier he'd been at another elementary school, in Rockford, Illinois, when a seven-year-old told him, "The notes you play on the piano sound so sad to me."

"Well," he told her, "you feel a lot better when you play those notes. That's what the blues is about, making you feel better to get them out."

Mr. Goering, born in French Canada and raised in Ohio, is, he notes, "50 percent Cherokee." But since first hearing a recording by Muddy Waters when he was nine years old, the blues became part of him. From his teens on, he worked as a blues apprentice in largely black clubs in the South and then in Chicago, learning from such classic mentors as Sunnyland Slim, Little Brother Montgomery, Pinetop Perkins—and Muddy Waters.

As he made the blues his own, Mr. Goering earned his professional name, Barrelhouse Chuck. In Debra DeSalvo's invaluable book *The Language of the Blues* (Billboard Books, 2006)—based on interviews with many classic blues bards—she explains: "A bar where whisky is served straight from a barrel is called a barrelhouse. The up-tempo blues that developed in these establishments came to be called barrelhouse, and those blues sped up the dancing."

Listening often to forty-eight-year-old Barrelhouse Chuck's CDs, *Got My Eyes on You* (Sirens Records, 2001) and *Prescription for the Blues* (Sirens Records, 2002), I want to dance, though I don't know any steps. And his singing reminds me of stories jazzmen used to tell me about rambunctious rent parties. But he can also make his "sad notes" tell the kinds of stories that later became known as "soul music."

The Sirens label is a passionate avocation of Steven Dolins, a tenured professor of computer science at Bradley University in Peoria, Illinois. Like Barrelhouse Chuck, Professor Dolins has been drawn to the blues since he was very young, and his way of helping keep the blues alive is through his record company.

In his notes for *Prescription for the Blues,* Professor Dolins tells how Barrelhouse Chuck became so deeply steeped in the blues and—as I've found out, talking to Chuck—such a vivid storyteller about the pantheon of blues makers and shapers he's known off as well as on the stand. Writes Professor Dolins: "Chuck would show up at his heroes' gigs, sit in and socialize with them. He not only trained with these musicians, he would also chauffeur them, live with them and ultimately care for them. He became their family. His recollection of special times with Little Brother and Sunnyland are vivid, hilarious and at times bittersweet."

For example, I was telling Barrelhouse Chuck how moved I was by his singing of the poignant "School Days" (on the *Got My Eyes on You* CD) by Floyd Jones, one of the original Chicago bluesmen, who could be found on Sunday mornings singing at the open-air Maxwell Street Market.

"I knew Floyd," Chuck told me. "I saw him just before he died in the hospital. I held his hand, saw him in the casket and I buried him. But his music stays with me."

Chuck believes that the blues he's lived can stay a living music if enough young people, who can't have the mentors he had, can feel those sad and barrel-house notes. In the schools where he has told and played his stories, the children encouraged him about the future because they clearly "do open up to the blues."

Of his gig at the elementary school in Highland Park, Chuck recalls with pleasure that he was very glad no one there "was trying to tell me about rap music compared to the blues. The kids took it all in. It's like they weren't spoiled by the garbage of today on the radio."

Those two weeks of blues at that school were generated by Professor Dolins, whose daughter was, at the time, in second grade there. He figured his daughter, too, needed to be educated in this roots music. "At home she hears blues all the time but mostly listens to Britney Spears."

There is a growing number of blues-in-the-schools programs around the country, but Messrs. Dolins and Goering feel strongly that there ought to be many more. Barrelhouse Chuck brightened when I told him that on December 7, when the president announced the recipients of the annual Presidential Medal of Freedom—the country's highest civilian award—B. B. King, an American blues legend, was on the list for his "distinguished service" to the nation—and, I would add, the world.

In 1999, jazz critic Peter Watrous wrote in the *New York Times:* "The wells that gave rise to so much American music have seemingly dried up. Blues culture is dead." But that same year, John Burnett of National Public Radio reported from the Mississippi Delta, the deepest fount of black blues, about a sixty-four-year-old auto mechanic and blues guitarist, Johnnie Billington, who'd become the Johnny Appleseed of the blues in the area's schools. At the Rosa Fort Middle School, he had put together a blues band; and as the youngsters played a slow blues, Mr. Billington pointed to a kid: "You see! He's feeling it, see!"

Barrelhouse Chuck tells me he'll accept any invitations he gets to go into classrooms. "That's where the future of this music is." It's too bad that Clear Channel and other corporate radio chains and stations have no playing time for Barrelhouse Chuck.

44 | Jazz's History Is Living in Queens . . .

No book on jazz history that I've seen includes the deeply rooted, living history of this music in the borough of Queens in New York City. Years ago, I interviewed Lester Young ("president of the tenor saxophone") in his home there; and I've visited the Louis Armstrong Home (a National Landmark, administered by Queens College) and the Armstrong Archives at Queens College. But until recently, I had no idea of the scores of jazz makers who have lived in Queens, and those who have died there.

The list is long, but among them: Count Basie; Bix Beiderbecke; Dizzy Gillespie and Louis Armstrong (close neighbors and friends); Ella Fitzgerald; John Coltrane; Woody Herman; Jimmy Rushing; Julian "Cannonball" Adderley; "Fats" Waller; James P. Johnson; Jimmy Heath; and Tony Spargo (he was a member of the white New Orleans Original Jazz Band that, in 1917, made the first jazz recording).

The fount of this research finally aligning Queens with New Orleans, Chicago, Manhattan and other storied centers of jazz is the Flushing Council on Culture and the Arts in Flushing Town Hall. Its regular tours of "The Queens Jazz Trail" include a large illustrated map of the icons and their addresses over the years. The lively map is the creation of Marc Miller, who has written a twenty-two-page guide that is further animated by tour conductor Toby Knight (a singer with the Chords, a doo-wop band).

Mr. Miller tells of John Coltrane tutoring children and teenagers in his St. Albans, Queens, neighborhood who showed musical promise. And he tells of a pivotal 1930s evening in jazz history when Benny Goodman first jammed with pianist Teddy Wilson at a party in the Forest Hills, Queens, home of Red Norvo and Mildred Bailey. The Goodman trio was birthed that night—one of the first, and the most historic, racially integrated groups to play in public. (There had been integrated after-hours jamming for years before.)

Mr. Miller has found that the first jazz community in Queens was formed by Clarence Williams—a successful record producer, music publisher and entrepreneur who in 1923 bought a home in Jamaica where "he planned to create a community of black musicians. . . . At a time when there were few hotels for African Americans, many out-of-town musicians stayed with the Williams family; among them Willie 'the Lion' Smith, Ma Rainey and Bessie Smith. Louis Armstrong probably got his first exposure to Queens visiting Williams."

The word got around of how welcoming Queens was becoming—and remained—for black musicians. Armstrong wrote, not long before his death, about how much he treasured the home his wife, Lucille, had bought for him in Corona in 1943: "Just think—through the 29 years that we've lived in this house we have seen just about three generations come up on this particular block. . . . Lots of them have grown up, married, had children, and they still come back and visit Aunt Lucille and Uncle Louis." And many of them went to the Louis Armstrong Elementary School and the Louis Armstrong Intermediate School in Queens.

Another Queens resident at the time, trumpet player Clark Terry, told me that Armstrong would occasionally invite Terry and other musicians to his home "to tell us the history of jazz."

The greatly respected bassist Milt Hinton ("the Judge," his fellow musicians called him) spoke for many in that community of black jazz creators about the effect being together in Queens had on their lives. "When I look back on it now, I realize what that house really meant to us. For the first time, Mona and I had something that was ours. It was our security and some new roots."

The roots continue to be fruitful. At the Flushing Council on Culture and the Arts—the curator of the past, and the generator of the future, of Queens jazz—producer Clyde Bullard has, for the past eight years, produced concerts with, among other jazz performers, Barry Harris, Marian McPartland, Dr. Billy Taylor and Randy Weston.

His father, C.B. Bullard—for twenty-seven years head of the jazz department at Atlantic Records—founded the jazz program at the Flushing Council, along with Jo-Ann Jones and Cobi Narita. Recently, Clyde Bullard applied for a National Endowment for the Arts grant to allow the creation of an 18-member resident Town Hall Jazz Orchestra to be directed by Jimmy Heath, known to his peers as "the complete Jazzman." The mission of this prospective orchestra, says Clyde Bullard, "will be to revitalize and rejuvenate the jazz heritage of Queens through concerts, lectures and performances of music created by the great legends that once resided here."

Among those who still do live in Queens is composer-saxophonist Heath. And of those who have died, buried in Queens cemeteries are Louis Armstrong, Dizzy Gillespie, Johnny Hodges, Charlie Shavers and Jimmy Rushing. And another seminal figure in American music, Scott Joplin, the master composer of the graces of ragtime, is buried in the borough's St. Michael's Cemetery.

The Queens Jazz Trails tour takes place the first Saturday of every month. Copies of the accompanying map can be obtained from Mr. Miller at Ephemera Press. There, too, is his celebrated illustrated map of the Harlem Renaissance that cites cultural historian Alaine Locke's 1919 first chorus to the abiding importance of Harlem: "Harlem is the precious fruit of the Garden of Eden, the big apple."

A story that climaxed in the Queens jazz community was told to me by alto saxophonist Phil Woods, designated this year a Jazz Master by the National Endowment for the Arts:

"Many years ago, at a club in New York, I was down. I was saying, 'I'm not going anywhere. I'm a white guy in this music.' Hearing me whining and crying the blues, Art Blakey and Dizzy Gillespie kidnapped me. They put me in a cab and took me to Dizzy's place in Queens.

"Dizzy sat me down and said to me about Charlie Parker, 'Bird gave it to everybody. To all races. If you can hear it, you can play it.'"

In countries all over the world, musicians of all blends of races are playing music created on the Queens Jazz Trail.

45 | Uncovering Jazz Trails

The headline in *Allegro,* the newspaper of New York's Local 802, American Federation of Musicians, heralded the presence of the jazz tribe—"over 8,000 educators, musicians, industry executives, media and students from forty-five countries"—attending the thirty-fourth annual conference of the International Association of Jazz Educators (IAJE). And when the annual photo of the National Endowment for the Arts Jazz Masters in the hotel's lobby got under way, there were so many paparazzi you'd think jazz is a popular music.

And a long piece by Nate Chinen in the January 7, 2007, *New York Times* was headed: "Jazz Is Alive and Well, in the Classrooms Anyway." The last phrase in that headline brought me back to reality. There have never been so many colleges, universities and freestanding teaching institutions on how to become a jazz musician. But where would all these graduates find gigs, let alone recording contracts?

Toward the end of the *Times*'s article, Bill Pierce, chairman of the woodwinds department at Boston's Berklee School of Music, said: "What I'm hoping, for the future of the music, is that the students who come to these schools go back to their communities to create their own scenes and develop their own audiences so the music can come back to some level, as it maybe once was."

It's an appealing vision, but how could it happen in real time? Dana Gioia, the then chairman of the National Endowment for the Arts (NEA), has done more for jazz than all of his predecessors and the rest of the federal government. So I sent him the beginnings of an idea—which I hope readers of this column will enlarge—on how to make the communities to which newly minted jazz musicians return welcoming and supportive boosters of the music.

I got this notion while researching a piece that appeared in the January 17 *Wall Street Journal:* "Jazz History Is Living in Queens." I've covered jazz in New York City since 1953, but almost entirely in the borough of Manhattan. I had no idea of the depth of the jazz roots in the borough of Queens. I knew Louis Armstrong and Dizzy Gillespie were neighbors, but not that among its residents had been Bix Beiderbecke, "Fats" Waller and Tony Spargo, a member of the New Orleans combo that made the first jazz recording.

Among those buried there are Scott Joplin, Johnny Hodges and Jimmy Rushing. Nor did I know that the first time Teddy Wilson jammed with Benny Goodman was at a party in the Queens home of Mildred Bailey and Red Norvo. That encounter, and Goodman's hiring Wilson, provided the momentum for black and white jazz musicians to play together in public, not only in after-hours sessions.

Dana Gioia was already sending NEA Jazz Masters to talk and play at colleges, jazz societies and other jazz-based organizations around the country. But if the NEA—or other sources—could fund research into localities around the country where jazz, as in Queens, has significant roots, present and future students from all these education classes could help form annual Jazz Pride Days and other continuing linkages to get radio and television coverage of the music (not only on Jazz Days), along with year-round support from civic boosters. (It's too late for the IAJE to work on it because the International Association of Jazz Educators played its final chorus in 2009.)

I keep being surprised—and I know others with similar experiences—at how many jazz buffs there are in all kinds of professions and other vocations: lawyers, judges, court bailiffs, taxi drivers, surgeons et al. A concerted movement in cities and other areas to dig into the jazz history and its personalities in those places could help create a living and growing jazz community with corollary gigs in clubs, concert halls, public schools and African-American churches where gospel music is still resoundingly alive.

I thought I knew all there was to know about the lively Boston jazz scene, of which I was a part from 1945 to 1953. But reading just parts of Richard Vacca's book in progress, *Making the Scene: The People and Places of Boston Jazz,* showed me how much I didn't know was happening then—as well as afterwards.

Over the years, I'd done some research on the Detroit jazz scene, but when I interviewed Congressman John Conyers (now chairman of the House Judiciary Committee), I discovered he had gone to high school with some of the later major figures of the music, and is otherwise a scholar of Detroit jazz. (Not surprisingly, he keeps certain jazz recordings in his office to energize him during the squalls and doldrums of Congress.)

What remains to be discovered and celebrated in Memphis, on Central Avenue in Los Angeles, regions of Oklahoma and Texas and, as I'm just finding out, Hawaii?

Survivors of these scenes, and of the regional territory bands, could unpack their instruments and join in the historiography along with getting paying gigs to bring the research to life. And, very importantly, they could meet and share with students—including recent graduates with formal jazz education—their experiences, along with what they learned from their elders. As Phil Woods told me, an important part of his early evolution was what he learned—on the band bus—from older players. Just from talking to them.

An impetus for jazz-curious folk living in or visiting Queens is a vivid, illustrated "Queens Jazz Trails" map, given out as part of the regularly scheduled "Queens Jazz Trails" tours—showing where these legends lived and other dimensions of the jazz scene there. In time, perhaps there will be jazz-trails maps and tours in other cities.

I would welcome information from readers in other cities or regions with jazz histories, however little known. Also, if the National Endowment for the Arts doesn't have the resources for, or interest in, this project, I'd appreciate other suggestions for getting jazz trails discovered and then populated by musicians, young and old, from these regenerated jazz scenes. I live in New York.

46 | Expanding the Map

With regard to "Uncovering Jazz Trails" (chapter 45), my hope is that as local newspapers, radio and television stations, and Web sites discover the depth of their cities' and regions' jazz roots, there will be more work for emerging local jazz musicians and for their elders who are still an active part of the scene. Along with more of the population, jazz players are lasting longer.

Maybe a consortium of freestanding jazz schools, like the Berklee College of Music in Boston, and the growing number of colleges and universities seriously involved in jazz education could coordinate further research expanding the map of cities that have made vital contributions to jazz, and still do.

For one of many such examples of how much I didn't know, I am indebted to Joe Mosbrook of Cleveland Heights, who, since 1988, has been conducting a weekly Cleveland jazz history radio series on Cleveland's NPR affiliate. He sent me a rare 252-page paperback book, *Cleveland Jazz History,* published by the Northeast Ohio Jazz Society.

One of its many pleasures for me is a chapter on the late Benny Bailey, an extraordinary trumpet player whom I was privileged to record for Candid (*Big Brass* and *Newport Rebels*). I hardly see him mentioned anymore. There at least ought to be a street named for him in Cleveland.

And Dr. Ronald Tikofsky wrote me about a city that is being awakened to its past and present jazz history through a group, the Milwaukee Jazz Experience, which, he adds, "supports jazz education in the public and private schools in the greater Milwaukee region, and also sponsors a jazz band made up from students from around the city."

The Milwaukee Jazz Experience puts out a newsletter. The city also has an enviable twenty-four-hour jazz radio station, WYMS, while many other cities remain bereft of that cultural stimulation heralded in a George Gershwin quote in the Milwaukee Jazz Experience's newsletter: "True music must repeat the thought and inspiration of the people and the time. My people are Americans and my time is today." Of course, since Gershwin's music is still being played, like Duke Ellington's, it's worth mentioning William Faulkner's "The past is never dead. It's not even past."

And from St. Louis, where my daughter, Jessica, directs and performs in Circus Harmony, featuring the only circus band I know of that includes jazz, klezmer, Japanese, Chinese and Persian musicians, Dr. Dennis C. Owsley has sent me a 200-page paperback: *City of Gabriels: The History of Jazz in St. Louis,*

1895–1973, with a foreword by Clark Terry. It's published by the Reedy Press in St. Louis. Owsley has a long-running jazz program on KWMU.

I suggest to *JazzTimes* or Jazz.com that they might publish Clark's concise but vivid foreword. And did you know that Duke Ellington discovered Jimmy Blanton in St. Louis when Rex Stewart ran to Duke's hotel and got him out of bed to hear that astounding young bassist?

City of Gabriels is an oral history, based on Dr. Owsley's interviews. As he says, "Going directly to the source can lead to the subject placing himself or herself in a favorable light, but sometimes the people on the ground have a better perspective than the professional historian."

More than sometimes. One of my greatest regrets is that after I got to be friends with Rex Stewart, Willie "The Lion" Smith, Frankie Newton and Jimmy Rowles, I didn't bring a tape recorder during some of our conversations.

Who but Clark Terry can tell us firsthand in this book about such very early jazz originals as the Mississippi riverboat trumpet players Charlie Creath, the "King of the Cornets," and Dewey "Squirrel" Jackson? (All parents knew it was time to pick up their kids because they could hear Dewey playing all the way down the river as the boat came in.)

And Milt Krieger is finding much jazz lore in the state of Washington. He's writing a jazz history of Bellingham, where he lives, and Whatcom County: "Mid-twentieth-century players, with stories of their predecessors, some on audiotape, join a host of currently active local musicians and other jazz people as sources."

I plan to contribute on these jazz trails, and I am eager to get works in progress from other cities and regions. There has to be a lot more source material in the Southwest (Ornette Coleman would be a prime source, but also the players who stayed home).

And not enough has been heard from musicians on the jazz scenes, then and now, in Memphis, Washington, D.C., Seattle, Atlanta, parts of Florida and more.

I'd also like to know more about city and state organizations devoted to this life force, such as Jazz in Arizona, Inc., in Scottsdale, celebrating its thirtieth anniversary this year. Its *Jazz Notes* newsletter includes a story on the Jazz in Arizona scholarships "to assist emerging jazz musicians ages 14 to 22, who have a goal of continuing the study and performance of jazz throughout their lifetimes."

There's a very active disability rights organization I write about called Not Dead Yet. Neither is jazz.

PART NINE

The Survivors

47 | The Thoreau of Jazz

When I was a teenager in Boston, one of my heroes—after Duke Ellington—was a fellow New Englander, Henry David Thoreau, who, as an unyielding abolitionist and opponent of the Mexican-American War, went to jail rather than pay six years of back taxes.

Years later, I learned that Martin Luther King, Jr., was first turned on to nonviolent resistance by reading Thoreau's 1849 essay "Civil Disobedience." King wrote, "Fascinated by the idea of refusing to cooperate with an evil system, I was so deeply moved that I reread the work several times."

Art Davis, who died of a heart attack at seventy-three on July 29, 2007, was, for me, the Henry David Thoreau of jazz. I've known many people in the jazz family with admirable integrity, but Art Davis's was fiercely unbreakable, whatever the cost.

As a musician, he was a total master of the instrument, always searching deeper into it—and himself. When Davis was with John Coltrane, at the Village Gate in New York, there were nights when John would turn a single song into a tumultuous microcosm for over an hour and a half. Art soared along with him, reaching climax after climax with, as Art remembered, "people shouting, just like in a holy-roller church."

Art Davis was a complete musician, as authoritative in a symphonic orchestra, a Broadway pit band, network studio assignment or accompanying, as he did, Judy Garland or country music comedienne Minnie Pearl.

He also became a pariah in parts of the music business for years because he insisted on breaking the color line in symphony orchestras. As I had reported in *The Reporter* magazine in the late 1950s, it was not only that Jim Crow managed much of that hiring. Also, as positions opened in an orchestra, the first-chair players (all of them white) would get management to hire their best students (also white) for those chairs.

For years, Art, having been turned down by leading symphony orchestras, challenged the conductors to pit him against any classical bassist they chose in an open competition. There were no takers. In the 1970s, he sued the New York Philharmonic for racial discrimination, and as the years went on, until the case was dismissed, Art lost a lot of the previous highly diversified work for which he had been sought. Obviously, the man was a "troublemaker."

But because of the lawsuit, the attendant publicity and Art's continuing challenge to put any symphonic bass part—however deeply traditional or unprecedentedly avant-garde—before him in competition for a gig in any world-famous orchestra, he became the major force that created "blind auditions." It became the practice, when there was an opening for any instrument, to audition the player behind a screen so that those judging his or her abilities—Art also protested gender discrimination—could hear the music but not see the musician. He lost the lawsuit, but won the battle.

During the years he was "blacklisted" (literally as well as figuratively) by many of his former employers, Art, with his customary determination, forged himself another career. While Ahmad Jamal sadly said that Art was becoming "a forgotten legend" in music, Art became a clinical psychologist. A formidable student at whatever interested him, Art earned master's degrees from the City University of New York. And then, always competing with himself, he earned a Ph.D. in clinical psychology at New York University in 1982. When he was asked about his lost years in music, Art, always an ironic pragmatist, said, "I wouldn't be Dr. Art Davis if it hadn't happened."

In 1986, he moved to California, where he continued counseling patients and also teaching the bass. He and I often spoke on the phone, talking not only about music—he had begun performing again—but also about politics, books, increasingly discordant world affairs and much else.

Art led his own jazz combos, made a few recordings, toured Europe and Japan and, as I wrote in *JazzTimes* ("The Mystery of Making It," March 2001), he set up "a nonprofit foundation, Better Advantages for Students and Society (B.A.S.S.), that awarded scholarships to students, in and out of music, who kept growing, but needed extra bread."

One of the last times we spoke, Art said he felt "his music abilities have still not yet been fully challenged." While he did remain active musically, he was no longer in as much demand as those abilities deserved, but I'm sure he kept challenging himself.

Art can still be heard on such recordings as John Coltrane's *Ascension,* volumes 1 and 2 of *The Africa/Brass Sessions.* And while I was producing albums for Candid Records, I was privileged to have Art on Booker Little's *Out Front.*

Booker was only twenty-three when he died of uremia soon after that recording. Booker, like Art, was a deeply thoughtful, venturesome musician who had not only a signature sound but very personal stories to tell in his music that kept resonating after the music stopped. Jan Jordan, a pianist who often played with Art during his years in California, said, "He always reached out to the people in the audience"—and connected.

In "Civil Disobedience," Thoreau wrote, "When a sixth of the population of a nation, which has undertaken to be the refuge of liberty, are slaves . . . I think that it is not too soon for honest men to rebel and revolutionize."

For Thoreau, rebellion was as natural as believing in himself. The same was true of Art Davis.

48 | A Living Memory of Dr. Art

A thirteen-year-old whom Dr. Art invited to sit in with him at a gig later sent me this letter about a musical—and human—experience he will not forget:

I can always remember the name Dr. Art Davis being mentioned by my teachers and family. Around the summer of 2004, my piano teacher Jan Jordan was playing weekly gigs with Dr. Art at both the Napa Rose restaurant and Ritz Carlton Hotel here in Orange County, California. Jan always talked about what a spectacular bass player Dr. Art was and what a pleasure it was to play with him. I was thirteen at the time and Jan invited me to come down to the Napa Rose and sit in with the band. I accepted, and a week later I was sitting at a table with my parents waiting to be called up to play a tune. The band was swinging, and I knew it would be a great experience. Dr. Art seemed to play his bass with less effort than anyone I had ever seen, and yet what he played sounded twice as good. When they called me up, I walked up to the bandstand nervously. So there I was with John Alessi on drums and Dr. Art on bass. "What you gonna play kid," asked Dr. Art. I told him Oscar Peterson's "Blues Etude." He seemed slightly impressed, and I counted it off and began the tune. I didn't play the best ever, but I remember how good it sounded as a whole. I looked up a few times during the tune to see Dr. Art playing effortlessly through the changes and playing so deep in the pocket that it was hard for me not to swing. When the tune ended, I got up to shake hands with the guys, but before I took a step away from the piano Dr. Art said "Where you goin' kid? Sit back down and play another." I looked back at my family, and Jan seemed fine with the idea so I sat down and counted off "All of Me." It sounded great and I had never felt more in the pocket.

Dr. Art seemed to let me take the lead but always was right on my heels no matter where I took the tune. I did a little interesting ending and got a little nervous as it was approaching that he might not follow it, but as it came I looked up, and he followed everything I did, plus more. I got up after the song ended but once again was told to sit down and play another. "You're not done yet, play another one with us," he said. I got a little nervous that I was starting to upstage Jan who was still sitting with my family, but I looked back and again he approved.

I called "Green Dolphin Street" next. The transitions between the Latin and swing sections had never been smoother, and it grooved really hard. I can remember loosening up and having a lot of fun. Before I knew it, I was calling the "tag" and the tune was over.

I stood up and this time was allowed to shake hands. Dr. Art had a nice grin and seemed to have had fun playing with me. He told me to keep playing and that I was welcome to come back anytime and sit in again. I did a few months later. What a great opportunity it was to play with one of the all-time jazz greats. Dr. Art taught me so much just by letting me play a few tunes alongside him. He taught through his playing, and I learned that jazz is all about listening, swinging hard and staying in the pocket. I'm always trying to apply what I learned from playing with one of the greatest jazz bass players to ever live. His advice to keep playing stays with me everyday, and I have no plan on stopping anytime soon.

Andrew Cedar, age sixteen
Tustin, California
February 4, 2008

49 | Barren Days

Having criticized National Public Radio (NPR) for cutting down its network jazz programming—some affiliate stations keep the faith—I have to commend the network for doing what no other radio operation, let alone broadcast and cable television, would have done: A four-part series by Felix Contreras on NPR's afternoon program *All Things Considered* about the problems that face older jazz musicians. (For jazz writers and historians, the dates of the series were April 19–21, 2005.)

Having been on the scene for so long, and having written here about the New York-based Jazz Foundation of America—which brings an increasing number of abandoned musicians back to active and playing life—I had some idea of the grim twilight of jazz musicians whose names abound in the cascade of reissues and in jazz encyclopedias but who are seldom working now.

It's so important that listeners, who have been given so much pleasure by these musicians over the years, know how these players often have to live. Until Contreras's NPR series, for instance, I had no idea that Wynton Kelly, who played with Dizzy Gillespie, Miles Davis and many others, died penniless. This NPR report, and other such investigations, should be widely circulated—and maybe record companies, club owners and other sources will be shamed into contributing money to the Jazz Foundation to make sure this stops happening.

Longtime Count Basie saxophonist Frank Foster is seventy-six, and three years ago a stroke left him paralyzed on his left side and unable to play any more. Contreras, a *JazzTimes* contributor, noted, "His monthly Social Security check and Musicians' Union pension don't cover his bills. But most elderly musicians don't even have that.... Pianist Danny Nixon says it has been and still is common practice to be paid at the gig in cash with no deductions for Social Security, Medicare, pensions or unemployment insurance."

Organist Nathan Lucas, whose father is tenor saxophonist Max Lucas, told another story in the NPR piece that I wasn't aware of. At ninety-four, Max plays with friends every week at Harlem's Lenox Lounge. Many of them, Nathan adds, should be home in bed: "They play from gig to gig, and they survive like that. Even when they're not able to really get around and function the way they should, they'll still be out because they have to make whatever it is they make that night. When we're sick we don't work, and that means we don't pay bills and we don't eat."

As for health care, Contreras notes that, like the working poor, many jazz players and their families don't have regular doctors, so in a crisis they wind up in emergency rooms. Some musicians know where they can get help before an emergency, for instance at Bronx-Lebanon Hospital Center, whose vice president, Bob Sancho, told this story:

"There was one musician called me up and said, 'Listen, I have a young boy. He's ten years old and he's been vomiting blood.' And I said, 'How long?' He says, 'Oh, many, many weeks now.' I said, 'Gee, you should have come in here a lot sooner.' They were embarrassed because they had no medical coverage, and they didn't want to ask for a handout."

Pride often delays musicians from going for help. Wendy Oxenhorn of the Jazz Foundation has told me of dire cases where she wouldn't have known aid was needed until other musicians informed her that one of their friends was too proud to ask her for what he would consider charity. She tells such players it's not at all a handout. Whatever they need is what they've earned all these years.

Contreras also spoke of musicians who have been internationally famous but are physically unable to continue their life's work and feel useless. On NPR, Dr. Billy Taylor tells of when Roy Eldridge "couldn't play those hot high notes and do what he used to do," but at the Jazzmobile in Harlem, which Taylor founded, people said, "'Here's a guy we love. We can't let him be sort of sitting at home and waste himself away.' So Jazzmobile was able to give him some gigs. He didn't need the money but it helped him get out with young kids and talk to them, realize that they respected him and that he was someone worth listening to. Made all the difference for him at that point in his life. Too many musicians didn't get that."

Too many musicians don't get that now.

Meanwhile, those veterans who never made the big time but still have to play to be who they are, have been enabled to work by pianist Danny Nixon. Contreras says Nixon "is able to get them into clubs in Harlem because the younger players usually don't come uptown. But even the few gigs that are there only offer on average $50 a night."

Nixon continues: "You go into the grocery with $50, man, you might come out with two bags. . . . By the time you buy cornflakes and some milk, and the orange juice and some eggs, that $50 is gone."

And even if these elders could find gigs on the road somewhere, Nixon says, "Older musicians can't travel as easily as younger players. They're physically less mobile, they have to keep track of medications and they're unable to keep up a demanding road schedule."

Also, there's not an abundance of jazz clubs around the country, and their owners are looking for those musicians getting written up in such magazines as *JazzTimes* or *Down Beat*.

Long after he left Duke Ellington, Rex Stewart was in exile in white farm country in upstate New York. A friend in that small town saw Stewart eagerly looking into the window of a place that sometimes had sessions. Not wanting to go in alone because he was black, Stewart asked his friend to walk in with him.

Sitting in, Rex was himself again.

50 | Keeping Jazz—and Its Musicians—Alive

In the moviegoing years of my youth, there was often, between double features, a short film showing ill and elderly entertainers with tuberculosis being regenerated in a residence named after Will Rogers. Ushers would then come down the aisles for contributions, and I'd put in my quarters. And the Will Rogers Institute still exists.

When I became part of the jazz scene and learned that very many jazz musicians do not have medical insurance or pensions, I often wondered why there was no place for players in need to go when threatened with eviction from their apartments or faced with medical emergencies.

The nonprofit Jazz Foundation of America (JFA) in New York and its Jazz Musicians Emergency Fund have provided musicians—many of whom have played with John Coltrane, Miles Davis and Dinah Washington, among other luminaries—with rent arrears; emergency living expenses, including money for food; and free medical care through Englewood Hospital and Medical Center's Dizzy Gillespie Memorial Fund in New Jersey.

When Dizzy was dying in that hospital in 1993, he asked his physician, oncologist and hematologist Frank Forte, to find a way for the hospital to provide the medical care he was getting to jazz musicians who couldn't afford it. Hundreds of them have since received free care there, ranging from operations by specialists to cancer treatment. Dr. Forte, a guitarist, is so committed to the mission of the Jazz Foundation that on Tuesday evenings he plays two sets of solo guitar at the Café Café on Highland Avenue in Tenafly, New Jersey. Donations from the customers to the Dizzy Gillespie Memorial Fund and the Jazz Foundation range from $100 to $300 a night. "That's more," Dr. Forte told me, "than I'd get playing for scale, if anybody paid me for a gig."

The executive director of the Jazz Foundation is the indomitable Wendy Atlas Oxenhorn, who is often on call day and night to deal with emergencies. At times, she has fed hungry musicians at her home. A foundation board member, Richard Parsons, then chief executive officer of Time Warner, says of Wendy: "She has the soul of a musician but the heart of a warrior." Wendy is a musician, a fiery blues harmonica player.

In 2004, the foundation was helping more than 360 musicians a year. "The average guy who calls in," Wendy says, "has not been to a doctor for twenty years. One hadn't been for fifty years." Often she first hears about clients from other musicians because, though in need, they don't want to feel they're getting handouts. Wendy assures them that she and others who have so enjoyed their music are giving the musicians what they have long deserved.

"There shouldn't have to be a Jazz Foundation," she says, "if they'd been treated fairly all these years." (In the interest of full disclosure, I'm on the Jazz Foundation board and, like all of its members, feel we owe these players for what they have meant to the lives of so many, including us.)

Wendy tells of a recent case: Johnny Mae Dunson, "a homebound eighty-three-year-old woman confined to a wheelchair. One of the first female blues drummers, she can sing like nobody's business. She wrote tunes for Muddy Waters and other blues masters but was never properly compensated. When we first met her, she had been without food for many days and was behind in rent and close to having her utilities disconnected. The JFA paid her back rent and prevented her being evicted. She now has enough food and a volunteer to do her grocery shopping. Her strength has returned, and she's writing songs again. We bought her a recorder and cassettes to make it easier for her to work. We talk to her several times a week, and it appears we have adopted each other. The Jazz Foundation family continues to grow."

On Thursday, October 28, 2004, at the Apollo Theater, the foundation presented its fourth annual benefit, A Great Night in Harlem, for its Jazz Musicians Emergency Fund. Among the hosts: Bill Cosby and Quincy Jones. The program included tributes to Ray Charles and Elvin Jones and performances from, among others, the Barry Harris trio, Jamie Foxx, guitarist James Blood Ulmer, Clark Terry and the Harlem Jazz Legends (all of whom are over eighty-nine years old).

Years ago, the myth among jazz enthusiasts was that it was a young man's game, its improvisers burning the candle at both ends. But the ages of the many survivors increase. As pianist-composer Cecil Taylor once told me: "Part of what this music is about is not to be delineated exactly. It's about magic and capturing spirits." For its players—and listeners—jazz is a magical life force.

At A Great Night in Harlem, the eighty-three-year-old spirit of the blues, who hails from Chicago, was on stage and rose from her wheelchair. As Wendy Oxenhorn predicted, she "set the place on fire."

Also on the program was the Jazz Foundation's president, Jarrett Lilien. The president of E*Trade Financial, he was in charge of a $15-million fund-raising campaign to establish the first Players' Residence for senior jazz and blues musicians. The building will be in Harlem. It will contain living quarters; on-site medical, dental and counseling services; a room for jamming; a recording studio; a communal kitchen; a phone number to call players for gigs; and the headquarters for the Jazz Foundation of America.

As might be expected, if this project—akin to the Will Rogers home that I used to feel good about when I saw it in the movies—is to become real, support will have to come from foundations, individuals and corporations, including those in the jazz industry. For example, the record companies profiting from the very welcome flood of jazz reissues should become important contributors. Sidemen don't get royalties, and among the sidemen on these scores of classic jazz sets are present and future clients of the Jazz Foundation of America.

Keeping the players alive keeps the music alive.

51 | In New Orleans, the Saints Are Marching In Again

The Jazz Foundation has been a lifesaver to so many musicians from New Orleans, giving them the opportunity to work and earn money with dignity. They've done more to help the New Orleans musicians than any other group that I know of. —DR. MICHAEL WHITE, NEW ORLEANS CLASSIC JAZZ CLARINETIST, BANDLEADER AND EDUCATOR

"It's hard for people to imagine what it's like to go through something like [Hurricane Katrina], and to then start over with nothing. The Jazz Foundation was there for us every time. . . . The light is coming back after so much darkness I thought would never end." —RODNEY ROLLINS, NEW ORLEANS MUSICIAN AND HURRICANE KATRINA SURVIVOR

Years ago in New Orleans, as I was going to Preservation Hall—with music swinging into the street from every nightclub on the way—I heard, coming from the hall, that joyous high-stepping jazz anthem "When the Saints Go Marching In."

Now, the devastation of Hurricane Katrina continues to lie heavily on the city—unstable levees, broken neighborhoods, broken families, and 250,000 residents still gone. But the spirit of the city—embodied in its music, long reverberating around the world—is rising. Many of the musicians, including brass bands, are back.

Much of the credit for their determined presence, so vital to the life force of New Orleans, is due to the continuing work of the New York-based nonprofit Jazz Foundation of America. On January 10, 2007, the International Association of Jazz Educators (IAJE), in its time the largest jazz organization in the world, for the first time included a special award in its annual conference: to the Jazz Foundation "in recognition of its incalculable efforts in support of the New Orleans and Gulf Coast musician communities following the Hurricane Katrina disaster."

Until Katrina, the Jazz Foundation of America (JFA), formed in 1989 by musicians—and by lay listeners for whom jazz is an essential, regenerating part of their lives—had been known primarily for its emergency help to the sick, elderly or out-of-fashion jazz musicians. Among them were once active players about to be evicted from their apartments and others in acute need of medical attention, including operations—which, through the foundation, they get free from New Jersey's Englewood Hospital and Medical Center.

Jazz makers, except for a very few, have no medical insurance or pensions; some, cited prominently in jazz histories and discographies, have died penniless and alone. The Jazz Foundation came into being to fill a crucial need. Its dauntless executive director, Wendy Oxenhorn, is always on call, and if a musician needs a meal, she's often the person to feed him. She once rushed to a hospital in the middle of the night to look after a newly admitted eighty-four-year-old percussionist.

Since Katrina hit, Oxenhorn says, "we've assisted more than 1,700 New Orleans emergency cases while still being there for some 1,300 new cases of our regular elderly musicians around the country."

For the displaced New Orleans musicians, she distributed more than $25,000 worth of new musical instruments. And among the foundation's key financial supporters, its president, Jarrett Lilien (his day job is as head of E*Trade Financial), has, Oxenhorn adds, "made it possible for the JFA to house and relocate hundreds of New Orleans musicians and their families—saving them from homelessness and eviction in 20 states."

Another special award from the jazz educators was given to another mainstay of the Jazz Foundation: Dr. Agnes Varis, president of Agvar Chemicals, "for providing funds for the foundation to employ more than 700 displaced musicians in eight states."

"Saint Agnes," as Oxenhorn calls her, paid for free performances post-Katrina by New Orleans musicians for thousands of children as part of her customary Jazz in the Schools program around the country. (The gigs for the New Orleans players included the elderly in nursing homes as well as the kids in schools.)

To enable the foundation to bring jazz musicians back to life in this tri-state area, New Orleans and throughout the nation, the proceeds from its sixth annual A Great Night in Harlem concert at the fabled Apollo Theater were absolutely vital.

As Oxenhorn said before the event, "It will be a night of living history." Among those onstage: Dr. Michael White and the Original Liberty Jazz Band from New

Orleans, Big Chief Donald Harrison and the Mardi Gras Indian Chiefs, Jimmy Heath, Frank Wess, Paul Shaffer (of *The Late Show with David Letterman*), Candido, Junior Mance, Ben Riley, Gary Bartz, Arturo O'Farrill, Henry Butler, Jimmy Norman—and, as happens every year, many surprises. If no one plays "When the Saints Go Marching In," they'll all embody the song.

The hosts were Bill Cosby, Gil Noble (of WABC TV's invaluable *Like It Is*) and Danny Glover. At a previous "Great Night In Harlem," I asked Cosby—and I was serious—to think about running for president. As Cosby keeps proving in the public square on such essential issues as education, he is a wise and fearless leader. Rejecting my invitation, he said, "What do you want me to do—bankrupt my wife?" I wished he'd reconsider.

At this May 17, 2007, concert, Dave Brubeck received a lifetime achievement award. And Roy Haynes, the continually evolving master drummer who has played with most of the major entries in the *Encyclopedia of Jazz*, soloed. Those who were there will be telling their grandchildren about Haynes's performance—and about the rest of the night of living history.

In the interest of full disclosure, I'm on the board of directors of the Jazz Foundation; but because of my day job, making sense of the news, I never have time to go to any meetings. All I do for the foundation is write about it—because, were it not for the creators of this music, my life would have been enormously diminished.

As Oxenhorn says of what the foundation does, "These are not handouts. It's a privilege to be of use to people who spent a lifetime giving us all they had."

When I was in my early twenties, Duke Ellington's tenor saxophonist Ben Webster gave me a lifetime credo: "If the rhythm section isn't making it, go for yourself!" But sometimes, you do need a rhythm section. Wendy is the rhythm section of the Jazz Foundation.

52 | The Beating Heart of Jazz

The Bush administration miserably failed New Orleans after Hurricane Katrina in 2005, but the Jazz Foundation of New York hasn't failed thousands of New Orleans musicians. On March 4, 2008, in recognition of how the foundation's Wendy Oxenhorn and other saints came marching in, Jazz at Lincoln Center awarded the organization a grant from its High Ground Hurricane Relief Fund: "Since Katrina alone, the Jazz Foundation assisted over 3,500 emergency [New Orleans] cases and has created employment for over 1,000 musicians in crisis with the Agnes Varis/Jazz in the Schools program."

Said Wendy, in gratitude: "We will be able to keep our beloved New Orleans musicians working, bringing free concerts to thousands of public-school children and hundreds of elderly residents in nursing homes throughout the New Orleans area. This allows the musicians to keep their dignity, heritage, music, and spirits alive."

Also, Adrian Ellis, Jazz at Lincoln Center's new energizing executive director, has committed to an annual benefit concert for the Jazz Foundation.

Meanwhile, back at the foundation's headquarters in New York, Wendy told of one of the many cases by which she and the foundation are regularly challenged. (Names are often omitted in the interest of privacy.) "Another great pianist," said Wendy, "who is only in her seventies, had just lost her husband this year. A few years ago, a car accident destroyed her face on one side."

New Jersey's Englewood Hospital, a pro bono Jazz Foundation partner in providing vital health services for musicians, "did all the reconstructive surgery for free. She spoke about how, when her husband was sick and dying, the foundation paid the rent for months to keep them from eviction and homelessness. After he died, our Agnes Varis/Jazz in the Schools [program] kept her busy, allowed her to pay the rent—and now she's doing so well, she's getting gigs all over the place. She tells me she feels 'life is beginning again!'"

Another story that Wendy has to tell among so many reminds me of a continually inspiring national disability-rights organization, Not Dead Yet, which I've been writing about for years. They never give up. Neither has a New Orleans musician, Steven Foster, and his son, Kwame, who was born with muscular dystrophy and has been on a life-support machine for the last eighteen years.

"Steve and his wife," said Wendy, "sent Kwame—now in his twenties and about three and a half feet in length—to regular schools and even to college, with all his challenges and with his life-support equipment."

His father, a clarinetist and alto saxophonist, was displaced by Hurricane Katrina and wound up in Tennessee, having lost his home and music school. Through its Jazz in the Schools program, the foundation has been helping to support Steve and his family, as well as footing the bill for Kwame's considerable expenses.

Wendy continued: "When the recent tornado knocked out electricity for twelve hours around the state, Kwame's respirator went down! His parents realized that to keep their son alive, they needed a generator in the house. We at the foundation immediately bought him one for $1,200. They are all breathing easy now."

That's not all about Kwame. This former A student at Southern University started his own foundation in 1991 to help, he said, "other young people with challenges to have hope and live a fulfilling life."

Kwame is also a flutist and often goes on gigs with his father and his mother (a bassist), bringing jazz to people in nursing homes and children in schools.

The president of the Jazz Foundation, Jarrett Lilien, a major planner and funder of a number of its programs, said recently: "Everyone is saying how times are getting tougher, and people are scared of what's happening out there. But imagine what it's like for the folks on the bottom of the pyramid. . . . They are in more danger than any of us, and this is a time when musicians need us at the Jazz Foundation more than ever."

The 2008 celebration—of what I call the spirit of Kwame—lit up the Apollo in New York on May 29, with Bill Cosby and Danny Glover hosting an evening filled with the joys and surprises of jazz.

Besides dealing with eviction notices, medical crises, and other acute needs, Wendy and the others involved in taking the Jazz Foundation to the next level are focusing, she noted, "on getting an endowment started so we can finally begin to explore longer-term goals such as the need for health insurance for musicians, the idea of online management and booking services, [getting them] income, and [the building of] the Players' Residence, so they can live independently and not have to go to nursing homes."

So far, "hundreds of lives have been changed, and will be—not just in crisis, as now, but with future programs to ensure that the ones who come later will never have to be in the situation that [others] now find themselves in today," she said.

Over the years, covering many different kinds of stories and people, I'm often unexpectedly told—by court bailiffs, surgeons, painters, architects, professional basketball players et al.—how jazz became an essential part of their lives. Recently, I interviewed an official of the American Association of Retired Persons (AARP) about its jazz program and exchanged stories with him about how, at times of deep loss, this music has had the power to bring us back among the truly living, reminding us how much fun there is in being swept into a swinging groove.

John Coltrane once said that the meaning of jazz "is the whole question of life itself"—not just for the players but also for those of us who can't live without it. Art Blakey, who was impelled to preach the gospel of jazz (and not only on drums), used to say: "You don't have to be a musician to understand jazz. All you have to do is be able to feel."

I keep writing about the Jazz Foundation to pay a small part of my debt to these musicians, who for so long have kept showing me how deeply and immediately I can feel. When I was a kid, sneaking into clubs before I was old enough to be admitted, these players seemed to be larger than I thought life could possibly be. Without them, my own would have been a lot grayer.

The Regenerators

53 | Bridging Generations

Having known jazz musicians off the stand from my teens on, I was struck—contrasting them with most of the adults I knew—by their dedication to their life's work. Louis Armstrong, for example, distilled how he and the music were one in an interview long ago with Gil Millstein of the *New York Times*. Armstrong said, "When I pick up my horn, that's all. The world's behind me. I don't feel no different about that horn now than I did when I was playing in New Orleans. That's my living and my life. I love them notes. That's why I try to make them right. Any part of the day, you're liable to see me doing something toward playing that night. You got to live with that horn."

I thought about that essence of the jazz calling when I heard a penetrating interview with Sonny Rollins on National Public Radio on April 28, 2007. It was by Howard Mandel, the seemingly tireless engine behind the Jazz Journalists Association and a valuable historian of the music. His conversation with Sonny ought to be anthologized.

Briefly included in the profile was Joanne Brackeen, whose passion for the jazz life so powers her intensely personal musical language that her insufficient recognition is inexplicable to me. Said Brackeen of Sonny, "He's got a sound that is him. You hear just a couple of seconds and you know who that is. Not only who he is but kind of how he is."

As Armstrong said of how music filled his days before he got on the bandstand, Sonny told Mandel: "If I'm doing a song, I practice it, I learn it. I learn the lyrics. I learn everything possible there is to learn about the physical piece of the composition or whatever it is I'm going after."

But that preparation is only prologue to the surge of spontaneity that makes the jazz life so worthwhile. Once Sonny is on the bandstand or on a concert stage, he continued, "I don't want to think about [all that]. I let the music play me. When I'm playing completely spontaneous, just something comes out of nowhere; that's my best work."

I got a glimpse of what that feels like—just a glimpse—when I wrote fiction: novels for young readers (including *Jazz Country*, still being read in some classes), novels about homicide detectives *(Blues for Charlie Darwin)*, and other fiction.

I'd do research, work out plots, but suddenly—when the writing started—the characters took over. I heard them speak. It was exciting, somehow starting a new world of surprises. But I never could do anything like that on the clarinet.

In the interview, Sonny went on to put into words why jazz musicians in their eighties and beyond never stop. "We're about creation, thinking things out at the moment, like life is," he said. "Life changes every minute. I mean, a different sunset every night. I mean, that's what jazz is about."

Or, as John Coltrane told me, "The music is the whole question of life itself." And Charles Mingus: "I'm trying to play the truth of what I am. The reason it's difficult is because I'm changing all the time. But I'm going to keep on getting through and finding out the kind of man I am through my music. That's the one place I can be free."

As for Sonny—keenly aware that jazz has to go beyond what he calls the "corporate culture" of past distribution of recordings—he has, as Mandel notes, "launched his own Web site with MP3s from his current album and video podcasts."

On sonnyrollins.com, Mandel continues, "You can see Mikayla Gilbreath, a thirteen-year-old saxophonist from Tempe, Arizona." On one of the podcasts, Gilbreath, who first heard Sonny's music in her grade school (I'd like to know the name of the teacher), is seen meeting Sonny backstage.

And she tells how she became committed to the jazz life. "I joined the [school] jazz band and we would, every Friday, listen to jazz music, just classic jazz," she says. "I heard Sonny Rollins, and I just loved it. I loved the way it sounded and I just—I wanted to play jazz instead of just music."

Mandel asked her if there was anything odd about having been "drawn to the music of someone whose background is so different from hers."

The same question could be asked of Sonny's admirers in Japan, Siberia, Iceland—all over the world. Wisely, the thirteen-year-old answered, "You know, I really don't think it matters. It's the music that kind of brought us together. It wasn't the fact that I was white and he was black, or that he was old and I was young. It was just—it was the music that we both loved."

Years ago, when rock music was exploding, I was gloomily telling pianist Teddy Wilson that when I was in my teens, I knew that there was a nucleus, however small, of other kids my age who were beginning to go deeply into jazz, no matter what was being played on the radio. But I see no sign, I told Teddy, that a hard core of lifelong jazz listeners is going to emerge from this new generation (this was at the time of Elvis Presley, the Beatles et al.).

"Something in music got to them," Teddy said, "and in time, some of them will want more from music than rock, something more meaningful to them personally than what everybody else is listening to."

He was right. And from what I hear going on around the country, there are more and more Mikayla Gilbreaths, kids whose own lives began to be enlarged when they heard someone like Sonny Rollins. Of course, there's no one like Sonny Rollins, and that's the point. Each listener he reaches connects in his or her own way, and wants more.

54 | The Rebirth of the Hot Jazz Violin

Until I heard the now legendary Stuff Smith (1909–76), I had no idea that a jazz violinist could more than hold his own in a powerfully swinging jazz combo's front line. Smith, who had played with Jelly Roll Morton, recorded with Nat "King" Cole and Dizzy Gillespie and toured with Norman Granz's dueling horn virtuosi, told jazz historian Stanley Dance: "You can swing more on a violin than on any instrument ever made. You've got all those octaves on the violin. You can slur like a trombone, play staccato like a trumpet, or moan like a tenor." As Jo Jones with the Count Basie band put it: "Stuff was the cat who took the apron strings off the fiddle."

Ardently exemplifying Stuff Smith's credo is twenty-year-old Aaron Weinstein in his first CD as a leader, *A Handful of Stars,* on Arbors Records.

This session should bring renewed interest to the often overlooked heritage of the jazz violin while heralding the advent of an unmistakably personal impro-viser who can be intimately tender (as on the Frank Loesser–Jimmy McHugh "Let's Get Lost") as well as so fiercely invigorating that you have to move to his music.

A third-year student at Boston's Berklee College of Music, Mr. Weinstein has already performed at the Wolf Trap Center for the Performing Arts and such jazz rooms as Birdland and the Django Reinhardt festivals in France and New York.

Starting at age eight, with lessons on a rented violin in a music-loving home in Wilmette, Illinois, Mr. Weinstein first began to find his vocation five years later when he came upon a cassette tape of Joe Venuti, the first internationally renowned jazz violinist.

"The power and authority with which he played," Mr. Weinstein happily recalls, "was so dominating that every note Venuti produced struck me as the absolutely definitive note to have been played at each given moment. It was the first time I had actively listened to a jazz recording."

He went on to the sunnily lyrical Stephane Grappelli, a colleague of the mer-curial Django Reinhardt in the Quintet of the Hot Club of France. Describing Grappelli's impact on his own development, Mr. Weinstein indicates he could have had a notable career as a jazz critic, though without having the much greater fun of being inside the music: "By the time he was in his musical prime, Grappelli had created a completely unique style epitomized by long lines of flowing eighth notes that he flawlessly executed at any tempo while always maintaining a feather-light touch."

Then Aaron Weinstein discovered what he calls Stuff Smith's "revolutionary playing." I asked him to elaborate on what he means by "revolutionary." What follows is the most penetrating description of that jazz master I have seen:

"Stuff Smith, more than any other jazz violinist of his day, blended rhythmic elements at the heart of the jazz idiom to the violin. At times, he used his instrument as a full big band, playing call and response between his violin's upper and lower registers. Every phrase Stuff played was pure jazz. He was first and foremost a jazz musician who happened to play the violin. Because of this, he broke the barrier that once separated violinists from other jazz musicians. He earned the respect of other jazz masters of his day, who treated him as a peer rather than an oddity. That is something to which all violinists should aspire."

The growing number of jazz musicians who have played with Mr. Weinstein—among them the richly lyrical tenor saxophonist Houston Person and the agelessly buoyant guitarist Bucky Pizzarelli on Mr. Weinstein's debut Arbors recording—regard him as a peer. As Mr. Person says: "Aaron will really go a long way because he's well grounded, and he really has a sense of jazz as it should be."

Among other established jazz violinists who helped ground Mr. Weinstein were Sven Asmussen, Johnny Frigo and Claude "Fiddler" Williams, who made jazz violin history with Count Basie in the 1930s and later with Jay McShann and beyond.

Eventually, however, Mr. Weinstein realized that "I needed to go further than the ideas of the idiom's greatest violinists. For me to understand the ideals at the heart of the jazz idiom, I began to look at many of my other favorite jazz musicians in the same way that I had reexamined the violinists who had made an impact on me."

Absorbing the self-discoveries of Zoot Sims, Lester Young, Bud Freeman, Warren Vache and Scott Hamilton, says Mr. Weinstein, "made me feel like my blinders had been removed. This was the beginning of my true development as a jazz musician."

Also part of that development is Mr. Weinstein's mining of the classic Great American Songbook, bringing back to life evocative melodies and moods far removed from the currently popular boiling cauldron of largely graceless rock, rap and hip-hop. Aiding him in this discovery of the quality of ballads that used to attract jazz improvisers is Houston Person, of whom the young violinist says: "He has an incredible respect for melody. Whether he is interpreting a Gershwin song or improvising on an Ellington tune, he's always playing some kind of a great melody—and he constantly seeks out interesting songs from the depths of the American Songbook and is always eager to share his finds."

On his CD, *A Handful of Stars*—the rewarding result of Mr. Weinstein's discovery of songs that, as he puts it, "have fallen through the cracks" or have otherwise faded from many musicians' memories—are "A Dream Is a Wish Your Heart Makes," "A Handful of Stars," "Someone to Watch Over Me," "If Dreams Come True" and "Pennies from Heaven."

This celebration of the timeless pleasures of jazz's sounds of surprise ends with the very definition of a jazz groove, a mellow musical conversation between Messrs. Weinstein and Person that transcends the players' ages and styles, achieving the joyous act of communion that has made this music an international language. Credit for this enduring recording is due Mat Domber, the owner and executive producer of Arbors Records, who not only immediately felt the need to record Mr. Weinstein but made this twenty-year-old the producer of his first album, in charge of choosing the musicians and the repertory. The rest of the Arbors catalog also reflects Mr. Domber's faith in what he accurately calls "classic jazz."

55 | The Newest Jazz Generation

Jazz has given me many unexpected startling pleasures. Years ago, at Basin Street East in New York, Sonny Stitt suddenly broke into a stop-time chorus, without the rhythm section, and all conversation stopped. It was as if time itself had stopped but was still swinging.

Five years ago, at Arbors Records' March of Jazz in Clearwater, Florida—a tribute to Ruby Braff on his seventy-fourth birthday—Sonny LaRosa's "America's Youngest Jazz Band, Featuring Musicians Ages 6 to 12" was scheduled first on one of the mornings. Remembering what Charlie Parker famously said, "Music is your own experience. . . . If you don't live it, it won't come out of your horn," I wondered how much these kids could have experienced.

I'd listen to a couple of numbers, I thought, and then take a walk on the beach. But the band hit with a "Bugle Call Rag" that almost knocked me out of my seat. I stayed for the whole swinging set, which included real lyricism in the ballads. Only a very young girl trying to sing of romantic love broke the spell until the return of the instrumentals. I've been following the odyssey of this band ever since. It won a gold medal at an international jazz festival in New Orleans, was convincing at the Montreux Jazz Festival in Switzerland and was the youngest band to have ever played at Preservation Hall in New Orleans, where it fit right into the jubilation.

During this year's Labor Day weekend, the world's youngest road band worked the Sweet & Hot Musical Festival at Los Angeles Airport's Marriott Hotel. In the audience was Rosemary Soladar, the longtime companion of one of the most joyous of jazzmen, the late trombonist Al Grey. (I'm eagerly looking forward to her book about him. He is—not only just was—in the jazz pantheon.) "The band," she told me, "had one of the few standing ovations for these merely astonishing youngsters, led by the eighty-year-old Sonny LaRosa—now in his twenty-eighth year as the arranger-conductor-mentor, and a model to these kids of how meaningful an educator can be to their lives."

As Jalon King, an alumnus of the band, wrote Sonny three years ago: "You have taught me the heart of passion and communicating through my music. . . . You are a true tower of inspiration to anything in my life that I do." Sonny, who played trumpet with the underrated band of Sam Donahue, among others—and for years after taught trumpet, piano and guitar in New York, moved to Florida in 1978, still teaching, and then started the nucleus of a band "with five or six kids who could play with good conceptions."

Duke Ellington once told me how he wrote individually for his musicians because, he said, "I know their strengths—and their weaknesses." In the November 7, 2000, issue of *The Floridian*, a section of the *St. Petersburg Times*, Lane DeGregory described the LaRosa method: "Most kids who come to him have never heard jazz. . . . Sonny shows them videos of Buddy Rich, Louis Prima, Billie Holiday. . . . He arranges all the songs himself. He writes out each part by hand, for every instrument, individualizing the approach to fit each musician's ability (or lack thereof). He draws the notes in black marker. The fingertips beneath in red. And he pencils the chord names in on top. He knows which kids can hold a long low C and who can hit a high F. He knows whose arms have grown long enough to extend a trombone slide and who still needs help counting."

Listening to the band at its various gigs, jazz musicians of renown have told Sonny, "Boy, I wish I had that when I was a kid!" As a failed musician able to read any piece of music but unable to speak jazz on my clarinet, I sure wish there had been a Sonny LaRosa when I was a kid. Maybe I could have eventually fulfilled my dream of subbing for Barney Bigard in the Ellington Orchestra.

Sonny is so eager to have his youngsters be heard that he'll split the expenses—and sometimes raise enough to pay them all—to fulfill a gig. It is utterly inexplicable to me that America's Youngest Jazz Band has never been invited to play at George Wein's JVC Jazz Festival in New York, at the annual International Association for Jazz Education events or even in their home area at the Clearwater Jazz Holiday. But for International Association of Jazz Educators (IAJE), especially, to have overlooked this band is what I call educational malpractice.

In Sonny's current band of twenty musicians, the age range begins at seven years, and there are two fourteen-year-old players ("to inspire the other kids," Sonny says). But that's the cut-off age. There are always openings in the band, and parents in the Tampa Bay area are invited to come hear the band with their kids who have shown an interest in music. The band's 2006 CD is titled *Sonny's 80th Birthday Edition: Keeping Swing and Big Band Jazz Alive!*

Sonny sometimes thinks of retiring, but as he told Lane DeGregory: "I never had the natural talent. I didn't have great ears. I wasn't a great improviser. God doesn't make everybody great. But the reward, for all my playing and praying, it's coming now." I've heard Sonny play his horn. He tells a story, his own story. Like every jazz player who's made it. And he's also made it as a teacher with big ears.

56 | Born in Israel

Randy Weston can't be mistaken for anyone else. As he once said, "I don't like the electric piano because my sound is my voice, and my voice is what makes me unique. A personal sound is the most difficult thing to achieve—it's an extension of yourself."

I have been listening often to the unmistakably personal voice of pianist-composer Anat Fort on her ECM CD, *A Long Story*. Like Anat Cohen and other Israeli musicians who came here from the lively Israeli jazz scene, Fort has worked New York clubs.

Fort assures me that she also does not play electric piano, and she feels constricted by the term "jazz." So did Charles Mingus, who insisted that he played "Mingus music." On her CD, while there is much deeply intimate and reflective lyrical music, there are bursts of forceful swinging. All but one of the tracks are her compositions, and each is an extension of her personal voice.

Born near Tel Aviv, she started on the piano when she was six, and though classically trained, Fort was always driven to improvise. "It drove my teachers mad," she says. "But I was far more into improvising on Chopin's music than just playing it straight. Some classical players are afraid of improvisation, but that's what makes me buzz." It wasn't until her late teens that she truly found her jazz calling. "I was listening to the radio [at] about three in the morning, and I heard John Coltrane playing 'You Don't Know What Love Is.' I couldn't go back to sleep."

I asked why Coltrane had so jolted her. "The sound was such a unique voice, so much like himself because it sounded like no other voice. It really spoke to me! It got me where it really mattered." The next day she bought the recording at a Tel Aviv music shop. Inevitably, Fort came to the United States to study jazz. Her teachers have included Rufus Reid and Harold Mabern, and a vital part of her education in this music of autobiographical improvisation came from her studies in the jazz program at the William Paterson University of New Jersey, one of the premier immersions into this music of insistent self-discovery. (Clark Terry is vividly associated with the program.)

Although Fort's reputation keeps growing on the New York scene, where she has been based since 1996, she is binational, often going back to Israel to perform and fulfill composing commissions such as her arrangements of Israeli songs ("my standards, in a way") for the Tel Aviv Opera House, where she also performed in 2006. Her American influences, she notes, include Bill Evans, Keith Jarrett and Paul Bley. (One day I'd like to see a penetrating study of Bley's impact on many players' lives over the years. His playing and writing are still underappreciated.)

For Fort, a key figure in jazz has been percussionist Paul Motian since she first heard him on a Bill Evans record. "I was blown away," she recalls, "and I dreamt of someday playing with him." Bassist Ed Schuller turned out to be the match-maker when, in New York, she started working with Schuller, who had been in many of Motian's bands.

That was the time to find out if her dream could come true. When Schuller called Motian to be part of Fort's ECM CD, "my first reaction," says Motian, "was to say 'no' because I didn't know her music." But Schuller persuaded him to come to hear her. And as in an Anat Fort dream, Motian was so surprised and pleased that, he says, "I liked the music so much that I recommended it to ECM. And I love the way the album came out."

So do I. Along with Schuller and Motian, yet another singular jazz voice is present: Perry Robinson on clarinet and ocarina. As Richard Cook writes in his invaluable *Jazz Encyclopedia* (Penguin), "Robinson is one of the very few to make a go of creating a place for the clarinet in the jazz avant-garde." Actually, whatever "avant-garde" means in the flow of fashion, Robinson plays what I call "soul music."

In Steve Lake's excellent liner notes for *A Long Story*, he says that Fort "is an intuitive musician firstly. . . . Israel being a complex melting pot, [her] memories may also include glimpses of an older Eastern European heritage." And Fort adds: "Sometimes I'll listen back and hear echoes of Gypsy music or Russian music." Also in her personal roots are echoes of klezmer improvisers that bring me back to the music I first heard as a child at Jewish weddings. One afternoon, after expressing delight to the clarinetist in the swinging klezmer band, he winked at me and asked, "Where you think Benny Goodman came from?"

Hearing Fort tell of how Coltrane's transformation of "You Don't Know What Love Is" changed her life, I also remembered what changed mine when I was eleven years old. Until then, the only music that had gotten me where it mattered was the improvising cantors in the synagogues and the klezmer players. But one afternoon, on a Boston street, coming from a record store, I heard Artie Shaw's "Nightmare" and yelled aloud in joyous pleasure. Years later, I found that Shaw had based "Nightmare" on a nigun, the kind of melody that the cantors used to improvise on. In Anat Fort's music, I also hear an imperishable flavor of niguns and, as Dizzy Gillespie used to say, the endless, flowing music of the universe.

57 | Theo Croker Arrives

I first got to know twenty-three-year-old Theo Croker after he returned from a gig in China (Shanghai's House of Blues and Jazz). He was so impressive there that he was later booked in the city's jazz club. On first hearing his trumpet on this immediately distinctive recording, I was struck by his "signature sound"—personal and indeed "in the tradition," but also contributing to its future.

It's a voice speaking directly to the listener, and his avoidance of showboating technique reminded me of what Count Basie once said to Buck Clayton: "I'd give a thousand dollars to find a trumpet player who doesn't play so many notes."

Furthermore, listening to Theo on ballads, it was at first hard to believe someone so young was able to sound as if he'd had extensive experience with affairs of the heart, gaining and losing love.

Croker has already appeared with such major players as Jimmy Heath, Frank Wess, Clark Terry and the Lincoln Center Jazz Orchestra, Jon Faddis and Benny Powell. Donald Byrd, with whom Theo studied at Oberlin College and Conservatory of Music in Ohio, said of him: "I would place Theo in a class of musicians who will redirect the flow, change and alter the current of today's New Jazz." If you think that may be somewhat hyperbolic, just listen!

Also, he will be an influence by his strong jazz roots as he keeps on learning about himself in the jazz life.

Theo is honoring his lineage as the grandson of the legendary Doc Cheatham. I was privileged to know Doc, who told me when he was in his eighties, "I find myself playing different every year . . . the new ideas still come to me." I expect Theo will also keep surprising himself.

Born on July 18, 1985, in Leesburg, Florida, Theo first picked up his horn when he was eleven—the year when, on a visit to New York, he heard his grandfather at Sweet Basil. (Doc Cheatham died, at ninety-two, in 1997.) Theo grew musically by listening to Doc's recordings: "a very appealing sound, the strength behind his sound, and always," Theo added, "a melody."

Relocating to Jacksonville, Florida, on his own when he was sixteen, his high school became the Douglas Anderson School of the Arts, where he stood out among his peers. By 2004, not yet twenty, he became the first artist in residence at the Ritz Theater (a formerly black movie house transformed into a museum with a performance space).

Expanding his wings, he led a seventeen-piece band there while also being commissioned to compose works for the band and his Septet as well as an eighty-member choir (The Ritz Voices). As if this weren't enough of a challenge, Theo conducted two concerts while there and taught a number of educational workshops for the young (not that he wasn't himself still young).

On to Oberlin College Conservatory, where he studied not only with Donald Byrd but also with Marcus Belgrave, Billy Hart and Robin Eubanks, earning a B.A. in Jazz Performance. Meanwhile he also worked professional gigs with Louis Hayes's Cannonball Adderley Tribute Quintet.

Especially important to his postgraduate education, Theo tells me, was "hanging out with such older musicians—Benny Powell, Jimmy and Tootie Heath, Billy Hart, Marcus Belgrave."

I asked him what he learned from them: "Mostly about how to live my life," says the quickeningly mature Theo. "Things not to do that they did; and things to do that they didn't."

Phil Woods and other musicians of his generation have told me that today's younger players lack—due to the paucity of big bands and their road trips—the special knowledge that came with being able to hang out and learn so much about the music and the jazz life from their elders.

Theo Croker demonstrates the benefits of that advanced jazz educational degree. Also as a musician of so many parts, Theo embodies what Duke Ellington told me many years ago: "Don't get trapped in categories." As deeply immersed in jazz as he is, Theo also writes—and produces—hip-hop, rap and film scores, along with ventures in contemporary classical music and other forms of music. I don't think he's yet planned to run for the Oval Office, but I wouldn't be surprised if one day he might.

After listening again to *In the Tradition*, I told Theo how moving his immersion in such ballads as "You're Blasé" was for me, and I wondered what experiences of his created the twilight in the music.

"My father, the man who raised me," he said, "died when I was eighteen. And other things I had to overcome in my youth changed my approach to playing."

Duke Ellington said to me once, "A musician's sound is his soul." And the soul can be jubilantly illuminated—and bruised—at an early age. For Theo's jubilation, swing along with him on "Struttin' with Some Barbeque."

I won't use the term "sidemen" for Theo's colleagues on this session because they are equal essentials in this celebration bridging the generations of jazz.

Pianist Sullivan Fortner, a New Orleans native, at the age of four was playing piano by ear, and five years later, nurtured by the strength of gospel music, became his church's organist. Like Theo, he moves in many grooves. He was in his high school jazz band and the pianist for the high school's concert choir as well as the Mahalia Jackson Mass Choir.

Bassist Joe Sanders, a graduate of the Milwaukee, Wisconsin, High School of the Arts was one of only five players offered a fellowship at the (Dave) Brubeck Institute at California's University of the Pacific. The artistic director there is the inspirational bassist Christian McBride. Studying with him, says Sanders, is "totally like living a dream." Says Sanders, whose dreams are multiplying, "I love classical music, but you can express yourself in jazz." He sure does.

Drummer Albert "Tootie" Heath, a member of a jazz royal family that includes brothers tenor saxophonist Jimmy Heath and bassist Percy Heath—has recorded with such masters of the music as John Coltrane, Dexter Gordon, Benny Golson, Art Farmer and Yusef Lateef. He now leads and produces The Whole Drum Truth featuring Ben Riley, Ed Thigpen, Jackie Williams, Billy Hart, Charlie Persip, Leroy Williams and Louis Hayes.

Trombonist Benny Powell, a luminous improviser whether on swingers or odes to romance, was with Lionel Hampton and, most notably, Count Basie's lustily swinging band. He also teaches a new generation of players on the roots of African music, including his work with New York's invaluable Jazzmobile. His appearances on two tracks of *In the Tradition* celebrate the continuing tradition.

A special treat here is Theo Croker's singing—as was the similarly intimate conversational singing of his grandfather, Doc Cheatham.

Theo's first CD for Arbors is due to the ever attentive ear of Arbors's creator, Mat Domber. Doc Cheatham's wife, Nellie, introduced Mat to Theo's mother when Theo was just starting on the trumpet and asked Mat to keep the youngster in mind.

"When he's ready," said Mat, "I'll record him."

Theo is more than ready. He has arrived!

58 | The Ladies Who Swung the Band

In 1776, not long before John Adams would help draft the Declaration of Independence, Adams's wife, Abigail, told the future second president of the United States, "Remember the ladies." Yet it wasn't until 1920 that the ladies gained the right to vote with the passage of the Nineteenth Amendment. And the battle for equality is still to be won by women in jazz, black and white.

For decades, the conventional, dismissive wisdom was embodied in the statement of the longtime dean of jazz critics, George Simon: "Only men can play good jazz." It was as if the black trumpet player Valaida Snow, much admired by Louis Armstrong, and Vi Burnside, tenor saxophonist for the all-female, largely black International Sweethearts of Rhythm, had never existed.

Women vocalists were admitted to the club—how could Bessie Smith, Billie Holiday and Ella Fitzgerald be kept out? And there was an occasional pianist. But as for female horn players, a male musician told me when I was a teenage jazz enthusiast, "They don't have the chops, the strength to hold their own in a combo or a band."

The pianist-composer Mary Lou Williams finally broke through in the 1930s with Andy Kirk's Dark Clouds of Joy big band in Kansas City. She was billed as "The Lady Who Swings the Band," astonishing her male colleagues. Harlan Leonard, another bandleader, said, "It was the first time we had ever seen a girl cat who could carve the local boys." Many years later, when Sherrie Maricle—who now leads the most swinging big jazz band on the scene, the all-women Diva—asked to sit in at a jam session in New York's internationally famous jazz club the Blue Note, a musician heading the session told her, "Well, you can play if you take your shirt off."

When I was in high school in Boston in the early 1940s, I was shocked into questioning my easy acceptance of the notion that jazz was a male preserve. Several of us cut classes to see a live performance of The Band That Plays the Blues, as Woody Herman's band was then called, at a movie theater. Having heard that Woody had committed the heresy of hiring Billie Rogers, a woman trumpet player, for his brass section, we were prepared to mock her flailing attempts at swinging.

Chicks just weren't built to roar and shout, we told one another, but Rogers had a big, penetrating sound, and that chick sure could swing! In Gene Lees's *Leader of the Band: The Life of Woody Herman*, Woody recalled that the twenty-two-year-old had more stamina than the rest of the section when the band played five or six theater shows a day.

But I still considered her an aberration, having no knowledge then and for years after of such joyously swinging big bands as the International Sweethearts of Rhythm—still left out of many jazz histories.

And there was the powerful soloist Valaida Snow, born in Chattanooga, Tennessee, in 1904. A star in Europe and Shanghai, Snow was virtually unknown in the United States. This changed in 2007 with the publication in Canada of a biography by Mark Miller, *High Hat, Trumpet and Rhythm: The Life and Music of Valaida Snow* (Mercury Press, Toronto). Along with the International Sweethearts of Rhythm, Snow embodied the truth spoken by the pianist Marian McPartland, who celebrates the role of women in jazz: "Each of us is an individual, unique, different. The kind of life we have lived comes out in our music."

The International Sweethearts of Rhythm were a product of rural Mississippi. There in 1937, Laurence C. Jones, the founder and president of the Piney Woods Country Life School for poor and orphaned children, organized an all-girl band to go out on the road and help raise funds. Within a few years the band outgrew the school and gained professional standing.

Sherrie Tucker, the author of *Swing Shift* (Duke University Press, 2001) writes, "In the 1940s the International Sweethearts of Rhythm enjoyed an enormous following among the African-American audiences who heard them on the black theater circuit; . . . at military camps both stateside and in Europe when the band traveled on USO tours; and over the airwaves courtesy of Armed Forces Radio broadcasts."

The band was "international" in that the reed section had Indian and Chinese saxophonists, not to mention a few white players. But since the great majority of the musicians were black, the white members had to wear dusky pancake during tours of the South. This wasn't a perfect disguise because, as a band member was quoted in Linda Dahl's *Stormy Weather: The Music and Lives of a Century of Jazzwomen* (Pantheon, 1984): "We couldn't paint their eyes."

The Sweethearts disbanded in 1948, with few white jazz fans or critics ever having heard their music. I knew of the band's blazing tenor saxophonist, Vi

Burnside, only because black jazzmen would tell me that she could stand on her own against Coleman Hawkins and other towering male saxophonists.

In the 1950s, as Sherrie Tucker has written, other all-women bands also proved that swinging had no gender: Ina Ray Hutton and Ada Leonard led their big bands of experienced professional female musicians on television variety shows . . . [But] only white women's bands were seen. Black all-women bands did not receive television exposure. An African-American women's combo led by the jazz violinist Ginger Smock was broadcast for six weeks on CBS but folded for lack of a sponsor. Black women's bands are forgotten.

The story of the trumpet dynamo Valaida Snow would make a great movie—a profitable one, too, here as well as in Europe and Asia, which the narrative of her life would need to cover. Mark Miller, in *High Hat, Trumpet and Rhythm,* describes her: "She stood just shy of five feet tall, but in the words of one of her many lovers, the influential Chicago pianist Earl Hines, 'had all the physical attractions you could want in a girl.' She used her wardrobe to particular advantage in that respect from elegant gowns that swept the floor to the shortest of shorts that revealed the longest—proportionately speaking—of legs."

But Snow's trumpet entranced musicians even more. In 1928, at a gig in Chicago, Louis Armstrong encouraged her to take a solo chorus when she played in his band. "I guess I needn't tell you," she remembered, "how proud I was to hear his hoarse but sincere encouragement while I was playing."

The Batavian guitarist Otto MacKenzie called her "a truebred artist. . . . She sang excellently, then played a solo on trumpet, on which instrument she could do all kinds of tricks and improvise tremendous breaks. After this, she would give out with some more choruses of dancing . . . tap-dancing too." The British jazz authority Richard Cook recommends the Valaida Snow 1935–1937 recording on the Harlequin label, to hear what he calls her "thrilling gaiety."

I have yet to see a solidly researched appreciation of Valaida Snow in an American jazz magazine or on television. The same is true of the International Sweethearts of Rhythm.

In 1958, I finally found a recording of the Sweethearts of Rhythm and wrote in the *Wall Street Journal:* "When I used to hear tales of the music created by these traveling ladies, I figured they couldn't have been that good. But [hearing] *International Sweethearts of Rhythm* on the Rosetta Records label reveals that they were better than their legend. So how come they're not even mentioned in 'definitive' histories of big-band jazz? Maybe because no one believed that women could do such things."

Part of the living legacy of that pathbreaking band is Catherine Russell, an authentic, warmly engaging jazz singer and the daughter of the influential bandleader Luis Russell. Her mother, Carline Ray, is an alumna of the Sweethearts of Rhythm, where she sang and played guitar and bass.

I've heard stories about the Sweethearts' triumphs from Carline Ray, who is still performing; she recently bought a new bass, and has been writing a musical. In a phrase her daughter likes to use, Carline Ray is still "in the pocket." Catherine Russell told me what that means: "A pocket means to me what the feeling was when on the dance floor, like at the Savoy Ballroom in Harlem. That's when the music reaches into you."

Like her mother and all the jazz women in this chapter, past and present, Catherine Russell embodies the quintessential effect of this music, performed when women and men are "in the pocket." As Russell puts it, and as Valaida Snow and so many other women personified it, "when the music is right, it heals everybody. It's all one energy—the band, the audience, the melody, the lyric, the swing. And when I'm onstage for two hours I feel like I'm sharing something that brings us all together."

The glass ceiling that segregated and marginalized women jazz players is finally being broken. For years now, the master trumpet player Clark Terry has had as his regular drummer Sylvia Cuenca. She could make an Army band swing! And a rising star on saxophone and clarinet is Anat Cohen, to whom I said when I first heard her, "You have the soul of Ben Webster," Duke Ellington's passionate tenor saxophonist. Actually, it's her own soul that drives her music—and her arrangement and compositions.

The most dramatic, indeed thrilling, evidence of the emancipation of women in jazz is the big band Diva, which plays throughout the United States and at prestigious festivals in Europe. Reviewing one of its recordings, *Live in Concert: Sherrie Maricle and the Diva Jazz Orchestra*, the British critic Geoff Burdett admitted in the magazine *Crescendo*: "I confess to being very surprised by the sheer power and spirit of this band, quite apart from the very high level of musical ability on display . . . Make no mistake, these girls can play—and I mean play."

As I wrote in *JazzTimes*, if there were still big-band competitions in ballrooms and after-hours clubs, these women "would swing a lot of the remaining big bands out of the place." On one of its European tours, when Diva played in Croatia, the stage was filled with bouquets at the end of the performance, a tribute to these dashing "chicks" who, as a *JazzTimes* review saluted them, "punched, kicked, roared and swung with a disciplined abandon and unaffected joie de vivre."

I wish those male musicians and the old-time critics who kept insisting that women don't have "the chops" to be jazz musicians were still here to confess how prejudice had closed their ears.

During an interview with Monk Rowe, director of the Hamilton College Jazz Archive in upstate New York, Diva's dauntless leader and drummer Sherrie Maricle emphasized that women jazz instrumentalists are breaking gender stereotypes globally: "The women in Diva are from all over the world. Our alto player, Karolina Strassmayer, comes from a tiny village in Austria. She's a brilliant jazz player. We have in our rhythm section two musicians from Japan, and on tenor saxophone we have a girl from Italy.

"I used to be looked at as weird, being the only girl drummer. Everybody in Diva has had the experience of people saying, 'That girl can play!' We're all [women] in Diva; suddenly none of us is a unique woman jazz musician. So now all of us have wider choices. It never occurs to me to worry about 'should I hire a man or a woman?' I just hire whom I like."

Another strong presence on Chicago's jazz scene today is Nicole Mitchell, a flutist and composer. For the past three years the *Down Beat* critics' poll has named Mitchell "No. 1 Rising Star Flutist." As her CD, *Nicole Mitchell's Black Earth Ensemble: Black Unstoppable,* powerfully demonstrates, Mitchell is an original rooted both in jazz and in other black world music.

The trombonist and Columbia University professor George Lewis states in a *Chicago Reader* article by Peter Margasak: "She has the broadest conception of herself as an artist and a human being . . . In her dazzling compositions she draws on variants of jazz from across much of the genre's history [as well as] reggae, African grooves, and Latin rhythms."

Among the life experiences in Nicole Mitchell's music is her becoming aware when she was eight years old of searing bigotry: "When I walked outside of my house [in Anaheim, California], I had neighbors actually tell me to move away from their property because I was degrading its value by standing in front of it." Adds Peter Margasak: "After the TV adaptation of Alex Haley's *Roots* aired in 1977, she was chased by classmates brandishing lengths of ropes like whips."

After initial instruction in classical music on flute and studies at Oberlin Conservatory, Nicole Mitchell today performs throughout the United States, Canada and Europe, while also winning commissions for her compositions. Her credo: "I think music is nurturing, and people need it. The type of music they listen to kind of holds their reality together. I wish for us to celebrate music that is truth for this moment that we live. A very unstable, interesting, horrifying and beautiful moment indeed."

Not all the early prejudices about women in jazz have vanished, however. Wynton Marsalis, the musical director of Jazz at Lincoln Center, is an accomplished trumpet player, composer, teacher and leading spokesman for the jazz community. But among women musicians, he has also long been known as never having had a full-time female member of the Jazz at Lincoln Center Orchestra, which tours worldwide from its New York base.

In June 2001, the singer Joan Bender organized a rally outside Lincoln Center to protest Marsalis's women-free orchestra. Demonstrators handed out fliers that were, I expect, very educational for the crowds of art lovers entering that shrine of creativity. "Women are in the Metropolitan, Philharmonic, and City Ballet

Orchestras," the pamphlets read, "because they have 1) job advertising; 2) blind auditions, in which unknown candidates perform behind a screen; 3) auditions observed by a committee [not just one man] . . . ; and 4) tenure process." And there was this revolutionary placard at the rally: TESTOSTERONE IS NOT A MUSICAL INSTRUMENT.

Since the adoption of blind auditions, "the number of women selected has risen dramatically to the point of equal representation in hundreds of orchestras," Lara Pellegrinelli wrote in the *Village Voice,* but "virtually none of the top mainstream bands—the Smithsonian Jazz Masterworks Orchestra, the ghost bands of Count Basie or Duke Ellington . . . currently employ any female players as permanent members."

As of this writing, there is still no permanent female member of the Jazz at Lincoln Center Orchestra, although concerts there have celebrated women in jazz. Diva has performed at Lincoln Center, and among the thousands of teenage hopefuls who enter the center's annual competition for high school jazz bands, many are young women.

Whether or not one of them eventually manages to breach the all-male barrier at the Jazz at Lincoln Center Orchestra, a growing number of these young instrumentalists will find that their way to jazz equality has been cleared by the Sweethearts of Rhythm, Valaida Snow and so many other swinging forebears. To paraphrase Duke Ellington, it don't mean a thing if it don't have those ladies in there swinging!

59 | Nineteen-Year-Old Saxophonist Verifies Future of Jazz

For more than sixty years, I've seen recurring obituaries of jazz. The threnodies are being prepared again—in the National Endowment for the Arts' latest survey on public participation in the arts and in such articles as "Can Jazz Be Saved?" (*Wall Street Journal,* August 18, 2009), in which widely respected music critic Terry Teachout wrote regretfully, "I don't know how to get young people to listen to jazz again."

Both the survey and Teachout's column attracted rebuttals in print and on the Internet, of course. But the most exhilarating one I've heard is musical— *Confeddie,* the debut CD of nineteen-year-old alto saxophonist Hailey Niswanger and a work with the joyous feeing of the first day of spring. More remarkable, Hailey is still a student, at Boston's Berklee College of Music. It's an institution that continues to have many active jazz professionals among its alumni. She wrote all the arrangements for *Confeddie* in collaboration with three impressive Berklee students: Michael Palmer, Greg Chaplin and Mark Whitfield Jr.

This self-produced, self-released quartet session, which is available on

Amazon.com, has such a vibrantly building thrust of swinging surprises that listening to it, I was suddenly a Boston teenager again, fantasizing, as I played my clarinet, that one day Duke Ellington would call and say, "We need a sub for Barney Bigard tonight. Can you make it?"

Hailey has already played at festivals, concerts and other gigs with such masters as Phil Woods, James Moody, Benny Golson, Wynton Marsalis and McCoy Tyner and with the Next Generation Jazz Orchestra at the Netherlands's North Sea Jazz Festival. In May of 2009, she was a featured artist at the Mary Lou Williams Women in Jazz Festival at the Kennedy Center in Washington, D.C. (where, the year before, she won the saxophone competition).

She plays with remarkable authority and drive considering her relative youth, and with the élan and dynamics of an unmistakable pro. But I asked her how it felt, at nineteen, to be onstage with such renowned, longtime headliners.

"It's a remarkable experience to be that close to all those years of experience in one person," she said. "I have only a fraction of that, with a whole lifetime ahead."

A growing realization she especially enjoys is "the feeling of connectedness with the people listening. I don't know them, never met them, but with my horn, we connect!"

Also, having been close to Benny Golson during a master class the tenor saxophonist and composer taught at Berklee and having been in his band at a concert, Hailey feels she learned about being in the jazz life by watching how "he so wanted to give—to give what he was feeling—and tell his stories, not to be famous but to invite people to be part of who he is."

I asked her reactions, however, to the prospect of spending a lifetime in this music that, according to the doomsayers, fewer and fewer young people are interested in hearing.

Her instant answer: "I go to a music school, surrounded by young musicians passionate to learn about this music. There will always be people who love jazz and want to give their lives to it. So how can this music ever die?"

Such thriving jazz elders as Phil Woods and Clark Terry have told me the same thing.

During the summer of 2009, Hailey performed in combos in and around Portland, Oregon, where she grew up and taught piano to children ages five to seven and woodwinds to the twelve-to-eighteen age group at a nearby camp. It was there, when Hailey was eight, that she played her first note on a clarinet. During her school years she also began learning the alto saxophone as teacher-mentors helped convince her, the only musician in her family, that she had found her calling.

"In high school, when I was fourteen," she told me, "I first learned how to transcribe solos, starting with [solos by] trombonist J. J. Johnson and then John Coltrane!" And, performing both with local bands and around the country, "finding how to do jazz, I discovered how much fun this is. It's always changing. I play a song on one gig, and on the next, it comes out so different!"

Why *Confeddie*? I asked of her title. She explained that it comes, in part, from "confetti," to mark the festive flavor of the music, and she added the first name of saxophonist Eddie Harris, whose spirit pervaded the sessions. Included are her personalizations of jazz canon standards by Herbie Hancock, Wayne Shorter, Kenny Dorham and Benny Golson—starting bravely with Thelonious Monk's "Four in One."

Understandably, in view of that challenge, she says she felt "a great sense of accomplishment once I had it under my fingers. I wanted my version to be different from the other versions of this song, so I decided to play the melody as a duo with piano and saxophone to add some flavor to the arrangement."

Having immersed myself in Monk's music, starting in the 1950s, and having gotten to know the composer, I believe he would tell Hailey, "You got it."

After two more years at Berklee, Hailey expects—while still performing— to do graduate work at the Manhattan School of Music, the Thelonious Monk Institute in Washington, D.C., or Juilliard. The last possibility reminded me, I told her, of sitting in Monk's living room one afternoon when Gigi Gryce—a passionately personal alto saxophonist and composer whom I'd known in Boston— burst into the room.

"Monk," he shouted, "I got into Juilliard!"

After a characteristically judicious silence, Monk said, "I hope you don't lose it there."

Hailey, having already deeply "got it," won't lose it anywhere.

At Berklee, her principal teacher and mentor is alto saxophonist Jim Odgren, who is assistant to the dean of the performance division. Among his own previous performance gigs were three years with vibraphonist Gary Burton.

"What sets Hailey apart, even from some players already in the business," Odgren told me, "is that she is a musician—not an apprentice. She's really playing—really focusing on—what she is feeling. Telling her own stories. And she does it with such authority that if you played her recording for an established jazz musician during a blindfold test, he'd never guess her age."

As for the current sorrowful portents of the last rites of jazz, there will be, as is already evident, new generations of musicians for whom this music will be as important as life itself—as John Coltrane once described it to me.

There will also be future listeners of all ages—as I can attest from phone calls I occasionally get from readers who require this music to lift their spirits when nothing else will break through lengthening shadows. I am one of those with this need, so I'll always know where to find Hailey Niswanger's *Confeddie*.

PART ELEVEN

The Master Teachers

60 | A Complete Jazzman

I am greatly indebted to Thomas Bellino, whose Planet Arts—a not-for-profit company involved in a network of educational and culturally awakening projects—includes Planet Arts Recordings. His 2007 release *Turn Up the Heath* by the Jimmy Heath Big Band, made me realize that in all these years writing about this music, I have ignored one of the most deeply satisfying and personal arranger-composers in jazz—especially evident when his instrument is a big band.

Jimmy Heath is hardly unrecognized. A 2003 National Endowment for the Arts Jazz Master, he is greatly respected by his jazz peers. As George Wein says in the course of the indispensable DVD documentary *Brotherly Jazz: The Heath Brothers* (brotherlyjazz.com), "If you have to have an arranger, you call Jimmy. And if you need a saxophone player for a session, Jimmy is there." But I wonder how many jazz listeners around the world know that, as Herbie Hancock emphasizes in the film, "Jimmy is a master composer." In his notes to *Turn Up the Heath*, Jimmy writes, "My first love has always been the big band, our symphony orchestra." But in his long and still vigorous career—encompassing his appearance on more than 125 recordings—he's had far too few opportunities to record his arrangements (which are compositions) and his original pieces with a big band.

I first heard this set after many grim hours at my day job reporting on the Bush Administration's grievously distorting the essential separation-of-powers harmony of our Constitution. But as soon as the first notes of *Turn Up the Heath* came on, my spirits lifted, and I still feel the deeply flowing pulse of the music.

Jimmy knows the value of space. He lets the music breathe; and, accordingly, the ensemble players and the soloists always sound like their natural selves—a multitude of individual voices cohering into a wholly distinctive conversation. Jazz, at its most enduring is, after all, constitutional democracy in action, with all of its individual stories becoming a mosaic of interdependence. And in Jimmy Heath's writing, as intensely swinging as it often gets, there is an implicit obbligato of singing lyricism. Anyone who can write like this knows what he was born to do in this world.

Dr. Billy Taylor says of Jimmy (who years ago used to be called "Little Bird"), "He was the guy who was very melodic, and he really learned a lot from Charlie Parker, but he also learned a lot from other musicians who were older and . . . after he got over his Charlie Parker fixation, he was able to incorporate some Ben Webster and . . . Lester Young and other people who played other styles."

In his composing-arranging as well as in his playing, Jimmy has indeed embodied jazz's rainbow of sounds and stories. One of the results is that he is technically a master of the language. Jazz is a craft before it can become an art. And in the *Brotherly Jazz* documentary, Jon Faddis—of whom Dizzy Gillespie was also a fundamental mentor—says, "What's amazing about Jimmy is he is one of the few guys who can, you know, tell you exactly what chord is going on, and what the voicing is, and you can sit on the bandstand next to him and learn."

On October 18, 2006, the Aaron Copland School of Music at Queens College, New York, saluted "legendary jazz artist and Professor Emeritus Jimmy Heath on his eightieth birthday." The concert consisted largely of Heath's compositions. And in a press release, the school pointed out that "for many years, Jimmy Heath, . . . Howard Brosky (trumpet) and Sir Roland Hanna (piano) were the foundation of our Master of Arts degree jazz program at Queens College." Extending his contributions to this global music, there is a Jimmy Heath Scholarship Endowment at Queens College. Dizzy once told Jimmy, "You've got to keep one foot in the past and one foot in the future."

In the liner notes, Jimmy also writes that he wasn't able to make a complete big-band recording until 1992 "with help from my friend, Bill Cosby," who produced the sessions. That Verve set, *Little Man Big Band,* won a Grammy nomination but has since been deleted. At last, this Planet Arts set "is a follow-up." It's a commentary on the jazz business that it wasn't until Jimmy was nearly eighty that he could go into a studio and make this ageless recording. And that was because Planet Arts, as a not-for-profit 501(c)3 company, was able to get funding sources such as the Aaron Copland Fund for Music and the New York State Council on the Arts.

"Jimmy has a lot more arrangements, including forward-looking ones," Tom Bellino tells me, "and I'd be happy to raise money for another Jimmy Heath Big Band recording. He's got more energy than anyone else I know, and it's an honor for me to be working with these guys. I grew up listening to this music." If only there were more Tom Bellinos in jazz. On the cover of the *Brotherly Jazz* DVD, Sonny Rollins says, "The Heath Brothers have made the world a better place. That's what jazz is all about." Tom Bellino understands that.

Jimmy Heath now has a joyous big band, based at the Flushing Town Hall in Queens, New York.

61 | The Lifetime Teacher

JON FADDIS

NAT HENTOFF: This is Nat Hentoff from the internationally renowned Blue Note Jazz Club in New York. The most exciting musical experience I've ever had, I think, any kind of music, was in 2003 when Louis Armstrong's home in the borough of Queens, which is in New York, was made a National Historic Landmark. All kinds of people were there from all over the world, the neighborhood—kids in the neighborhood—when Louis was there the kids knew him, they talked to him. All of a sudden above the crowd, from a balcony next to where Louis's den used to be, I heard "West End Blues." A cappella, no accompaniment, played by—well, played by my guest here—Jon Faddis. It was stunning. So, our guest here tonight is Jon Faddis, master trumpet player, composer, conductor, educator. Now, I know, as everyone in the jazz community knows, that Dizzy was your chief mentor. The story has been told by you, but for the audience, tell us briefly about twelve-year-old Jon Faddis meeting Dizzy Gillespie.

JON FADDIS: Twelve-year-old Jon Faddis was a big, big, big fan of Dizzy Gillespie's, and growing up in Oakland, California, there were a few jazz clubs in the area. My parents, seeing my love for Dizzy and his music, took me to hear him one night at a club called Basin Street West in the North Beach area on Broadway of San Francisco. Dizzy was playing, and he had a great group at the time with Kenny Barron, James Moody, Chris White, Rudy Collins, and I went to hear Dizzy, and Dizzy was strolling between the tables and my father says "Diz, my boy really digs you! He's a trumpet player!" Dizzy looked at me and said "You a trumpet player?" and I froze. And could not say one word, 'cause it was Dizzy, and Dizzy was my hero. So, I said to myself, the next time I meet Dizzy, I'm gonna talk to him, and that actually happened three years later, at the Monterey Jazz Festival. My mother took me down to the Monterey Jazz Festival, and I decided to bring all of my Dizzy Gillespie records that I had collected, which at that time was about fifty LPs—a big stack of Dizzy Gillespie records.

NH: Lucky they weren't 78s.

JF: Those would have been heavy. But my mother and I were in the fairgrounds looking at all the trinkets and things they were selling, and my mother said "There's Dizzy!" I said, "Mom! Go get the records!" So she ran to the car, which was in the parking lot, got the records, and came back. By the time she came back I was sittin' there talking to Diz. I said "Mr. Gillespie—Dizzy, would you sign my records?" And he sat down right in the grass, and I sat down in the grass, and he started signing records. And then he said, "I don't remember this one!" And I said, "Yeah, that's the one where your solo goes 'Whee doo-doo'" and I'd start singing his solo to him. He looked at me like I was crazy or dizzy, and he remembered me. A couple of weeks later, he was playing at another club in San Francisco called the Jazz Workshop, and again my mother took me to hear Dizzy, and I brought my horn this time. So during the bass solo on "A Night in Tunisia"—the bassist was Jimmy Merritt from Philadelphia—and during the bass solo, Dizzy walked—it was a long narrow club—and Dizzy walked by my table, and I said, "Diz, you gonna do the ending?" He looked at me and said, "You got your horn, you do it!" So I ran down to the dressing room where my horn was and I got my horn and I'm sittin' in the back of the club. And Dizzy was playing a little cadenza on the end of "Tunisia," and he was signaling me with his eyebrows. I don't know how—he was maybe one hundred feet away, I couldn't see his eyebrows moving from the back of the club. So he took the horn down and—"Okay!"—and I played (sings) "Dah Daaaahh, Doo Dahhhh!" He invited me up to play two tunes with him, and from that moment on I knew that I wanted to become a trumpet player.

NH: You know, when the time comes for the JON FADDIS movie, that is the best opening. You have to find a fifteen-year-old who can do it! (Laughter)

JF: I remember Dizzy announcing me that night. He said, "This young man is fifteen years old and he's been playing the trumpet for sixteen years!" (Laughter)

NH: Now, speaking of young players, I read in the current issue of *Jazz Improv NY* magazine, you spent an afternoon with second graders at the Harlem Academy. How did you and the second graders and the music interconnect?

JF: Well, one of the things I did was I brought a gift [of this music] to all the second graders in the class of my latest CD. So when they see a gift like that they get all excited 'cause it's a gift. I also think, seriously, that I have, and my wife can verify this, that I have many of the qualities that second graders have, you know, I like to tell jokes, I like to fool around—

NH: I was going to say, it sounds so fun—

JF: I like to have fun—to look at something with the curiosity of a child is something I like to do, and these kids had drawings on the wall and all these different things, and I was talking to them about their musical interest, who plays the drums, who plays the piano, does anyone play the trumpet—"I do!" Here, let me get a mouthpiece, and then they go "fhew," nothing comes out; I say, "Make your lips buzz, 'fhhhhhht,'" then the sound comes out, and all the kids, like, wide-eyed, oh, and I'm saying it's not that difficult. But the main thing that you have to do is practice—groans, you know. But we got along famously, we had a great time, and I look forward to going back and spending some time with the kids when they're a little older.

NH: Well, you're doing that, I gather, in Chicago, with the Jazz Institute of Chicago's Jazz Links program with high school students. What is that program?

JF: Well, the Jazz Institute—I'm very good friends with the head of the Jazz Institute of Chicago, Lauren Deutsch, and when I was chosen to become the artistic director of the Chicago Jazz Ensemble—which was the big band that was started by the late Bill Russo, um, let me see, maybe forty-one years ago now—I called Lauren, and she knew that I was coming into Chicago and I was going to spend a significant amount of time there, and I wanted to check with her and find out what I could do to help whatever it was she was doing. And one of the things that she had established is the Jazz Links program, which is—it has kids, different ages, up through high school, and they get together and have jam sessions with professionals. So it's sort of like on-the-job training for them.

NH: Do they record any of these? So the kids can hear them?

JF: I'm not sure.

NH: I'm just curious. Might be part of the instruction.

JF: Probably not yet, but I think they're hoping to document this whole process. And I've hosted a couple of pizza parties for these Jazz Links kids and had them come over to the room, and we sit there and have pizza—Chicago-style, but you know I prefer the New York myself—but we have the pizza, and then have a jam session and I talk to them about some of the things that they can do and some of the things they're practicing sometimes, like when they don't understand theory, I'll send them a theory book that they can read and try to understand it a little bit better. One of the great things we just did in Chicago is we started a program for middle school and high schools students called the Louis Armstrong Legacy Program and Performance, and we had about eight schools come and perform transcriptions that I did of "West End Blues," "Wild Man Blues" and "Struttin' with Some Barbeque." And for those that were younger, from middle school, and the music was a little bit too difficult for them, we did "When the Saints Go Marching In" and "What a Wonderful World." And it was supported by the Louis Armstrong Educational Foundation with Phoebe Jacobs.

NH: I know Phoebe, yes.

JF: And also, yeah, I think the Polk Foundation? And there was a young kid, maybe in the eighth grade, his name was Methuselah.

NH: Methuselah?

JF: That's his first, that's his name, and—he came over, I think, a couple of years ago from Africa—he came out, and he started to sing "What a Wonderful World," and there were tears flowing in the audience, it was so beautiful. And when I started going to Chicago and performing, a lot of the schools that we would visit and perform [at], and the clinics, were in the suburbs. But through Lauren Deutsch [and] Dick Dunscum at Columbia College we had a meeting with Chicago public school teachers, and they were telling us some of their needs. And we helped to set up this program. Because, unfortunately, with budget cuts—

NH: And with No Child Left Behind, so you have to test for the test all the time—

JF: Yeah, jazz programs are getting dropped, music programs are getting dropped, art programs are getting dropped left and right.

NH: Now, have any of these teaching [and] playing sessions that you're talking about ever been filmed? Because if they have been or could be, it would be great to send around to the schools and maybe stimulate some of the principals or division chairmen to have—there's nobody like you, but other people doing that sort of thing.

JF: Well I believe one of the parents brought a film camera the last time we had it, and there's a blind pianist that I think was twelve years old who is incredible, and his mother wanted to film him, so I said, "OK."

NH: This should be on PBS, or something like it, because the more people who see this, especially the more young people who see this, seems to me, it'll inspire them, and that's where your jazz audience and players are gonna come from.

JF: Of course the future of the jazz audience is from getting to these kids when they're young.

NH: Yeah. Now, we started this conversation with Louis Armstrong. When did his playing begin to mean something to you?

JF: Well, I think from a young age, when I started playing the trumpet, I was always aware of Louis Armstrong's music; he used to appear quite often on television, on the *Ed Sullivan Show* or something like that, but also in films. And, you know, if it was a trumpet player on television, I wanted to watch it. When I was ten years old, my trumpet teacher, Bill Catalano, introduced me to Dizzy Gillespie's music, and part of my study, and my lessons, was to practice excerpts from Dizzy's solos until I could eventually, after several weeks, put together a chorus of a Dizzy Gillespie solo. When I was, I don't know, probably thirteen or fourteen, my parents would have parties in the house, and [when] I would come out, "John, do 'Hello, Dolly.'" And I would do my imitation of Louis Armstrong singing "Hello, Dolly." At that time I wasn't really aware of the Hot Fives and the Hot Sevens or the recordings he did with his all stars or the things he did with Duke Ellington or the big band things that he did. I did a recording session for Bob Thiele, after I'd gotten to New York, I was probably in my early twenties. And written down was the introduction to "West End Blues." And I said, "What is this," [and] he says, "Are you kidding, this is Louis Armstrong's 'West End Blues,' from 1928. This is one of the greatest trumpet solos ever recorded." So, after I finished the recording session, I went to—

NH: Tower Music.

JF: Not Tower, maybe King Carole, they had a place in Times Square, on Forty-second and Sixth or somewhere like that, and I went in, "Do you have 'West End Blues,' by—and I knew the buyer—do you have 'West End Blues' by Louis Armstrong?" "Oh, of course, here you go." And I went back, and then I learned it, and a few years later, after that, I recorded it on one of the albums I did with Ray Brown and Mel Lewis, Kenny Barron. Then I started to get into Louis

Armstrong's music. And what was happening by this time was [that] I started to do master classes and clinics, and I read something that Dizzy said, because at this time in New York, whenever Dizzy would appear somewhere, I would always come and sit in with him. And I read an excerpt—I read something that Dizzy said to Fats Navarro and Benny Harris, who would always challenge him and try to get him. And Dizzy said, "Look you guys, I can go back farther than you, and I can draw from that so you're not gonna get me."

NH: That's what you're doing now at Purchase University, you're teaching as well, right?

JF: Yes, exactly. A lot of students really start to learn the history of the music and start to respect the stylists, the great stylists that have come before them, and some others are really hesitant to do that because they think they have their own voice and that they don't need to listen to anyone else.

NH: Or else that jazz started with Charlie Parker, so why do they need the other stuff?

JF: Well, it's much later than that now; now it's Coltrane and Wayne Shorter and Joe Henderson, someone like that, Michael Brecker—

NH: What happens to them when you expose them to Chick Webb and, you know, all the other people you bring them back to?

JF: It's funny, because some of my best students come from other countries. And when they come to this country, they become very serious about studying. So when I say "Look, you have to know the history of this music, especially on your instrument. If you're playing the drums, you should know something about Baby Dodds. You should know something about Chick Webb, Papa Jo Jones. It's not only Tony Williams and Jack DeJohnette and Brian Blade and people like that. You have to go back, because that way you'll have a foundation. You'll know how to use your bass drum, you'll know how to use your high hat properly. You'll have to know how to shade for different artists." Then I show him a video of Papa Jo Jones and he has a snare drum, a bass drum, one tom-tom, a high hat and one cymbal, and they say, "How can he play like that?"

NH: Can I just interrupt for a second? I saw Papa Jo once at a club in Boston. He got off the stand with just his sticks. He played all over the room, swinging in time, his times, on the floor, the ceiling—well not the ceiling—but it was astonishing! He never broke stride, and it was musical!

JF: Actually, now there are some very interesting videos of Papa Jo on YouTube. I tell my students, and I say "Look, I want you to learn these Papa Jo Jones solos." He uses his hands. He uses sticks, and it's a brilliant solo construction that's on YouTube. And I do that with all of the instruments whether it's bass, drums—

trumpet, of course; you know, I have my trumpet students learn Louis. You have to learn some Louis. I have a couple of very talented students now, and I have one of them—I'm pushing him to push himself, because he's very adept in his comfort zone. But once he goes outside of that comfort zone he gets nervous, and I want him to go outside of his comfort zone, and I have him do "Rockin' Chair" by Roy Eldridge. "Heckler's Hop"—and these are difficult solos. Those solos aren't even easy for me. I have him going, and when he gets it, I say, "There you go!"

NH: You know, there ought to be a series of you teaching. It would really be a contribution. Get some intelligent television producer on this.

JF: You know, there are so many videos out on "teaching jazz." But one of the things that I found and one of the things I'd talked with Dizzy about is the importance of learning the instrument. Period. Just being able to play the instrument. So a lot of the things that I do—for example, when I was playing here, like three days ago, Sunday night, there were, like, five or six trumpet students from Israel who came to the show. So one of them came up; it was Sunday night—it was the last night—we were between shows, and one of them says "Oh, I wish I had brought my horn, I could have a lesson with you." So one of my students from Purchase was there, and I said, "Can I borrow your horn and mouthpiece?" The student from Israel started playing, and it was very interesting because when he played jazz, all of his fundamentals went out the window. I think, I'm surmising, but I think that he felt that if he were to feel free, he had to get rid of the proper technique, and I told him, "No, you have to use that technique to inform your jazz playing. No one's gonna want to listen to you if you're missing every other note," which he was, so I just took him through a couple of exercises. "Now, learn how to play this," then his tonguing started to get better, his slurring started to get better, and I said, "Now, you apply that to your jazz playing." I said, "Play me something pretty." He really couldn't think of anything, so I said, "the other thing you have to do is start memorizing music. You have to listen to Louis Armstrong and the Hot Fives and Hot Sevens and Dizzy and Bird and Miles and Fats Navarro and Clifford Brown and Freddie Hubbard. Listen to all of these guys and put it in your computer."

NH: It reminds me, Lester Young once told me something about when he plays. I was at his home in Queens, and he said, "I always learn the lyrics to songs I'm going to play." So I said, "Where do you learn them?" and he pointed to a stack of records by Frank Sinatra.

JF: There's a story about Ben Webster playing a beautiful ballad. He's in the middle of this beautiful ballad, and all of a sudden he stopped playing. And someone says, "Hey Ben, why'd you stop?" He says, "I forgot the lyrics."

NH: Ho ho! You know, Ben Webster once taught me something when I was in my early twenties that's lasted me all my life, as a writer and a person. He had left Duke, and he couldn't get club owners to hire his regular musicians with the money they had, so he was trying to make a Boston group swing, and he was making it, but sitting there at the bar he said to me, "You know something? When the rhythm section isn't making it, go for yourself."

JF: Well, you know, along those lines, there's—I read this in some book—but there was a question posed to Louis Armstrong about how he could play with mediocre bands. And Louis looked at the questioner and said, "Well, there's the band that you're hearing," and then he pointed to his head and said, "There's the band I'm hearing." And I tell my students that constantly, that you have to listen internally to the music that you want to play in and that you're hearing. You have to hear; you know if you're a horn player, you have to hear a great rhythm section of Walter Page and Count Basie, Freddie Green and Papa Jo.

NH: Then how are you getting that not-so-good rhythm section out of your mind?

JF: I think the mind is strong enough to do many, many things. One of the things that it can do is overcome one's environment and surroundings. That happens when you're playing with professionals, or sometimes I'll go and play with a school group. They don't really know how Papa Jo approached drum fills with the Basie band or Sam Woodyard, how he might have chopped wood, or kept the thing going, they don't really know those things. Sometimes I'm hearing different things than what's going on onstage. I really took what Louis Armstrong said to heart, or to ear! (Laughs)

NH: Well, Dizzy Gillespie taught me something. He was talking about himself, but it certainly helped me as a writer, I hope. He said, "It's taken most of my life to learn what notes not to play."

JF: This is something that I've thought about quite a bit, because when Dizzy was young and he hit the scene with Bird in 1944 or 1945, the recordings, you know, but there are no recordings with him in Earl Hines's band—that was an exciting time, like when Louis Armstrong was hittin' those Hot Fives and Hot Sevens. In the Earl Hines bands, they were young and very exciting. But one of the things that really speaks to me is hearing the development of artists like Dizzy, who came out on the scene when they were young. Like Louis Armstrong, who hit the Hot Fives—and hearing them years later when they are much older and much more mature. For example, the recording of Louis Armstrong just playing the melody to "Azalea" when he played with Duke Ellington is some of the most beautiful music that I've heard, and there's so much in each note that he plays. There was a night one time at the Village Gate—just a few blocks over—and I was sittin' in with Dizzy, and Dizzy decided for whatever reason that he wanted to play "I Can't Get Started" that night. And he played "I Can't Get Started" like I'd never heard. And I said,

"Dizzy! Wow! What was that you were doin'?" He said, "Aw, it wasn't nothing." He sort of dismissed it. But in listening to his first recording of "I Can't Get Started" or subsequent recordings with his big band in 1956, or from the album "Something Old, Something New" in 1963, and that moment at the Village Gate, I would have to take the Village Gate. Because I think that was one of the instances where Dizzy the trumpet student and the musician student—he's always learning and seeking new things—that sounded to me like one of the nights where it all came together. It wasn't high and flashy, or loud. It was very, I thought, very emotional and very spiritual. That was something that Dizzy was talking about. It took him that long to learn what not play. And when he said that, he was seventy years old!

NH: Oh my! In all of your teaching—you have no spare time, I gather—one question, which may not even be a fair question. It's been well known among musicians that to last for yourself you have to have your own sound, your signature sound. Can that be taught? How do people evolve as you're talking about, so that once somebody with ears hears their first ten or even fewer bars, they know who it is?

JF: I think that in the development of our music over the last century or more, younger musicians have always had someone that they looked up to and were inspired by and tried to sound like, whether it's John Coltrane, whether it's Sonny Rollins, whether it's Hank Jones, whether it's Dizzy Gillespie or Charlie Parker, whether it's Lester Young, whether it was Louis Armstrong. All of them had someone that they imitated, that they studied, that they learned every note on their solos, on their records. Dizzy looked to Roy for that. Roy looked to his older brother, Joe. Benny Carter, Coleman Hawkins—a little bit of Louis. Louis looked to King Oliver. Coltrane, when he was twenty years old sounded like Charlie Parker. When he was in the Navy Band he was playing alto and was trying to sound like Charlie Parker. I think getting your own sound is not something that happens immediately, and I don't know whether it can be taught, but I do think that it's something that the younger musician has to want and they have to really strive to do that. But I think it's almost frivolous to try and do that before understanding other styles. I think they have to have the background of some Louis Armstrong, some Roy Eldridge, some Cootie Williams, some Rex Stewart. Even Harry James or Bunny Berigan. That singing, that cantabile style of trumpet playing. Some Dizzy, some Fats Waller, some Clifford Brown, some Miles. Then you have a foundation. And it's not so much that you want to sound like them, because one will only sound like one's self anyway. But it's that you want to have a foundation so that you can develop your own sound. Sound is, for everyone, different. The sound of Miles Davis's trumpet sound is very different from Roy Eldridge's trumpet sound. I think one's sound is a reflection of one's persona, one's personality, or what's in one's heart. It also depends on the environment in which one is playing, and it also depends on the sounds, like Louis Armstrong said, the sounds that one is hearing. Because playing an instrument, you have to have a concept of sound first here, in your mind here (points to head), otherwise it's not going to happen. A lot of mistakes are made, just note mistakes are made, because one is not hearing the music.

NH: That reminds me that a trombonist once told me that [on] his first night with Duke Ellington, Duke was going to call a tune, and this new musician said "I don't understand. What are the chords to this tune?" And Duke said, "Listen, sweetie, listen." The other thing I remember of Duke, talking about sound, he said, "The sound of a musician is his soul," which is pretty much what you were saying.

JF: Well, something you mentioned earlier about hearing a band of students, and all of them sounded the same. That was one thing that was really extraordinary about Duke's band. So many individual sounds, yet there were times when the whole was greater than the sum of its parts. That the band really was more together than a lot of people thought, and it had that really, really great sound. When I listen to something like "The Far East Suite" and I hear Johnny Hodges soloing on "Isvahan" and I hear the band in the background, I'm not hearing Clark Terry playing a trumpet part, I'm not hearing Cootie Williams playing a trumpet part, I'm not hearing Britt Woodman playing a trumpet part, or Laurence Brown playing a trumpet part, or trombone part, rather. I'm hearing music.

NH: And yet, that came about in part because, as Duke used to say, "I write for each player in the band." He once said, "I write for their strengths and their weaknesses." But then there came a time when there weren't any technical weaknesses.

JF: Well, I always kind of regret—I got a call when I was about nineteen years old to join Duke Ellington's band. At the time I was a member of the Thad Jones-Mel Lewis Orchestra, and I decided to stay with Thad and Mel. I was young, I was nineteen, I didn't know that Duke would be gone in just a few years. I didn't know. We never know. That's one of the things I try to impart to my students. When Frank Wess goes to play at the Vanguard a few weeks ago, you go hear him! You go to listen to what he's doing! He's your link to Marshall Royal and Lester Young and Ben Webster. You go listen and study with him and ask him questions.

NH: Phil Woods once said that one of the things young players may miss unless they have you as a teacher occasionally, he said, "On the band bus, and playing with the older musicians—" when he broke in, "you learn so much by what they say and do."

JF: There's always been a mentoring aspect to jazz music. When a new kid came on the band, you have somebody like—someone sitting next to him who's much older, he'd say—"Look, don't spend your money there. You gotta send some money home every week to your mom." And they would take him aside, and some people followed that advice and others didn't. But there was always that mentoring aspect, and I remember one time asking Dizzy. Dizzy was always very open—not even just with me, but with all musicians who came to him and wanted to talk about music—he would sit down at the piano for hours.

NH: I remember he used to say, "It's all there on the piano!"

JF: He'd be right in the middle of an interview and say, "What's this?" and he'd sit there at the piano, and sit there. So I asked Dizzy, when you were younger, who showed you these things? He said, "Nobody." I think it was because Dizzy was curious about music. One of the stories he used to tell is he went to a jam session once and they played a song in a different key from the key Dizzy knew it in, and Dizzy thought he knew the song and said, "Every note I hit was wrong. Wrong!" He went home and he cried, but he vowed to learn music in every key.

NH: So what you have to have to begin with is a curiosity and a determination.

JF: Determination, curiosity, perseverance, and I think a passion, a passion and a love for this music. If a student, if a young musician is into jazz because he wants to make a lot of money, he's in it for the wrong reasons. It probably won't happen. But if you're in it because you love this music and you'll play it no matter what, you're on the right track.

NH: It's like one of my mentors as a journalist, Izzy Stone, once said, "If you're becoming a journalist to change the world, find another day job. You've gotta do it because you have a passion for finding out things."

JF: Same thing with jazz. Same thing. It's one of those elusive art forms, you know, it's not like looking at a painting by Matisse or Renoir. You hear these sounds, and then, if they're not recorded on record, they're here in your head, but—sometimes the memory can be faulty. I like to try—sometimes I have trumpet students, I don't play a lot at my trumpet lessons—but sometimes I like to try to let my trumpet students get a little bit full of themselves. And if they're working on a Roy Eldridge solo or working on something by Dizzy, even something from the Abrin's book. Here's how we want to get sound out of the instrument.

NH: One of the many players you worked with was Charles Mingus, and I'm interested because he was an old friend of mine. What did you learn, if anything, when you worked with Mingus?

JF: Let me first say that the first time I met Mingus, I called him Charlie, and he got so mad! And of course, when I was growing up I would read stories; I liked to read about jazz, and I read about how angry and violent he could get, so I thought he was going to hit me in the mouth, and I got scared!

NH: He did that once to somebody!

JF: Yeah. But I joined Mingus when I was eighteen. It came about through Roy Eldridge, Snooky Young and Clark Terry. I met Clark Terry in California when I was seventeen, and I talked to him about moving to New York, and he said, "Call me when you get to New York." I called him when I got to New York, and he was on the way to *The Tonight Show,* and he said, "Come on by!" So I went to *The Tonight Show,* and he introduced me to Snooky Young. He introduced me as this young trumpet player, "He's playing with Hamp's band now, he's got everything going for him!" But Clark had never heard me play, and he was introducing me to all of the *Tonight Show* staff, Jon Frost, Doc Severinsen, Dick Perry, Jimmy Maxwell, Snooky, without having heard me. So, about me and Mingus, he had written a piece for Roy Eldridge, and Roy's doctor wouldn't let him play it because he had just gotten ill.

NH: You mean it was just too demanding, huh?

JF: Mmm hmm. So Mingus said, "I'll get Snooky Young for this concert coming up." And this was in December or January—the concert took place in February of 1972. Snooky was in the process of changing locations. He was moving from New York to California with the *Tonight Show* band, and Snooky said, "Why don't you call this kid JON FADDIS?" So he did. Mingus did. He called me to come in and play this piece, and I looked at the piece, and I was scared to say anything to this guy because of his reputation. He said, "You think you can play this?" and I said, "Yeah, I think it will be OK." We had a rehearsal with the full band, and the band had cats like Gene Ammons and Charles McPherson, all these guys in the band. The concert was—I think the concert was that night. And between— during a break at the rehearsal—I didn't know that you could leave tickets at the box office for someone. We were rehearsing at Carrol's or somewhere like that and the concert was at Philharmonic Hall. So my roommate at the time was Lew Soloff, and he wanted a couple of tickets, so I went to the box office and bought a couple of tickets and tried to drive in a taxi across town to his place and get back in time for the rehearsal. We had an hour break, and I was late. Mingus had sent the band home, and when I walked in, it was just Mingus, and he looked at me, and he said, "You f—'d up my rehearsal!" and he started screaming at me. "I'm sorry, Mr. Mingus, I'm sorry! I had to go give—" and he was mad. But then, when we played the concert that night it was very successful. It was like Mingus's homecoming, and here was this young kid playing this trumpet piece. Bill Cosby was the MC. Dizzy had just gotten out of the hospital, and he came up to me and said, "Boy, I came out of my deathbed to hear you." Lee Morgan was there, Jimmy Owens, Donald Byrd—there were all these trumpet players there! And that was sort of my coming out. After that, Mingus asked me to do some gigs with his small group. I went to Chicago with his group, learned the music, and then I went to Europe with his group. While this was going on, my father was saying, "You got to go to college. You need to have something to fall back on in case you don't make it. You need an education." My father grew up during the Depression. He was very involved in the civil rights movement. Education was very, very important to him. But I was sort of living my dream. I did tell Mingus, "Mingus, I have to leave early from the tour because I'm going to go to Manhattan School of Music and study music." And he looked at me and says, "Boy, you in the best college you could be in now!" I didn't understand what he meant at the time. Now I understand what he meant.

NH: That reminds me, I was in Thelonious Monk's apartment when Gigi Gryce came in, you know the young alto player, the arranger. He said, "Monk, I just got into Juilliard!" And Monk had one of his pregnant silences and looked up and said, "I hope you don't lose it there." But you don't advise that to your students.

JF: No, because the scene has changed, and jazz education is a very important part of the jazz scene. One of the things that is difficult for jazz musicians, and one of the reasons why the Dizzy Gillespie Fund at Englewood Hospital is so important and why the Jazz Foundation of America is so important—

NH: I should say to viewers—the Jazz Foundation and Dr. Forte at Englewood Hospital arranged—when Dizzy was dying, he said to Dr. Forte who was his oncologist, etc., "I want jazz musicians to be able to have the kind of treatment that I'm having," and they worked it out. And because of the Jazz Foundation, musicians get everything free at Englewood Hospital.

JF: And often, musicians who are just playing in clubs don't have insurance or medical plans or anything like that, so it's unfortunate, but one of the things becoming a teacher can do is it can allow you to have a pension fund. It can allow you to have medical insurance. And I tell students, "You never know what's going to happen in your life." But not only teaching to have insurance or pension, but teaching to try and impart the correct information to students. Because there is a lot of—we were talking earlier, speaking earlier about editors and misinformation that is in a lot of books—we have to try and make sure the right information gets to the up and coming, the other generations. So teaching and jazz education is an important part of the scene now.

NH: That's very important to say. By the way, speaking of miseducation or misinformation; Mingus did not take what he considered ignorant music criticism lightly. He not only wrote to the publications, he once in a while went to their offices. Have you ever had that feeling when you read something about you?

JF: No. I mean, yes, I've had the feeling, but I've never acted on it. Well, Mingus tended to act out. I was once preparing with David Sanborn, we were going to play together in Cannes, on the French Riviera. He was going, "What are we going to play?" I said, "Well, we can play 'A Night In Tunisia,'" I say. So I sit at the piano and say these are the chords. And we started, somehow we got on the topic of reviews, and he had scathing reviews, but I respect David because he really wants to learn this music. He studies with George Coleman, and even though he's successful playing another type of music that wouldn't really be considered jazz, he's into the music. And reviews are something, both good and bad, that I tend to take with a grain of salt.

NH: Now, if you were teaching jazz critics, what would you tell them they ought to do before they write?

JF: Before they write.

NH: Before they dare write!

JF: I would tell them to get a hold of the *Modern Language Association Handbook* and learn about grammar and word choices. I would have them read a book of critical reviews of the classical musicians, and a critic would say, "So-and-so's music will never amount to anything," and they're talking about Stravinsky's *Rite of Spring*. The book is *The Lexicon of Musical Invective*.

NH: Slonimsky, yeah.

JF: And I'd have 'em read those reviews and say, "OK?" But I'd also tell them, "Look, with jazz, one review can make or break someone, and you're really affecting not just them but you're affecting their band mates and families."

NH: Yeah, [you're] talking about what made me feel very timorous about that aspect of the business, yes.

JF: So even if you do not like what the person is playing, or you don't like the way the band sounds, with jazz music you should put as positive a spin on it as you can, because it's, one, a very small part of the music business; and two, many people don't understand what jazz is. And a person may be just glancing through the paper, and it says up top, "Jazz Review," and they read this negative review, and they'll say, "Just like I thought! I don't want to hear any jazz," and they'll never go out and hear jazz.

NH: The way I ended my guilt after I left *Down Beat,* is that since then I've only written about musicians whose music I liked and felt I could understand.

JF: I think that's an admirable quality that you have.

NH: It just made me feel better!

JF: Because I've read about reviewers reviewing concerts that they weren't even visiting, or weren't even listening to.

NH: You spend a great deal of time teaching, and in view of the fact that every once in a while there are writers, so-called critics, who declare the obituary of jazz or say unless you get to the cutting edge it won't last, how optimistic are you about the future generations of jazz listeners?

JF: When I go to festivals, not only in Europe or Japan, but in this country, sometimes what is being passed to the audience as jazz isn't really jazz. I think the listeners have a responsibility, though. It's not just a background music. It's not just a music that's used on radio and television commercials. A lot of musicians, a lot of people have died and fought very hard for this music. It's a music that has some parts of it that are scripted, but most of it is made up on the spur of the moment. There's no other music really like that, and I think the listener has a responsibility to study the music and understand what it is and understand what the different styles are. What is the difference between New Orleans jazz and that polyphonic music, and bebop. What is free jazz and how is that different from New Orleans jazz? And I think the key is getting to the young early. Getting to the youth of today. Because when they grow up and their peers are all listening to pop music, R&B, rap, hip-hop, jazz has to fight that much harder to be respected.

NH: One thing I tell journalists about interviews, always when it's almost over, say to the person, "Is there anything I haven't asked that I should have?" Or, "Anything that you want to say that I didn't ask about?"

JF: Well, let's see, is there anything? Well, I am very involved in education, in jazz education, and one of the things I would say that you didn't really ask about is some of my mentors aside from Dizzy. Dizzy took me under his wing, Snooky Young took me under his wing, Thad Jones took me under his wing, Mel Lewis took me under his wing, Clark Terry took me under his wing, Sweets Edison took me under his wing, Buddy Tate was one that sorta took me under his wing, and all of these musicians that had nothing to really gain by being encouraging to this young trumpet player who used to love, and still does, love to tell corny jokes. But they did it of their own volition because they were looking at the big picture, and they were trying to see the future of the music, and they did it without any ifs, ands, or buts when I asked them questions. One of the best pieces of advice came to me from Sweets Edison. We were playing the *Sammy Davis Jr. Show* together, and I was twenty-two or twenty-three, I don't know. I was playing first trumpet sitting next to Fip Ricard, who played with Basie's, and Sweets is in there, and he says, "Save your money and don't mess with Uncle Sam." And what he was saying to me, I didn't understand until much later, when I got in trouble with Uncle Sam. But these musicians never charged me a penny for a lesson, and that is why today, if someone asks me for a lesson and I have time, I won't charge them. I will say something [like], "Well, if you really insist on putting out some money"—I will say, "Make a donation to the James Moody Scholarship Fund at Purchase College, or the Jazz Foundation of America," or something like that.

NH: That reminds me of a trumpet player few people talk about anymore, Frankie Newton, and Frankie once told me that he was teaching and somebody didn't have the money and he said, "That's OK. Anybody who wants to know about this music, I'll teach." So there's a phrase I've used a few times about all you people, "the Family of Jazz." I have that sense, and it's certainly international.

JF: And unfortunately, many of our fathers, mothers, brothers and sisters have passed on. And then, before you know it, you have young musicians looking up to you, and this came about with me—I wasn't trying to do that—but I became aware of my role in jazz and the future of jazz. It doesn't matter the style one chooses to play, whether one chooses to play New Orleans music, one chooses to play swing, one chooses to play bebop, but you really, really have to be sincere in your approach to the music, and you really have to love it. You have to love it.

62 | A House of Swing—for All Ages

When I became the New York editor of *Down Beat* (then the "jazz bible") in 1953, Birdland, named for Charlie Parker, proclaimed itself in its advertising "the jazz corner of the world." Now, a half century later, the multidimensional Jazz at Lincoln Center (JALC) in the Time Warner Center could well become the hub of the global jazz community under Adrian Ellis, its exceptionally creative and pragmatic executive director as of October 2007.

"The purpose of Jazz at Lincoln Center," Mr. Ellis told me, "is to help secure a vital future for jazz," and that requires "an informed and receptive audience. That's where we can probably make the biggest difference in the longer term."

Adding sudden urgency to his mission was the 18 April, 2008, filing for bankruptcy of the largest organization in the history of jazz—the International Association for Jazz Education—which represented 10,000 educators in fifty-six countries while being involved in hundreds of jazz programs at American colleges. Its effect was to considerably increase the study and appreciation of jazz and its history, and thereby to add to its listeners.

I have known the two most successful enlargers of the international jazz audience, impresarios Norman Granz and George Wein; but neither of them had Mr. Ellis's wide-ranging experience in strategic operations planning. He has worked for such cultural organizations as the British Museum, the Pew Charitable Trusts in Philadelphia and the New York City Opera, among others.

An economist by education and training, Mr. Ellis founded AEA Consulting, a management firm with offices in New York and London. He has also advised the

Royal Shakespeare Company, the National Gallery in London, the San Francisco Opera and the Doris Duke Charitable Foundation.

As a boy in North Wales, he was a dedicated listener to Voice of America programs hosted by Willis Conover, the single most effective jazz evangelist in the history of the genre. And, in furtherance of spreading the gospel to his own nine-year-old son, Nathaniel, and twelve-year-old daughter, Rebecca, Mr. Ellis has taken them to Dizzy's Club Coca-Cola, one of the performance spaces at Jazz at Lincoln Center.

In its twenty-second year of programming (the last five at the Time Warner Center), the organization that Mr. Ellis heads produced more than 3,000 events in the 2008–09 season at its "House of Swing"; in schools; and during the national and international tours of the Jazz at Lincoln Center Orchestra (headed by the center's artistic director, Wynton Marsalis).

To Mr. Ellis, however, Jazz at Lincoln Center has only begun to swing. "I do not want this to be an isolated, self-regarding institution," he told me. He wants, for example, to increase JALC's already considerable involvement with the students of New York City's schools and to ultimately become a "national pilot for other school systems."

He also is hoping to get into more of the city's neighborhoods, including Harlem. Accordingly, a search started for a Jazz at Lincoln Center Manager of Community Engagement.

An indication of how JALC has already reached into communities nationwide came in 2000 when I visited my alma mater—Boston Latin School. Founded in 1635, the school has long been classically traditional in all its curricula. So it was a revelation, on my return there, to hear a band of youngsters in the music department playing Duke Ellington's "Things Ain't What They Used to Be." Duke's music is not easy to play; but that performance, I told the high schoolers, would have pleased him.

The bandmaster, Paul Pitts, told me his appreciation for JALC's annual Essentially Ellington competition, entered by high school jazz bands across the country. Mr. Pitts explained to me: "We get original charts with a recording of the Jazz at Lincoln Center Orchestra playing them. And after the students study them, we send a recording of our interpretations to the competition in New York." I saw that the original charts had informal instructions from Mr. Marsalis to each high school bandmaster, such as "Make sure they get the proper human and vocal quality to their sound." In 2004, when I attended Boston Latin's alumni dinner as alumnus of the year, the jazz band played Ellington throughout the evening—thanks to the outreach of Jazz at Lincoln Center.

But Jazz at Lincoln Center gets kids long before high school. WeBop! classes are offered to children from eight months (I kid you not!) to five years, along with their parents. They experience the surprise and self-discovery of improvising through scat singing and playing in very elementary instrumental combos. The participants are identified as hipsters (eight to sixteen months); scatters (seventeen to twenty-three months); stompers (two to three years old); the Gumbo Group (three to five); and syncopators (four to five). I've heard several of the scatters, and I can easily imagine Ella Fitzgerald's delight in joining in.

Mr. Ellis's educational vision also includes an internationally available jazz civics class to demonstrate the interactive essence—the gestalt—of the music. Master drummer Max Roach used to tell me that jazz is like the Constitution—individual voices listening attentively to each other and creating a distinctive, invigorating whole.

Mr. Ellis believes this is a vital part of jazz education: "Jazz requires each member of a group to improvise, but it won't work for a soloist or an ensemble if the musicians don't play in balance. For example, the drummer can't play too loud or you can't hear the bassist. These group dynamics teach the importance of choice. Some choices require sacrifice . . . to achieve the ultimate goal of an ongoing swinging groove. At any given point you are forced to accept something you really don't like. And that's the truth of swing too. You might not like the time someone else is playing, but to sound good as a group and play together you have to work with it and make all your times come together."

Mr. Ellis hastens to add, though, that the mission of this jazz education is "securing a vital future for the music." "Jazz is an end in itself," he notes, "an absolute value, at its best an extraordinary and beautiful manifestation of human potential. But the music also has a role in helping each of us understand how to play a fulfilling and creative role in the complex, structured, improvisatory project that is American democracy."

To enable anyone in the world with a computer to be part of the learning experience, Jazz at Lincoln Center has—with Veotag Inc.—created "Education Events Online" (www.jalc.org/jazzED/streamin). You can click on "Trombone Master Class" with Wycliffe Gordon and Joseph Allesi; "Jazz Talk: Walkin' and Swingin': Mary Lou Williams"; or "Master Class with Gerald Wilson" on his history with Duke Ellington, Ella Fitzgerald and Jimmie Lunceford.

But Mr. Ellis would also like to bring people—especially a younger, more diverse audience—to the House of Swing itself at the Time Warner building. Thanks to Mr. Ellis's plans, "The atrium and adjacent areas will contain thematic exhibitions, more jazz-related retail shops, an enhanced Jazz Hall of Fame, café and bar." It will be, he tells me, "an information and orientation point for jazz in New York City."

The first Saturday of most months, audiences can listen for free to the "Jazz Battles": two jousting musicians on the same instrument. And, to further lower the financial barrier for jazz, there are $10 "hot seats" for each Jazz at Lincoln Center production in the Rose Theater. They're available to the general public on the day of each performance.

The House of Swing is grooving—an exuberantly evolving force in the international jazz community.

63 | Inside the Jazz Experience

RON CARTER

NAT HENTOFF: This is Nat Hentoff from the internationally known and visited Blue Note Jazz Club in New York City. Our guest has been rightfully described as the musician's musician. He's a bassist, cellist, composer, leader. Now, to start, John Coltrane told me once that he always wanted to know more of how his music affected the listeners. Does that ever occur to you at all? *Is* that a factor in your reaction?

RON CARTER: Well my feeling is it's always nice to know whether the listener takes something away from the performance. A melody, a rhythm, a certain intensity. But my first responsibility is to make the musicians that I'm playing with play like they wouldn't play if I were not standing there.

NH: That's the key!

RC: For me. Yeah. You know, of course every musician, every artist—dancer, painter, sculptor—they hope the viewer or the listener to their art leaves there feeling a better person, more in tune to their specific art, painting or song. I think the artists' real first commitment is to make the people around him, as a bass player, better.

NH: That's it.

RC: You know, when Trane plays ninety-five choruses and sits down he's basically done for that tune. But the band is still going! Like the rhythm section is still the people who make the stuff happen.

NH: Now, in an interview recently in *Jazz Improv* magazine, a very good magazine, the New York issue, you said something that reminded me of conversations I had years ago with a remarkable poet and expert on the blues, Sterling Brown. He taught at Howard University for about fifty years, and he told me he was not allowed to include jazz in his courses because they thought it came from an unsavory background. What he did was he brought in Stravinsky's *Ragtime [for Eleven Instruments]*, some pieces by Milhaud, who was influenced by jazz, and said to the students, "Now, I'll show you where it came from," and he put on some Luckey Roberts and Duke Ellington. Also, some years later Adam Clayton

Powell had a paper in New York in competition with *Amsterdam News.* I knew the editor. He knew jazz—I saw him at jazz clubs—but he never used jazz, and the implication was [that] it wasn't right for the image. So what you said in that interview was that "the black press, the black media, has a great deal of responsibility in the lack of, and the possibility of, increasing the visibility and viability of jazz." Is that still pretty much the case?

RC: The only difference is that if I were writing it verbally I would underline all of those words. I think that the media in general tends to look at jazz sideways, and they're more inclined to give a sound byte to any kind of music, you know. All the current talent shows they have on TV now, they're all hyping music from a genre that really isn't broad—

NH: Or deep!

RC: To say the—yeah, deep! (motions with fingers to show small amount and laughs) But I think that the black media, in particular, I think, have a responsibility to make the public aware. Not more aware, but aware that there's an art form out here that is their country's hue and cry. The State Department, for all that they do that's not so hot, what they do in jazz, that's very good, as often as they do it, or as seldom as they do it, is to sponsor tours of jazz bands to all these countries. You know, for years Willis Conover got the music from uptown—

NH: I wish we had Willis Conover now, because he made the music known all over the world.

RC: Absolutely, and today when I travel to Eastern Europe, Poland, Czechoslovakia, we hear stories of knowing our music through the Voice of America!

NH: That was Willis!

RC: Yeah, yeah. My feeling is still the same, that if papers like the *Amsterdam News,* like the *Chicago Defender,* like the *LA Sentinel,* like the *Pittsburgh Courier,* if they still exist—it's their responsibility not just to advertise Kangol hats and the latest wedding and church service but to say, "This music, which is your contribution to more than your neighborhood—"

NH: It's interesting, because when I was in my teens and beyond, I would read the black press for civil rights news and I would never find jazz in it! Currently, perhaps the major figure in the media is Oprah Winfrey. Has she heard much jazz?

RC: No, the story is that she's not a fan of the music. I've been threatening to start a rumor—you know, rumors sometimes come true—and the rumor I'm thinking of starting is that my quartet will appear on the Oprah Winfrey Show for Thanksgiving. That gives them three months to catch up to my rumor. Again, people like that, who have such power, really, I mean she'll say, "This is my favorite book of the month," and it'll sell a million copies in two weeks! Or, "This is my favorite diet product, or this is my favorite"—and man, because of her viewership, she makes stuff move! It would be nice to know that she feels that she can help this music, which is also a part of her music, available to more than 400 people in a nightclub in a week.

NH: Well, maybe if Obama becomes president you can tell her that, if he knows anything about jazz!

RC: Well, the story is that he's got John Coltrane on his iPod, so we'll see if he has any interest in anything other than John Coltrane.

NH: Well, Coltrane isn't bad to start with!

RC: Absolutely not! There's no question about that.

NH: Now, you're a leader, and you've also been a prominent sideman with prominent leaders. Miles Davis, Chico Hamilton, Herbie Hancock, Eric Dolphy, Wayne Shorter. At first, when you're with a band with a strong-willed leader, and you're pretty strong-willed, what are the problems, if any, of adjustment?

RC: Well, I think my first job is to see—now, I hate this kind of term—where he's coming from. I have to find out what works for him and how long am I willing to do this knowing that it works for him. When I've done these gigs with these strong-willed leaders, Joe Henderson for example, I'm inclined to play—if I've got a two-set night—I'm inclined to play what I know—from listening to them and playing with them before—what works for them. So for me, the first set is for them. If I've kind of doped out what works for them, the second set is what works for me. The second set is my job, my feeling, my determination to play something that they're not expecting to hear. If I can get them to give me their attention for the second set, hopefully my different notes and my different rhythms will make them go a direction that is not on that normal path. Sometimes they like it, sometimes they don't.

NH: What happens, if it ever happens, if the drummer and the pianist aren't quite attuned to your rhythms?

RC: Well, then I'll do it 'cause there's only but three of us. I'll say this to my students who come in complaining about what a drag the gig is, and I'll say, "Listen, you know, every job you play is like going to school free. If the music isn't your personal taste but you can make it through this gig, however long it lasts—a week, two nights—your job is to play the best half note you can find. Or the best pitch you can find. Or if you're playing a bass part, can you play this bass part correct every time you have to play it." So on those gigs where the level of rhythmic curiosity and harmonic daring is not to the level that I'm able to go in doing that, then my job is to find what kind of notes can I play to make the piano player feel more comfortable. And maybe I shouldn't be so rhythmically aggressive with that drummer whose interest is not that. For example, to play with Connie Kay is different than playing with Tony Williams. They both have different comfort zones. My job is to see how comfortable I can get playing in their comfort zones. Then if I can pull them a little more to my zone for the next night, hey, we're in business!

NH: Now, how much time do you have these days for teaching? I know you've been a professor in residence at various places. Are you still with City University?

RC: No, I retired from City College three years ago. But there I taught more than just bass, I taught jazz composition, I taught arranging, I had two ensembles and listened to the seven bass players who were there. But right now I'm on the road so much, my teaching is limited to five private students who come weekly.

NH: When I once asked Duke Ellington, "What do you look for when there's—which was rarely the case—a vacancy" in his band, he said, "I want somebody who knows how to listen." What qualities do you look for in a student, or try to bring out. Is that one of them?

RC: One of the first things I try to get them aware of is intonation. You know, Nat, bass players are, for me, the low men on the band totem poll. Generally speaking, they take lessons later in life. The lessons are generally not by a bass player, they're just kind of filling in for lack of a teacher. They're in an ensemble, and since they're so far behind, generally speaking, everybody else in the band, as far as harmony, keyboard playing—they don't get the kind of attention they need in that band, to be able to make their harmony level, their compositional skills, get better, their sense of form improve or understand what form is, intonation, playing the same notes a different place on the bass, knowing the instrument—most of them don't have that kind of help internally.

NH: Yeah, that's interesting, you mean, internally that has to be—

RC: In the band. No one says, the trumpet player won't say, "Hey why don't you play this note here rather than here," or the drummer won't say, "You know, that A is kind of out of tune with my bass drum. Can you fix that note?" So I make them aware, first of all, of those kinds of situations. Secondly, I have what I call "bass 101," and I try to explain to them that the bass is a chamber, a box, three feet by two and a half feet by maybe eight inches with a stick in between, the sound post, and your job is to make this box sound as well as you can, sound as resonant, sound as beautiful as you can, and these are the facts to make this box work. The next thing that we get to is reading music. Now I don't mean F chord or C chord. Can you read a bass part? 'Cause composers, ya know, they're writing real bass parts for bass players. Now a Gil Evans chart, man, or a Don Sebeski arrangement, they've got notes all over the place, man, and you gotta know where these notes are, ya know? And then we do exercises and etudes to increase their skill level.

NH: Ya know, Mingus once told me, when he was coming up, he was studying with a bass player in the symphony orchestra out in Los Angeles, and he was practicing all the time, and then he said, "Suddenly, the bass became part of me and I became part of the bass." Does that make any sense to you?

RC: I can understand how he could feel that, especially being Charles. For me to express that feeling out loud, it kind of takes the mystery that ties me to the bass. I kind of like not knowing that it happens. I like knowing and being a part of it, but I don't want to know it.

NH: Now, another thing you said in your interview in *Jazz Improv* magazine was when you were coming up but already very proficient, you were told by, of all people, one of the icons of classical music, Leopold Stokowski, conductor of the Philadelphia Orchestra, that classical music audiences weren't ready yet for black players.

RC: Mmm hmm, I think what he said was the board, the people who do the hiring—

NH: 'Cause that reminded me of Art Davis, who fought that for a long time, and he filed a discrimination suit against the New York Philharmonic, and it finally was dismissed after a long time, but I wonder, part of the pressure that was being put on after that happened, and other people pointed it out, they started using blind auditions. Is that still the case?

RC: As far as I know, but whenever this topic comes up, I kind of duck it because it's still kind of painful for me, even at my age and sixty years later, but I ask these questioners—is that the right person?—these interviewers. I say, "Look, before I answer this question, whatever happens, that'd be my answer to you. I would like you to have taken any of the five top orchestras and then look through their photographs for ten-year periods of time. You tell me since 1960 how many additions to the orchestra they have of African Americans. And they will talk about my answer to you. It hasn't changed much, you know, and my concern— one of my concerns—is that these music schools continue to turn out African-American players with no jobs in sight in the orchestras. Now, not only is there still a discriminatory base, I feel, but when orchestras have hirings, those players stay there twenty or thirty years, man! They don't do a two-week stint and quit. They're there, man! They're there till they get tired of being there. And to know that you're walking in to a field where the turnover is pretty slim after spending four or five years practicing seven hours a day in that kind of heated atmosphere, looking for a job that doesn't exist is shameful! Especially harmful to an African American whose chances of having a successful solo career as a violinist are not great, and these orchestras he's looking at [that] are not the top flight that he's spent his dreams and time to prepare himself to be a member of, are not available to him. Now what are you going to do?

NH: You know, that's something for viewers of this to think about, 'cause every time I see a symphony orchestra on public television I do the same thing, I look [to see] how many black players are there? There are very, very few.

RC: My comment about when the [New York] Philharmonic goes uptown to play the Abyssinian Church for Thanksgiving holidays—every year they play a service up there, at Thanksgiving or Christmas—and I say, keep the buses running so they can get out before the last note dies out, you know? I mean, what kind of cultural exchange is that, man?

NH: Now, we were talking about how difficult it would be if there were black players in any quantity about their getting gigs. This is a chronic question these days; there are so many schools, not only places like Berklee, but in universities that prepare and teach jazz musicians to be musicians, like North Texas State. What about the job problems now, because there are practically no territory bands, very few big bands—where do they break in? How do they break in?

RC: Well, you know, given—the other problem is, there are fewer major recording companies. CBS doesn't do much anymore—only really Blue Note Records that has a major recording company mentality. But there are enough of what I call pocketbook labels, that produce some really good jazz records. But I think the survival of those jazz school graduates depends on how aggressively they are willing to make their gigs. To create work for themselves. There are a lot of small rooms around New York, man, that we see around in the newspapers—in the *JazzTimes* and in local jazz magazines—there must be twenty or thirty rooms in New York that have duos or trios playing. They work a couple of nights a week, you know, and if their presence proves to increase the customership of that restaurant, then they stay another two weeks! So I think it behooves those people who walk into a field where there are no longer tremendous major label jazz recordings, and there are no territory bands, and the big bands only work in your imagination—they have to make a place for themselves to play.

NH: You know that goes back to what you were saying about the media as a whole. The *New York Times* has two jazz writers, and they're good. But how many papers around the county, even metropolitan papers, have that much coverage?

RC: Not that many, and I kind of get disappointed in the *New York Times* on occasion, because I don't like to use the bandstand verbally for political format, a political forum. I'll ask the guys in the band if they mind my saying the following thing: "Ladies and gentleman, I just bought the *New York Times* today, at an increasing price I might add, and their banner says over here is the weather, and here it says 'All the News That's Fit to Print.'" Now we've been working at this club, this is our sixth night. We played two sets, and certainly our first night is played in time before the newspaper is put to bed, as they say in the business, and able to be prepared for reviews the next day. Well, we haven't made it yet. So that tells me that this music's not fit to print—in their view!

NH: If you were still a professor, and in the curriculum you chose you had a class of people who wanted to become jazz critics, jazz writers. What kind of a curriculum would you set for them? What would you be looking for in them that you could reach so they would know what they were doing?

RC: Well, the first thing I would do is have them go to two nightclubs a week. I would have them write a review of that band for class to see if they'd be able to pick out things in this group, or this music, or individual players who caught their attention, to see if they have the writing skill to write a review of this group with those elements that they felt impressed them enough to write enough about for an audience who clearly could not get there. The second thing I'd do is to go to a record date a week to find out how do they make records. That what you have on your turntable at home is the product of X number of hours of work. The prerecording, the hiring of the band, getting the live recording, getting the arrangements, getting the sound, I mean, there's a whole process before you open up this package and play this record. Well, most reviewers they review the sound on the disc without knowing what it takes to make it work. I think that's important to understand what makes a record a record. Good or bad, it's a process. And next I'd like them to take up an instrument. I don't care what it is, man, saxophone, piano, drums, to find out what kind of skill level it takes to get past the squeaking stage. If they can do these three items for me in the fashion that shows they are capable of making these kinds of critical decisions, which affect not only the musician's career but the people who come to the club to make the club sustain itself, we will talk about it.

NH: You know, you've laid out the proper curriculum. I've never heard this before, but it is so exact and precise, I'm going to write about it and see what'll happen—if anyone will do it!

RC: Please! Yes! Well, you know we all complain about critics, and I'm sure every art field complains about a critic who's never been a dancer or who's never been a sculptor or a painter. Well, that's what that is! And until they sit down at some point along the way and devise a way to enlighten these people as to what their responsibility is, the best way to be placed in a position to really have a view of what it takes to make this product—dance, theater, acting, jazz, and earn a living at it! It's a whole other story, you know?

NH: Speaking of making a living, both of us are involved in the Jazz Foundation of America, and I don't know how many people who really like the music and collect the records know how many musicians who are no longer in fashion or are sick or whatever, have problems paying the rent! Let alone, I don't think many jazz musicians have pension plans or medical insurance. So what the Jazz Foundation does is take care of people like that, and they even have—because of Dizzy Gillespie, they provide free surgery and free medical care. But still, there must be many musicians who have never heard of the foundation. How serious is that for people who are no longer able to play regularly.

RC: Well, it's a problem that everyone's facing in these days and times, with the economy and the situation the way it is. But I think what I'd like to see happen is for this foundation—again, speaking of the media, and since the primary players who have expressed a need for this kind of service are African American—why doesn't the *Amsterdam News* do a weekly story on someone that they've helped with a little thing at the bottom: "To join this Jazz Foundation, contribute this much money as a tax write-off." I think people who don't even know the music understand that situation. Those who are able to make a contribution to that kind of worthwhile organization would do it if they knew it existed. And again, the black media could very well do that. Why aren't they stepping up to the plate?

NH: Now, one of the ideas that Wendy Oxenhorn, who is the executive director of the Jazz Foundation, has is that she is trying to get financing for a musicians' residence. You know, when I was a kid I used to go to the movies and see the trailers and the actors' residence where people who were out of work would get taken care of. Does that sound like a pretty feasible idea to you? It could also be a place where they could get gigs and the like, and they or the media could help?

RC: I think it's necessary. I've been looking at rents skyrocketing. I drove down an area the other day where there was a parking lot near a studio. It's now a big hole in the ground and they're going to put a big apartment building now. As you know, several studios in New York have literally disappeared off the face of the earth. These residences are necessary for the jazz musician who, as you mentioned before, is having a difficult time maintaining his status given the difficult times. And clearly there are needs for this kind of housing for the arts in general. Again, the media needs to step up and say, well this is a worthwhile organization, another one, and what we can do for you is give you a plug on the six o'clock news or have a two-minute spot featuring this need and see what kind of interest we can raise. Of course, the bigger problem is that we're spending ten billion dollars in this [Iraq] War, man, and money's going down the tubes.

NH: Yeah. And now as we're talking, we're spending domestically about billions on what's left of the economy at the moment.

RC: Please, really.

NH: Now, something else that could be done, it seems to me, but isn't being done in many of the schools around the country, the public schools. Because of the No Child Left Behind Act, which is well intentioned, the kids are being taught to take tests in reading and math, which of course you need, but hardly any of the schools any more have courses in music, or arts, etc., and one of the things that bothers me: the Constitution. Most kids don't know what the Constitution is about, but why not music classes, 'cause that's a great way of getting people interested in school!

RC: Well, I just read this morning that our mayor, during this budget crisis, has determined on a number of percent cuts for school music budgets. I mean, that's another music class that maybe still existed that's gone. That's been the case throughout these financial crisis times. The first thing to get cut is music—sports always has a life—and I think—

NH: That's because there's an audience for sports, and we haven't been able to create enough of an audience for music!

RC: A big enough audience, yeah. I think what we're looking at now is the possibility that another Bird, another Charlie Parker, didn't get a chance to try his wings out because there's no music in school. And that really frightens me, that we're passing up the chance for another genius to come along, or a Miles, or a Monk—kids who could develop to that mindset if they had enough encouragement when they were eight or nine years old in the public school system.

NH: That reminds me, when Charlie Parker died, Art Blakey said the next day, what really saddened him was not only the death, but, he said, "how many kids in school, not only blacks, but how many kids even know who he was?"

RC: Yes. It's a tragedy, yeah.

NH: I once went to a school in Harlem. I brought them some Duke Ellington records. To them it was exotic music.

RC: Yeah. Well, you know, the problem again is that there are no facilities and no money to allow these kinds of programs to take place. The local union here does what they can for school concerts, and you play for the kids and they love it, but you're gone. It's not a half hour a day for music. Until we get into that mindset, music in general and the arts in general will continue to scuffle, not just to find an audience, but to find creators for that audience.

NH: Now, getting to the music itself again, I found a very inspiring close to Oscar Peterson's autobiography, *The Odyssey*. He spoke about, there are times when you're playing and everything's working. The people you're playing with, you yourself. He said, "It's a transcendent experience. You feel there's nothing you can't do!" How often does that happen?

RC: Not often enough, but I know the feeling. When I had my seventieth birthday party concert at Carnegie Hall, June 24, 2007, when I walked on the stage, just me, no one else on the bandstand on the stage, just me—in a nice-looking tuxedo, by the way. I got this tremendous applause and I was ready to go home, man. I had done all I could do, I was ready to leave. I understand that feeling, I think we all look for that moment, when anything is possible.

NH: Now, for the first time in its existence, the National Endowment for the Arts, the guy in charge now, Dana Gioia has actually tried to do something for this music. He's leaving next year! Suppose the next president, whoever he may be, makes the really important decision to make Ron Carter head of the National Endowment for the Arts. What would you do with the scope, depending on if Congress came up with the same amount of money, what would you do in terms of spreading the word.

RC: That's not a tough question to answer, it's a tough question to verbalize, and the two aren't the same. I think the first thing I would do is find someone who could tell me how many music programs have been taken out of the schools. The next step would be, how can I get it [them] back in there. I think the third thing I would try to do is have increased funding for the arts programs, because you know [the cost of] travel is going through the roof, and these places that are not on the immediate travel path need to have this exposure, but the cost of getting the band from point A to point B is ridiculous! And it's getting higher. I'd like to have an increase in funding for travel. Not for the business necessarily, but the cost of getting from point A to point B. I think the last thing I'd try to do is to try to find some air time with this radio or television to present one important artist a week.

NH: Let's say public radio would be the place to start with!

RC: Well, I'm not sure. I kind of read the polls and the newspaper and stuff like that, and talking to public radio station people, I say "Now look, I see this record on the charts, 4 or 5 or whatever the number is, and according to the sound scan these records aren't selling that number of copies to be in this location. And they tell me that people who listen to NPR stations are great listeners, but they aren't necessarily supporters of an item. You know, all of them like jazz but all of them don't go out and buy that record. So I would rather try a major nonpublic radio station.

NH: Yeah, if you could get one that isn't so part of a corporate scene.

RC: But that's part of the process, though, man. You gotta get past that first door, man.

NH: Now, there's a member of Congress, I think, who would work enthusiastically with you on this. He came up in the Detroit jazz scene when he was in high school. He told me in his office he has recordings by Miles and Coltrane 'cause when he gets way down he needs a lift, and that's John Conyers.

RC: Yes, I know John very well, and he's been a staunch supporter of this music for years. In fact, he's the one who got written into the Congressional Record how important jazz is. He comes to New York for the ASCAP Convention and IAJE when he has time. Of course, he has his hands full with his primary job, but he's been supporting this music as long as I can remember John being in the area.

NH: As you say, miracles can happen, and maybe one day there will be Ron Carter as head of the National Endowment for the Arts.

RC: Well, I'm not sure I'd take it, but I certainly would be on the advisory committee.

NH: Is there anything I haven't asked about all the time you've been in music— you've created so much, you've worked with so many creators—[anything] that I haven't asked that would be pertinent to people to get more out of this?

RC: My recommendation to an audience who doesn't know this music would be to get three records, three discs. Any one by Duke Ellington, any record by Louis Armstrong, and any record from Miles Davis 1963 to 1968 to understand how music has progressed from point A to this point. And I think if I could get them to sit down long enough to hear, for example, Miles Davis's *Kind of Blue,* or any Louis Armstrong, or Duke Ellington playing Jimmy Blanton. Any of those series of records to introduce them, that this is the music that all the stuff over here is based on, but it starts right here. The last thing I'd try to do is get a radio show and have someone make a weekly program concerning the broad history of this music. Just to make those people who are not aware of all of the influences. I mean, I would have a program saying, this is the theme of John Coltrane but it's over here in this hip-hop record. Or, it's over in this score from this movie, or there's a snapshot of it from this symphony orchestra, just to see that this music, this jazz that they've been kind of not allowed to hear, really, is a part of this whole big picture of music. If I could get that done for them, I'm sure the audiences would improve in size, because now they'd see there's a relevance not just to this music but to music that they'd like.

NH: You know, I've written about this recently. There's a teacher in Queens, an elementary school teacher, who has an idea in teaching that different students have different main interests, or could have them, so she teaches them about art, even in the second grade, and music. And she started playing jazz for them, and they seemed to really take to Coltrane. Something about the music hit them, and they found out through her that the Coltrane home in Queens was about to be sold to a real estate guy who would of course tear it down. And there are people in the area who are working to prevent that, and the kids got very interested, and they started having bake sales, and they had a whole program of Coltrane music in the auditorium. And that's an example. Who would have thought that [of] a bunch of second graders! I think this will last with them a while.

RC: But it was introduced to them in the second grade. All I'm asking, there are a lot of second grades in this country. Not just near Dix Hills, but there are second grades in Detroit, there are second grades in Chicago. Get it to them, and let them decide that this is what they want to listen to for the next twenty years or so.

NH: Yeah, I remember Milt Jackson once said to me, "They talk about jazz isn't popular music, well how could it be when they don't get exposed to it!"

RC: And given that context, if you look at certain ads, there's jazz in the titles—jazz cologne—jazz is a common word in advertising. Whether we hear it or not the word is there. Let's have some music to make it work.

NH: That leads to the usual question. We've been talking about things that have to be done, should be done. How optimistic are you about the survival of the music here. It's already survived a long time in Europe, and I've heard bands from the Soviet Union in the remote areas there. What about this country?

RC: I think three things are helping jazz's survival in this country. One is that the schools of the higher educational level, colleges and universities, are still teaching it. There's still jazz summer camps where kids who maybe don't have a band in their neighborhood go to the summer camps every summer, two. And number three, there are some wonderful players out here, Nat, who are determined to make this music theirs. And as long as they can maintain that focus, given all of the detrimental facts that come their way, as long as they are determined to make this music theirs, personal, we're going to hear the music and be with it for a very long time.

NH: Now, you've accomplished so much. What if anything, what things would you still like to do?

RC: One of my phrases is, "find the best note." I'm still looking for the best set of notes. I think when I lay the bass down, if there would be an epitaph written across the bass, it would be that people thought of me as a "wonderful bass player, but also a great friend." I think the third thing I'd like to do is be able to walk into an airport with the bass and someone knows what it is. (laughs)

NH: Now we were talking about that sense of transcendence, when everything is working. Has anything leaped to your mind about a gig, an experience you had on the stand that keeps resonating every once in a while in your experience?

RC: You know, there was a club in New York called Sweet Basil. It's got a new name now, but it's still there. I was working there with a trio one night in the summer. As you know, the Village in the summer gets very active and people come in from everywhere just for the Village. I'm in this club, Sweet Basil, and we're supposed to start at 9 o'clock and it's now 9:15 and the pianist hasn't shown up. Well, people are getting restless, and they want their money and they're starting to complain about no music and the food isn't right and they're starting to really get antsy. It's now 9:30 and no piano player, and the place—it's Friday night, man—and the place is full. The club owner says, "What do you want to do?" I said, "I got this one," so I went up there by myself and played for forty-five minutes, solo bass. I think people were so stunned to see this guy do that, that I had their attention. When everybody gets frustrated, maybe not finding enough of the right notes or not getting this particular audience's attention, I go back to that zone because I know that it is possible to get that done.

NH: Again, that reminds me that back in Boston, Jo Jones got off the stand and all by himself, he went around the room, I guess he was feeling frustrated with the group or something, and he played on the walls, on the tables, and it was just astonishing, and then he got back, and he had said what he had to say.

RC: Yeah, he was an amazing drummer, too, and a very nice man.

NH: He was also—you probably know this—he was very intent on taking care of young musicians so they would do the right thing for this music. He called them his kiddies.

RC: He called them his "young talent." Yeah, I used to see him at the Vanguard all the time.

NH: And when he died, there was a service for him at St. Peter's Church, and Max Roach, who was one of his kiddies, said that he was playing in Chicago once and he suddenly saw Jo in the audience, and he really put himself all out on the stand, and when he got through he went down there where Jo was and expectantly waited for what Jo would say. And Jo Jones said, "All I could hear was your watch."

RC: (laughs)

NH: And the other thing, I've learned so much from musicians. Dizzy Gillespie told me once, "It took me most of my life to learn what notes not to play." And as a writer, it took me a long time to know that, too.

RC: I can understand that feeling. I mean, one of the things I used to hear Miles do night in and night out is play not a great note tonight but find that same note somewhere else tomorrow night. Make it right.

NH: You know, I had some long interviews with Miles, and he had a very exacting criteria about music. How was he to work with?

RC: Well, you know, there are a lot of, as you know, stories and rumors and things that are not complimentary about him, and I never saw any of those events take place, not in my five years. I found he was a very intense musician. He came to work to play every night no matter what his physical pain was. I mean, every night! That kind of presence demanded the same kind of intensity from the remaining four. He seldom told us what to play or what not to play. He kind of trusted that we were bright enough and intelligent enough and curious enough to know when it wasn't happening and make some adjustments. He was very politically aware. He did various fund-raising benefits for various social organizations. He was generous with his money and time, and it was a great experience for me. And I would like to think that me playing with him was a great experience for him!

NH: One thing I didn't know until I read an interview with you was that they asked you who were the bassists who influenced you as you were starting? And you answered that it wasn't a bassist, it was trombonist J. J. Johnson! What was it about J. J. that hit you?

RC: Well, you know the trombonists of his time, they were really going like this for all of the notes [reaches with hands like trombonist]. I've seen videos of trombonists back at that time, and they were really going as far out there as they could go, and as far as they were allowed to go. I worked opposite J. J. at a club in Rochester for a week, and I noticed he never went this much [holds his hand close to his face] past the bell, it's all in here, you know, and having studied trombone in school—you know the overtone series and what notes are here and what notes are here—and he just had such a command of this series of notes and each range that it was not necessary for him to go out here for those same notes that are right here. I said, "Well if that's possible given the trombone and knowing this overtone series, is it possible to have the same kind of instrumental knowledge on a string that goes like this [motions like a bassist]. Can I find the same notes here, what I call playing horizontally, that I can playing it vertically. And there was a great awareness, like, "Wow, check this out, this is—I can do this! I just gotta get it done!"

NH: Well, the last question. What to you has been the least fulfilling in your choice of a vocation? I can imagine you wouldn't have wanted to be anything else unless I'm wrong.

RC: No, you're right.

NH: What about the jazz life as you've lived it has been the most satisfying, the most challenging—well, Duke has a song I've always liked, "What Am I Here For"—and you answered that in terms of your vocation. What was it that you were here for?

RC: That's a lot of questions all in one paragraph! One of the things I've enjoyed as a member of the jazz community is I've met some great, great people masquerading as musicians. I've met some wonderful players who as people were just stunning to me. Art Farmer, Benny Golson, I love all those guys, man, if they didn't play music I wouldn't care! They're just fabulous to me, and if I were to look to find an image to imitate, that thirty or forty guys who I could take some of each of to help me be a complete person as I envision me being a complete person. The other thing I'm happy to be a part of in this career is that I've been able to see other people in their own environment, their own cultures, whether it's Japan, China or the States, man! Each state's got its own culture. Each state has their own specific culture involved in it. To have the capacity, the facility to travel to all of these various cultural units has been an enlightening time for me. And I think the final thing for me has been I've been happy and lucky to play with people who've allowed me, because they've trusted my musical judgment, to experiment with them and come out pretty much on top.

NH: Well, I recently wrote, ending what may be my last jazz book after having been sixty years trying to be on the scene: In my day job I've met all kinds of people, supreme court justices, defense lawyers, whatever, but the people I've learned the most from, not only in their music, and that's a lot, but from themselves, are musicians, and you, sir, are one of them. And thank you for the time to come today.

RC: Oh, thank you, sir.

NH: Ron Carter, from the Blue Note. This is Nat Hentoff.

RC: Thank you.

64 | These Little Kids Think Coltrane Is Cool

At Harvard's Graduate School of Education, Howard Gardner has long taught his theory of multiple intelligences to enable his students, when they enter their own classrooms, to understand and nurture these various strengths in the youngsters they teach. As explained by a Gardner practitioner, second-grade teacher Christine Passarella, in last fall's Adelphi University newsletter: "In the past, if you had linguistic intelligence, if you could read and write, you were smart. If you had mathematical and logical intelligence, you still got credit for that. But what if you had musical intelligence or what if you had kinetic intelligence? You see that with musicians and athletes. So Howard Gardner says there are gifts in all of us and it's up to us to teach to those."

Teaching in the Holliswood School, Public School 178 in Jamaica Estates, Queens, she says, "I have worked on wonderful projects on artful thinking with the Metropolitan Museum of Art. Children studied paintings not just about the artist and his style but to look at the relationships between the characters in the painting, and the setting. It's a way of developing thoughtful dispositions."

Ms. Passarella told me that she teaches "in a looped classroom that gave me two years to develop my program with the same children, starting in the first grade. I began mixing great works of art with classical music; and over time I introduced rock, the blues and jazz."

A childhood friend, blues guitarist Joey Leone, had at first introduced her to the music of John Coltrane, and when she played his recordings "the children were drawn to the range of feelings in the songs as I gave them the backgrounds of the compositions.

"'Alabama,' for example, was about Martin Luther King and racial discrimination; and while 'My Own True Love' concerned a man and a woman, John Coltrane's *Love Supreme* expressed a love for humanity."

This reminded me that in one of my conversations with Coltrane he said he was searching for the sounds of what Buddhists call "Om," which he described as the universal essence of all of us in the universe. He also told me regretfully, "I'll never know what the listeners feel from my music, and that's too bad."

Ms. Passarella's second-grade students, she says, would have told him how moved they were by not only the ballads "but the more avant-garde recordings, such as 'Interstellar Space.'" She notes that, through her teaching, "I have discovered that young children have open, welcoming minds, and the more pure and emotional the music, the more they connect. Soon they were hooked on John Coltrane's music."

The children learned that Coltrane lived in Dix Hills—a hamlet on Long Island not all that far from their school—from 1964 to his death in 1967 (his family sold the home in 1972). And they were saddened to discover that the house—where he composed *A Love Supreme* and all his last works—had been in danger of being demolished by the real estate developer who now owned it. But they and their teacher soon were excited by the news that a resident of Dix Hills, Steve Fulgoni, a longtime jazz enthusiast, had come to the rescue of the Coltrane home.

Mr. Fulgoni, at the time the historian for the Half Hollow Historical Association in the Dix Hills area, contacted the developer, who didn't know much about Coltrane but was quickly and extensively informed. He told Mr. Fulgoni that he would be willing to sell the property.

Starting what he calls a "grass-roots effort" to save the house—aided by news coverage in New York City and Long Island newspapers and on television—Mr. Fulgoni eventually persuaded the town of Huntington, of which Dix Hills is a part, to make the building a local landmark; in 2005, the town bought the home from the developer. It has since been listed on the New York State and National Registers of Historic Places—with the ownership transferred to "Friends of the Coltrane Home," whose board includes Coltrane's son, Ravi; Ravi's wife,

Kathleen Hennessy; and Mr. Fulgoni. Before her death, John Coltrane's widow, Alice, was an enthusiastic proponent of restoring the house.

But the structure, left untended for years, requires much fund-raising to become what the Coltranes would like it to be—"a place of learning" where, for example, Coltrane's meditation room would change into a multimedia room for schoolchildren.

Among the more dedicated recent fund-raisers were Ms. Passarella's second graders. They engaged in raffles, cake sales and a book fair. Then, their teacher tells me, on May 23, 2008—at a special assembly program in Coltrane's honor— "they sang their original songs and choreographed ballroom dances." One dance was named "Chasin' the Train" (Trane was Coltrane's nickname).

The school's principal, Diane Hobbes, and assistant principal, Patrick Klocek, in their review of Ms. Passarella's—and her class's—performance, said: "During the past few months, you have given your students a wealth of prior knowledge they could not have received anywhere. Throughout the assembly program, every single one of your students smiled from ear to ear and walked with their chests pushed out and their heads held high. They will never forget this day when their teacher made them feel larger than life."

The teacher says, with pleasure, that her second graders "are now being called Kids for Coltrane." With their moving into the third grade, she will no longer be their teacher. But she plans to start a Kids for Coltrane Club once a week during lunch. "We will invite these students already familiar with his music and also new members."

She also will continue to share with her future students "the work of other jazz musicians, and other genres of music—as well as connecting music to visual art" in association with the Metropolitan Museum of Art.

"I hear in John's music a direct message to me as a teacher, and that is to go on teaching children in a way that respects their individuality. His music tells children to be who they want to be, that it is OK to be different, it is OK to feel, and that we all need to be able to express who we are in our own way to find what writer and philosopher Joseph Campbell called 'following your bliss.'"

Coltrane, trying to put into words the actual experience of playing jazz, once said: "When you're playing with someone who really has something to say, even though they may otherwise be quite different in style, there's one thing that remains constant. And that is the tension of the experience, that electricity, that kind of feeling that is a lift kind of feeling. No matter where it happens, you know when that feeling comes upon you, and it makes you feel happy."

That kind of happiness can lift listeners too—listeners of any age, including second graders.

EPILOGUE: MY LIFE LESSONS FROM THE JAZZ "SOULS ON FIRE"

John Coltrane once described for me the meaning of his existence: "This music is the whole question of life itself." My first sense of how my own life would be formed by music was when I was a kid, sitting next to my father in the synagogue during the High Holidays as the cantor (the *chazan*)—in his black robes and high black skullcap—took over the service.

In my memoir, *Boston Boy,* I told how his music went all the way through me: "What he sings is partly written, largely improvised. He is a master of melisma—for each sacred syllable there are three, four, six notes that climb and entwine." In the continuous dialogue with God—he's sometimes arguing with God, I thought—there was "The cry! The *krechts,* a catch in the voice!" (I was later to hear "the cry" in black blues singers.)

"A cry summoning centuries of hosts of Jews. A thunderstorm of fierce yearning that reverberates through the *shul* (the synagogue), and then, as if the universe had lost a beat, there is a sudden silence—and from deep inside the chazan, a soaring falsetto. The room is swaying; his soul, riding a triumphant vibrato, goes right through the roof."

Years later, in New York, I'd hear John Coltrane at the Village Gate, where, as his then bassist Art Davis recalled: "He'd play a tune for an hour, or two hours, same song. People would just be shouting, like you go to a holy roller church. John had that spirit. Despite the critics who tried to put him down, the black brothers and sisters would be there!" So was this white guy.

Elie Wiesel, writing of the Hasidic sages, called them "souls on fire." In eighteenth-century Poland, the Hasids created their identities within Judaism, celebrating their faith in joyous music and dancing. And I've been drawn into their exhilaration in one of their synagogues in this country.

But the souls on fire I've gotten to know personally for more than sixty years have been jazz musicians, and they've not only lit my soul but also taught me about much more than music. The often volcanic Charles Mingus became one of the closest friends I've ever had. Like Duke Ellington, he did not use the term "jazz." It's "Mingus music," he'd declare. "I'm trying to play the truth of what I am. The reason it's difficult is because I'm changing all the time."

And their own truth was what he demanded of the musicians who played with him. As one of them told me: "You had to keep stretching yourself while you're with Mingus. He just wouldn't let you coast. Even in public—you've seen it—you'd be in the middle of a solo, and he'd yell at you to stop playing licks and get into *yourself*. He had more confidence in what we were capable of than we had."

And in my conversations with Mingus, I had to stretch myself, and learn. In the 1950s, when I was still trying to find out what I was here for, Mingus—acutely conscious of Jim Crow, to which he sometimes reacted explosively—told me:

"It's not only a question of color any more. It's getting deeper than that. People are getting so fragmented, and part of that is that fewer and fewer people are making a real effort any more to find exactly who they are and to build on that knowledge.

"Most people are forced to do things they don't want to most of the time, and so they get to the point where they feel they no longer have any choice about anything important, including who they are. We create our own slavery. But I'm going to keep on getting through, and finding out the kind of man I am, through my music. That's the one place I can be free."

Charles died of Lou Gehrig's disease in 1979. Almost until the very end, although he could no longer speak or move his hands, he was—the last time I saw him in his apartment—humming a new melody into a tape recorder to be orchestrated by a colleague. The continuing, and indeed growing, impact of his music—and his life that was its content—was reported on National Public Radio (August 2008) by Robert O'Mealley, founder of the Center for Jazz Studies at Columbia University: "My students almost jump out of their chairs when they first hear Mingus. And then they want to go, they want to play like that. They want to play for real!"

That reminded me of Mingus's stories of the music that first went all the way through him when he was a child: "My stepmother," he told me, "would take me to a Holiness church. The blues was in the Holiness churches—moaning and riffs between the audience and the preacher. People went into trances."

Then, as soon as he could, the youngster would hear all the jazz bands that came through Los Angeles: "I almost jumped out of the balcony the first time I heard Duke Ellington. One piece excited me so much that I screamed."

I miss Charles, including the phone calls early in the morning. There was no voice, just spirit-filling gusts of music. Then Mingus would come on: "What did you think of that? I just wrote it." From the first notes of the first bar, I knew who it was.

There were other jazz souls who had gone through such searing fires of rejection that their stories of recovery buoyed me when I was far down—after, for example, marriages so discordant that the equivalent musical notes for them haven't been named yet. (I'm now in my third: however, that has lasted fifty years, thanks in part to Dizzy Gillespie's advice to me on how to keep a marriage together: "If she is determined never to be wrong, just let her be right all the time. Just say, 'Yes, dear,'" said my marriage counselor, Mr. Gillespie.

But in my life there was a considerable period, for a time, of cyclical clinical depression—much harder to recover from than shattered marriages and other broken yearnings for companionship. These bottomless black sites can't be imagined by anyone lucky enough never to have experienced them.

I have also been summarily fired from some of the most prestigious publications in the nation—after more than twenty-five years at the *New Yorker,* more than fourteen years as a columnist at the *Washington Post,* more than fifty years at the *Village Voice,* and there are others. As jazz musicians know far better than I, having to live from gig to gig can drag you down.

But when I'm so far down that hardly anything will lift me up, one of the ways I get moving again is by the stories of their abandonment told me by jazz musicians who so unyieldingly insisted on listening to their own drums that, for years, other musicians treated them as untouchables.

Having come to New York from Boston around the same time I did, Cecil Taylor found it so hard to get gigs that he survived by delivering sandwiches for a coffee shop. But at night, in his loft, he told me, he would stage concerts, playing an extensive repertory for audiences that were not there.

Getting his music into the air lifted his spirits. But during that period, when one night he was allowed to sit in at Birdland in New York, the revered Jo Jones, known for encouraging young players (he called them his "kiddies"), reacted to Cecil's wholly unexpected sounds and cross-rhythms by throwing a cymbal at Cecil, speeding him off the bandstand.

Cecil went on to continue to be only himself, becoming—as jazz encyclopedist Richard Cook put it—"a feted member of a world-wide avant-garde, with festivals in his honor."

Ornette Coleman had an especially hard and harsh road to earn respect from most established jazz musicians. In 1958, I was at his first recording session. It was for the Contemporary label in Los Angeles.

After getting to know Ornette, I wrote the liner notes for his second album. As his music instantly made clear, Ornette, believing that jazz could express more and deeper feelings, wanted his alto saxophone to "reach into the sound and warmth of a human voice."

One well-known jazzman, drummer Shelly Manne, who was on Ornette's second Contempory release, did understand that he was in the presence of a powerful new way of speaking jazz: "Ornette sounds like a person crying or a person laughing when he plays. And he wants *me* to want to laugh and cry. Although he may be flying all over the horn and doing weird things metrically, the basic feelings are still there. And when you're working with him, he makes you listen so hard to what he's doing that he makes you play a whole other way."

But many musicians didn't want to feel uprooted. In Los Angeles, before he came to New York, when Ornette showed up at jam sessions, the other players would sometimes walk off the stand. What particularly hurt him, as years after, in 1966, he told *Newsweek,* was when "four very famous jazzmen in Los Angeles let me play with them. Five seconds later, they all walked off and left me alone before 500 people."

In 1959, after Ornette broke tumultuously onto the New York jazz scene, where I heard him many nights—being one of the very few critics who tried to champion him—I was sitting at the Five Spot one evening next to Roy Eldridge, who said: "I think he's jiving. He's putting everybody on." And pianist Red Garland, a respected Miles Davis sideman, said: "I like to see a struggling cat get a break. But Coleman is faking. He's being very unfair to the public."

Miles Davis disagreed: "He's not playing clichés." And pianist-leader-composer John Lewis became a Coleman enthusiast. But most of the musicians who came to the Five Spot were so dismissive of Ornette that, as he told me, "all I got was a wall of hostility. I could feel their anger."

However, while almost invariably, in my experience, it is the musicians who first appreciate and validate a truly singular newcomer before the critics do, Ornette—who was absolutely not going to change who he was—said to me:

"We never did have a night at the Five Spot with a cold audience. A listener need have no trouble with what we do if he reacts only to what he hears and what he *feels* as we're playing. Some people get so involved in trying to figure out what we're doing that they don't pay attention to their emotions."

That made me feel good too. Some musicians have put me down because I can't tell what chords they're playing, or when they go outside the chord. But Duke Ellington also reassured me that I could be of use to the listener when he said during one of our conversations: "I don't want anyone listening to our music to *analyze* what we're playing. I want them to open themselves to all of the music as they *feel* it."

And Ornette persevered until now, when—for many around the world—he is on the Mount Rushmore of jazz.

Back at the Five Spot long ago, Ornette gave me a way to answer those who have shied away from jazz as being "difficult." We were talking after even the magisterial Coleman Hawkins—one of the first of the giants to welcome the "difficult" Thelonious Monk into the family—had said of Ornette: "You know I never like to criticize any musician publicly. Just say I think he needs seasoning. A lot of seasoning."

Unfazed, the then fiercely controversial newcomer responded to his musician critics: "Music is a free thing, and any way you can enjoy it, you should. Jazz is growing up. It's not a cutting contest any more—seeing which man can outplay another. More and more, people are listening not for what a man knows about a horn but for what he expresses through that horn."

Phil Woods put it even more succinctly: "Dizzy once told me: 'If you can hear it, you can have it!'"

The late Whitney Balliett of the *New Yorker* also concisely understood why this international language has become so personally essential to so many of us when he described jazz as "the sound of surprise."

It was also at the Five Spot that four of five nights a week I'd stay until closing during a long engagement by Thelonious Monk's quartet with tenor saxophonist John Coltrane. Every night, musicians who didn't have a gig elsewhere were lined up, two or three at the bar.

Coming home, early one morning, I wrote in my day book: "I never was in Chicago when Louis Armstrong played with his Hot Five, but it must have been comparable to this. Monk and Coltrane were exhilarating because you never knew what was going to happen next. You did know that whatever that would be would never happen again. And you might well remember how those moments felt for the rest of your life."

I keep having these regenerating feelings. Around when I reached eighty—still writing on my day job as a reporter—I was way low one of those days, meeting deadlines on the genocide in Darfur and about those parts of the Constitution here in the United States being on life support. That night, I went to the Blue Note club near where I live in New York's Greenwich Village for a tribute to my friend Clark Terry.

A mentor to Miles Davis and Quincy Jones when both were barely known outside their neighborhoods, Clark—born in 1920—has survived a number of formidable ailments. That evening, having been helped out of his wheelchair, he was making it up to the bandstand as someone in the audience shouted, "How are the golden years, Clark?"

Terry, trumpet in hand, turned toward the voice and said, "They suck!"—and beat off the first number of the set. He played as if he were in his twenties. The gloom and the feeling of futility about what I'd been doing during the day wholly lifted. I was almost skipping on the way home. Jazz again had refilled me with life.

I don't know a single jazz musician who has ever retired because he or she was convinced they had no more to say in their music. Many years ago, I saw Duke Ellington on one of his few days off. For years, he had been on the road for 200 or more one-nighters a year, with such jumps as between Toronto and Dallas.

That afternoon, he looked worn out, and I said, "You don't have to keep on living this way. You can retire on the standards you've composed—on your ASCAP income." He looked at me as if I had become a stranger.

"Retire?" he almost shouted. "To what?"

As time goes on, there is no quotation I repeat more often.

A tenor saxophonist and composer I recorded for the Contemporary label many years ago, Benny Golson (born in 1929), brought a new group in the summer of 2008 into a New York club, Smoke, just before going into a recording studio with it and his new compositions and arrangements.

"Creativity never retires," he told the monthly *All About Jazz–New York*. "Anybody who's worth their salt never says, 'I've done this and I've done that, now I'm finished.' Music is open-ended; there is no end to it. Hank Jones put it this way: 'The horizon is always ahead.' That's right. It's perpetual. You want to go on, you don't want to stop."

Will *jazz* ever stop? At seventy-six, Phil Woods was performing for the BBC in England in 2009, the year in which I wrote this. He had recently been designated a Jazz Master by America's National Endowment for the Arts and was working on new commissions, with more playing gigs to come during the year.

Between concerts and broadcasts in England, Phil told John Watson of *Jazz Journal:* "I've had pulmonary ailments, and soprano sax and clarinet are now a little difficult to play, but alto sax is still my friend." And as I've heard him play recently, a resoundingly joyous friend.

Asked about the future of the music that keeps him thriving, Phil said: "The young musicians keep coming, and I'm very optimistic because the music is so strong, and so many good men died for it; and so many people love it, and it's such a strong, vital social force, so I have hopes. I do have hopes."

The term "social force" reminds me of my favorite story about Dizzy Gillespie. In one of his "jazz ambassador" tours for the State Department, Dizzy and the band were in Ankara, Turkey, ready to play at a lawn party at the American embassy.

"While I was signing autographs," Dizzy recalled, "I happened to look at the fence surrounding the grounds. A lot of street kids were pressed against the fence. They wanted to come in and hear the music. One of them actually climbed over the fence, and a guard threw him right back over it.

"I asked what was going on. Why did they do that? Some official said, 'This party is for select people. Local dignitaries and important Americans in the city.'

"I said, 'Select people! We're not over here for no select people! We're over here to show these people that Americans are all kinds of people.' I had a girl in that band, and almost as many whites as blacks. We had a good mix.

"The ambassador comes over and asks, 'Are you going to play?' I say, 'No! I saw that guard throw a little kid over the fence. Those are the people we're trying to get close to—the people *outside* the fence.'

"So the ambassador said, 'Let them in, let them all in.'"

I was very privileged to have known, and learned from, Dizzy and all the other musicians in this book. For two years, 1960 and 1961, I did more than write about them. Archie Bleyer, who owned a then successful popular music label, Cadence, decided, as he put it, to "do something for jazz." Asking me to start a new label, Candid, he promised me free reign, and he kept his word. I told him up front that the releases would not measurably add to his income for a long time. He might not even have heard of some of the leaders of the sessions.

Having been at recording sessions where the producer actively and insistently tried to shape the music, once I had chosen the leaders, I gave them free reign. Most of what I did was to write down the time of each take, send out for sandwiches, and make sure that the leader was at the final editing session. It was his or her byline, not mine.

On rare occasions, when the players got stuck in dense arrangements, I did leave the control room and suggest that they just move into a blues—and they were liberated again.

Being part, however marginal, of the actual making of jazz was one of the most satisfying experiences of my life. We released some forty albums by, among others, Charles Mingus, Max Roach, Abbey Lincoln, Cecil Taylor, Clark Terry, Phil Woods and blues bards Otis Spann, Lightnin' Hopkins and Memphis Slim.

A session that brought me back to my boyhood—when I used to listen again and again to a Mound City Blues Blowers 1929 date by Pee Wee Russell and Coleman Hawkins—was *Jazz Reunion: Pee Wee Russell and Coleman Hawkins.*

Working directly with them was a fantasy come true. After the session ended, Hawkins, the inventor of the jazz tenor saxophone, in whose presence I was somewhat in awe, pointed to Pee Wee and said to me: "For all these years, I've been listening to him play those funny notes he used to think were wrong. They weren't. They didn't have a name for them then."

Another date was led by a Texas tenor, Booker Ervin, who wasn't well known and is hardly mentioned any more. He had been a sideman with Charles Mingus, who had said to me: "Nearly everybody I've worked with whom I've liked seems to get into a trance when they're at their best. When Booker was really going, I'd say something to him, and he just didn't hear me. He was somewhere else—inside the music."

Booker Ervin died in 1970, just short of his fortieth birthday, of kidney disease. The title of his Candid album came from what he said in the studio, listening to a playback: "That's It!" I was so glad to send his signature room-filling sound and daring unpredictability out into the world.

The Candid recording that means the most to me was made in 1961 by twenty-three-year-old Booker Little, a trumpet player and composer. As soon as I heard him on a previous session led by Max Roach, I knew he'd be a shaper of the future of jazz because of his vision as a player and composer. And his sound reminded me again of what Duke Ellington had told me: "A musician's sound is his soul."

A few months after the session, Booker died of uremia. The last time I saw him was at the final editing session in the studio, where he told me of his plans for a future Candid date. He never mentioned his illness.

Booker's influence keeps growing among instrumentalists and composers who have absorbed his vision—described by him in my liner notes for his *Out Front*: "My own feelings about the direction in which jazz should go are that there should be much less stress on technical exhibitionism and much more on emotional content—on what might be termed humanity in music, and the freedom to say all that you want to. There are a number of people who are making contributions toward that freedom, and it will all work out, as it always has in jazz, in many different ways.

"For some people," Booker Little continued, "Ornette Coleman was an awakener. There were some things missing in what he did when he came on the scene, but the one thing he did have was a feeling of freedom. He didn't stay within the conventional tonalities, and he played harmonic patterns against each other. Technically, he didn't know which ones he was working with, but that wasn't important.

"The important thing was that he played them the way he *heard* them."

Candid went out of business in the United States because Archie Bleyer's own label, Cadence, fell on hard times. But from then on, musicians coming back from gigs in Europe, Japan and other nations around the world would tell me that they had seen Candids in record stores. Alan Bates, owner of the Black Lion label in England, took over distribution of the label globally. (There is one label he licenses, Pure Pleasure, which releases recordings only on vinyl—for those demanding collectors who prefer that historical sound.)

On his Candid set, Booker Little startled me by dedicating one of his originals, "Man of Words," to me. It was his description—in sounds, dynamics and rhythms—of the writing process. As I paraphrased in the liner notes what he told me, there is first the all too blank sheet of paper (to this day, I still use a typewriter); followed by the uncertainty that the piece might not be going anywhere; and eventually, at least in Booker's music about me, an unexpected resolution.

Once again, there were the sounds of surprise in my life in "Man of Words."

The exuberant cornetist Jimmy McPartland once told me of a conversation he had, as a jazz apprentice, with Bix Beiderbecke, who will always be legendary.

"I like you, kid," Bix said. "You sound like me, but you don't copy me. One of the things I like about jazz, kid," Bix went on, "is I don't know what's going to happen next. Do you?"

No, I don't, Bix. (These musicians and I still converse.) And these continuing surprises keep brightening my life. It's not only the musicians who feel about jazz as I wrote long, long ago: "Once you're inside the music you'll want to keep going deeper and deeper, because it's impossible to get enough of it."

Chapter 1, "Who Owns Jazz?" was first published in *JazzTimes*, August 2005.

Chapter 2, "My Debt to Artie Shaw," was first published in *JazzTimes*, April 2005.

Chapter 3, "The Family of Jazz," was first published in *JazzTimes*, May 2004.

Chapter 4, "Beyond the Process," was first published in *JazzTimes*, December 2004.

Chapter 5, "Playing Changes on Jazz Interviews," was first published in *JazzTimes*, April 2007.

Chapter 6, "Inside the Ellington Band," was first published in *JazzTimes*, October 2006.

Chapter 7, "Duke Ellington's Posthumous Revenge," was first published in *JazzTimes*, November 2004.

Chapter 8, "Essentially Duke (and Wynton)," was first published in *JazzTimes*, March 2005.

Chapter 9, "Ellington's Band Is Heavenly in these 'Live' Forties Recordings," was first published in the *Wall Street Journal*, March 28, 2007. Reprinted with permission of *The Wall Street Journal* © 2007 Dow Jones & Company.

Chapter 10, "Is Jazz Black Music?" was first published in *JazzTimes*, June 2008.

Chapter 11, "No One Else Sounded Like 'Pee Wee' Russell," was first published in *JazzTimes*, June 2008.

Chapter 12, "Just Call Him Thelonious," was first published in *Down Beat*, July 1956.

Chapter 13, "Remembering Dizzy," was first published in *JazzTimes*, September 2004.

Chapter 14, "Oscar Peterson: A Jazz 'Behemoth' Moves On," was first published in the *Wall Street Journal*, December 27, 2007. Reprinted with permission of *The Wall Street Journal* © 2007 Dow Jones & Company.

Chapter 15, "A Great Night in Providence for Jazz and Snow," was first published in the *Wall Street Journal*, March 30, 2005. Reprinted with permission of *The Wall Street Journal* © 2005 Dow Jones & Company.

Chapter 16, "The Perfect Jazz Club," was first published in *JazzTimes*, December 2005.

Chapter 18, "The Music of the 1930s Is Back in Full Swing," was first published in the *Wall Street Journal*, August 2, 2006. Reprinted with permission of *The Wall Street Journal* © 2006 Dow Jones & Company.

Chapter 19, "The Expansive Jazz Journey of Marian McPartland," was first published in the *Wall Street Journal*, March 18, 2008. Reprinted with permission of *The Wall Street Journal* © 2008 Dow Jones & Company.

Chapter 20, "Going Inside Jazz with Wynton," was first published in *JazzTimes*, January/February 2009.

Chapter 21, "Memories Are Made of This: A Conversation with Clark Terry," was first published in *JazzTimes*, June 2007.

Chapter 22, "Man, I'm So Lucky to Be a Jazz Musician: Phil Woods," was first published in *JazzTimes*, July 2008.

Chapter 23, "Conventional Unwisdom about Jazz," was first published in *JazzTimes*, May 2006.

Chapter 24, "Are Krall and Monheit Jazz Singers?," was first published in *JazzTimes*, December 2001.

Chapter 25, "Billie Holiday, Live: A Biography in Music," was first published in the *Wall Street Journal*, February 12, 2008. Reprinted with permission of *The Wall Street Journal* © 2008 Dow Jones & Company.

Chapter 26, "This Daughter of Jazz Is One Cool Cat," was first published in the *Wall Street Journal*, June 14, 2006. Reprinted with permission of *The Wall Street Journal* © 2006 Dow Jones & Company.

Chapter 27, "The Springtime of Frank Sinatra," was first published in the *Wall Street Journal*, December 5, 2007. Reprinted with permission of *The Wall Street Journal* © 2007 Dow Jones & Company.

Chapter 28, "Sinatra Sings in Vegas, and You Are There," was first published in the *Wall Street Journal*, May 22, 2007. Reprinted with permission of *The Wall Street Journal* © 2007 Dow Jones & Company.

Chapter 29, "She's on the Road to Renown," was first published in the *Wall Street Journal*, September 5, 2007. Reprinted with permission of *The Wall Street Journal* © 2007 Dow Jones & Company.

Chapter 30, "Bing and Guests Swing on the Air," was first published in the *Wall Street Journal*, August 9, 2005. Reprinted with permission of *The Wall Street Journal* © 2005 Dow Jones & Company.

Chapter 31, "The Joyous Power of Black Gospel Music," was first published in the *Wall Street Journal*, March 29, 2006. Reprinted with permission of *The Wall Street Journal* © 2006 Dow Jones & Company.

Chapter 32, "The Healing Power of Jazz," was first published in the *Wall Street Journal*, December 29, 2005. Reprinted with permission of *The Wall Street Journal* © 2005 Dow Jones & Company.

Chapter 33, "Old Country Jewish Blues and Ornette Coleman," was first published in *JazzTimes*, September 2008.

Chapter 34, "The Jewish Soul of Willie 'The Lion' Smith," was first published in *Jazz.com*, October 2009.

Chapter 35, "Satchmo's Rap Sheet," was first published in *JazzTimes*, December 2007.

Chapter 36, "The Constitution of a Jazzman," was first published in the *Village Voice*, September 2007.

Chapter 37, "How Jazz Helped Hasten the Civil Rights Movement," was first published in the *Wall Street Journal*, January 15, 2009. Reprinted with permission of *The Wall Street Journal* © 2009 Dow Jones & Company.

Chapter 38, "The Congressman from the Land of Jazz," was first published in the *Wall Street Journal*, June 24, 2004. Reprinted with permission of *The Wall Street Journal* © 2004 Dow Jones & Company.

Chapter 39, "Jazz Musicians in the Public Square," was first published in *JazzTimes*, March 2006.

Chapter 40, "Quincy Jones—Past, Present and Future," was first published in the *Wall Street Journal*, May 12, 2004. Reprinted with permission of *The Wall Street Journal* © 2004 Dow Jones & Company.

Chapter 41, "King Oliver in the Groove(s)," was first published in the *Wall Street Journal*, July 25, 2007. Reprinted with permission of *The Wall Street Journal* © 2007 Dow Jones & Company.

Chapter 42, "Giants at Play," was first published in the *Weekly Standard*, December 10, 2007.

Chapter 43, "Barrelhouse Chuck Goering Keeps the Blues Alive," was first published in the *Wall Street Journal*, January 3, 2007. Reprinted with permission of *The Wall Street Journal* © 2007 Dow Jones & Company.

Chapter 44, "Jazz's History Is Living in Queens . . . ," was first published in the *Wall Street Journal*, January 17, 2007. Reprinted with permission of *The Wall Street Journal* © 2007 Dow Jones & Company.

Chapter 45, "Uncovering Jazz Trails," was first published in *JazzTimes*, June 2007.

Chapter 46, "Expanding the Map," was first published in *JazzTimes*, October 2007.

Chapter 47, "The Thoreau of Jazz," was first published in *JazzTimes*, November 2007.

Chapter 49, "Barren Days," was first published in *JazzTimes*, September 2005.

Chapter 50, "Keeping Jazz—and Its Musicians—Alive," was first published in the *Wall Street Journal*, October 21, 2004. Reprinted with permission of *The Wall Street Journal* © 2004 Dow Jones & Company.

Chapter 51, "In New Orleans, the Saints Are Marching In Again," was first published in the *Village Voice*, April 10, 2007.

Chapter 52, "The Beating Heart of Jazz," was first published in the *Village Voice*, May 20, 2008.

Chapter 53, "Bridging Generations," was first published in *JazzTimes*, September 2007.

Chapter 54, "The Rebirth of the Hot Jazz Violin," was first published in the *Wall Street Journal*, February 21, 2006. Reprinted with permission of *The Wall Street Journal* © 2006 Dow Jones & Company.

Chapter 55, "The Newest Jazz Generation," was first published in *JazzTimes*, January/February 2007.

Chapter 56, "Born in Israel," was first published in *JazzTimes*, July/August 2007.

INDEX

Italicized page numbers refer to illustrations.

TEXT
10/12.5 Minion Pro

DISPLAY
Minion Pro

COMPOSITOR
BookMatters, Berkeley

INDEXER
Sharon Sweeney

PRINTER AND BINDER
Maple-Vail Book Manufacturing Group